Franz Holford
Doppelgänger

Musician unmasked

Francis Ravel Harvey

Freshwater Publications

busybird
publishing

First published by Busybird Publishing 2025

Copyright © 2025 Francis Ravel Harvey

ISBN
Paperback: 978-1-923216-36-5
Ebook: 978-1-923216-37-2

This work is copyright. Apart from any use permitted under the *Copyright Act 1968*, no part of this publication may be reproduced, stored in a retrieval system or transmitted in any form or by any means, electronic, mechanical, photocopying, recording or otherwise, without the prior written permission of Francis Ravel Harvey.

The information in this book is based on the author's experiences and opinions. The author and publisher disclaim responsibility for any adverse consequences, which may result from use of the information contained herein. Permission to use any external content has been sought by the author. Any breaches will be rectified in further editions of the book.

Cover Image: Portrait for Franz (William) Holford, reimagined by Francis Ravel Harvey

Cover design: Busybird Publishing

Layout and typesetting: Busybird Publishing

Freshwater Publications

Busybird Publishing
2/118 Para Road
Montmorency, Victoria
Australia 3094
www.busybird.com.au

By the same author

The Canon: Australian Music Journal Sub-Ed. 1950-1959

After the Dream: Life of Charles Chauvel (MS) 1959

Australian Theatre Yearbook, Founding Ed. (Australian Elizabethan Theatre Trust, FP Publications) 1959

Theatregoer, Monthly, Founding Ed (FP Publications) 1959-61

Theatre, Arts in Australia (Longmans Green) 1960

Australian Encyclopaedia One-Volume – Theatre, Contrib. Ed. (Horwitz) 1961

Design Australia, Quarterly, Founding Ed. (Ure Smith) 1967-70

Tales of Many Lands, 20 min. Radio Series (ABC Radio Drama) 1970

The Theatre of Bertholt Brecht and *The Caucasian Chalk Circle* by F R Harvey (Tutortapes, National Library, 1976)

The Poetry of Gerard Manly Hopkins, by F R Harvey (Tutortapes, National Library, 1976)

Australia Council – What it Is and What it Does (Australia Council) 1981

Chapel of Ease (Freshwater Press) 1992

The Letters of Lachlan Macquarie, (Thesis, Mitchell Library 1993)

Traveller to Freedom: The Roger Pryke Story (Freshwater Press 2011)

In the Salon of Franz Liszt: Musical Play for the Live Theatre (Musica Viva 2016)

Mata: Play for the Live Theatre (MS) 2020

'Roger' Film Script (MS) 2020

The Captain Film Script (MS) 2022

Memories of an Orphan Boy Audiobook (Author 2, 2023)

Francis Ravel Harvey

Journalist and author, Francis Ravel Harvey was born at Homebush, New South Wales in 1930 and began his career as a cadet journalist on (the now extinct) *Sun* newspaper in 1947. In 1950 he worked for almost ten years as producer of the independent monthly music journal *The Canon*. He worked as a freelance journalist in the live theatre in Sydney, wrote scripts for the ABCs *Tales of Many Lands*, and founded his own monthly magazine *Theatregoer*. He was theatre critic for the *Canberra Times* in the 70s and published the first theatre yearbook for the Australian Elizabethan Theatre Trust (1959-60).

He worked as an editor and writer for Horwitz Publications and Ure Smith, founding the first magazine in Australia on industrial design, *Design Australia*, for the Industrial Design Council of Australia, which was commended by the late Duke of Edinburgh. He edited various trade magazines for Horwitz in the bookselling, food and restaurant industries.

Mr Harvey worked as a senior journalist with the departments of Health and Social Security in Canberra, editing the quarterly journal *Health* which he founded, and then transferred to Sydney as a Senior Project Officer for the Australia Council, editing the magazine *Artforce*, producing annual reports and advocating for the arts through lectures. He remained with the Australia Council for eight years, producing publications, exhibitions and seminars. From 1981 he spent ten years as head of the Information and Publications Unit at Macquarie University, from which he retired in 1991. In 2012 he published *Traveller to Freedom* the life of ex-priest Roger Pryke. Having recently completed *Doppelgänger,* he published an Audiobook *Memories of an Orphan Boy* in 2023. He holds a Masters in Literature and Public History at the University of Sydney and is a member of ASA.

Franz (William) Holford, an Australian pianist and composer who remained an enigma for the greater part of his professional life. (Photograph courtesy John Champ)

Prelude One

When I was sixteen I used to travel by ferryboat from Woolwich to Sydney each day to attend high school, which was located in the old colonial gaol at Darlinghurst. My travelling companion was a swarthy French fellow schoolboy François (Frank) Mommaerts, who chose to call me by my middle name - Ravel. He liked the French connection to my mother's name and the fact that both our ancestors seemed to come from Tours, in the heartland of France.

As the ferry approached Circular Quay one morning Frank and I were sitting in our usual place on the outer deck of the ferry *Karingal* and as we passed under the Harbour Bridge my friend suddenly grasped my arm and pointed to a ship moored at East Circular Quay. It was an old tramp steamer and Frank was excited.

'See that ship, Ravel? Tied up at the Quay there, 'See it?'

'Sure,' I replied. 'So?'

'My grandfather owns it...it's from France - see the tricolour? It's sailing today and guess what? I'm going with him...!'

This totally unexpected announcement partially explained why my friend was dressed so casually and was toting a bulging canvas kitbag.

'I'm going as a deck boy - to France, Ravel - *to France!*' He paused and then pressed my elbow urgently.

'...Come with me.'

'What? Just like *that?*' I gasped.

'...Yes, just like that. As a deck boy. My grand-pére will pay you. He's paying *me!* C'mon Ravel!... come with me, just us two. It'll be amazing fun!'

He could see I was hesitating, and I was. I hated school. I reflected that my own father had jumped on a boat from England to Australia in 1914 to avoid the Great War. Could I do the same? The ferry had docked, and we stood on the Quay. I looked at my friend's smiling, eager face and shook my head sadly. 'I can't, Frank. I'd love to, but I can't.' Then he was gone, and we never saw each other again. I often look back across those 75 years and ponder how different my life might have been - how radically different. Amongst a host of other things, I would never have written this book. Perhaps that might have been a good thing.

- Francis Ravel Harvey, Sydney, 2025

Prelude Two

*Love taught me how to beauty's eye alone
the secret of the lying heart is known*

- DRINKWATER

It was one of the cleverest hoaxes in Australia's musical history and outranks the Ern Malley Affair for its longevity, sheer audacity and for the number of so-called 'experts' fooled for over sixty years. For decades in the mid-20th century a Sydney musician, masquerading as an important international musical identity, managed to convince his colleagues, the public and notable contemporaries such as Sir John Barbirolli, Sir Eugene Goossens, Dr Edgar Bainton, Sir Bernard Heinze and the great German conductors Felix Weingartner and Karl Rankl that he had studied with the great masters of piano at famous music centres in Europe and England.

He also illegally declared himself a Doctor of Music, of Medicine and of Philosophy in three separate disciplines for more than fifty years in Australia without ever being challenged to produce his credentials.

It is a strange, sad and at times humorous tale of a gifted but narcissistic man caught up in a fantasy of his own devising. The Australian musician Franz Holford, who died in 1994, and whose birth and background have remained a mystery to the musical world, was variously described throughout his professional lifetime as German, German/English and German/Australian; said to have been born in Heidelberg in 1907 of a father who, he claimed at different times to different people, was either a surgeon and private consultant to Kaiser Wilhelm, or was the conductor Felix Weingartner.

Claiming to be a piano pupil of the French master Alfred Cortot, of Edwin Fischer and Robert Teichmüller, he was hailed by certain Australian musicologists as a musician who 'mixed in Europe with some of the finest musicians of his time'.[1]

The title 'Doctor' used by Franz Holford from 1940 until the end of his life was undoubtedly self-conferred. The closest he ever came to achieving a doctorate was a negotiation (which failed) for an honorary degree from Melbourne University through the efforts of his friend and colleague Sir Bernard Heinze.

In an Australian era famous for its 'cultural cringe', Franz Holford experienced the full weight of an expectation prevalent at the time, that it was obligatory for a musician in Australia either to be European or at least to have studied abroad, and to have the relevant professional qualifications. To study abroad is an expectation which unfortunately still drives many young Australian musicians overseas. Holford's solution to the problem was simply to adopt a false persona and title and carry off the deception by the sheer weight of his own charismatic personality. Such a feat would nowadays be very difficult, if not impossible to achieve.

In fact, the man who deceived some of the most eminent musicians, musicologists and scholars both in Australia and overseas for so long - was not European born and educated, but was thoroughly Australian being born and raised in Petersham, Sydney, the illegitimate grandson of a humble horse-collar and saddle maker. It was a dark shadow which hung over his life and a secret he carried to his grave.

The *raison d'être* for this book is that the myths which Franz Holford promulgated during his lifetime have begun to take more tangible form since he died. In 2001 a scholarly monogram was published by the Centre for Studies in Australian Music, University of Melbourne entitled *A Franz Holford Miscellany: including his Middle See* compiled and edited by Jennifer Hill and Kerry Murphy.[2] This was followed by a major article in the *Music Teacher Magazine*[3] entitled simply '27' by Phillip Wilcher, who also wrote a book about Franz Holford, entitled *Soft voices die*, and James Murdoch, founder of the Australian Music Centre[4] compiled an impressive obituary in *The Australian* newspaper.

'Official' biographies of him are filed in the library of the Australian Music Centre in Sydney, and a large collection of papers and manuscripts exist in the National Library Canberra and in The State Library of NSW. A growing number of entries exist on the internet, many of which are filled with misinformation about Franz Holford's life, and they often present – to say the least – a fanciful depiction of the man.

For almost ten years of my life from the age of 20, I was the equivalent of an unpaid amanuensis to Franz Holford, and lived and worked at the house 'Norwood' in Hunters Hill with the Holford family, mainly engaged upon editing and producing his music journal *The Canon*, which ran for almost nineteen years. At various times I undertook other work to sustain myself, but most of my time was spent producing *The Canon*, a niche market music journal, for which I received no salary and little recognition.

This is a book I have struggled with for many years, and which has been deliberately left until late in my life for several reasons. Franz Holford lived to be almost the same age as myself, but chief among my reasons for this book is that hopefully most of the dramatis personae who inhabit the following pages are no longer living, or are in a situation where the subject no longer causes pain or embarrassment. I know it to be a painful subject still among some of the key witnesses I wished to speak to – and who declined to be interviewed. That is a risk I have decided to take, but I should point out that my most compelling reason for publishing this personal account is that a great deal of misinformation continues to grow and circulate which needs clarification, especially in an era where the internet is such a powerful medium for accumulating and disseminating misinformation.

Upon my retirement from Macquarie University in 1991, I engaged with a genealogist Dr Marjorie Newton to trace Franz Holford's lineage. Newton's husband Don was himself a musician and had been a Holford pupil, who sang in the same choir as I did, called *The Warwick Singers*, which Franz Holford formed and conducted for several years in the 1950s. Don died in 2018 aged 90 (an additional spur to this book), and the research papers of the Newtons are now lodged in the NSW State Library.[5] The discovery of his roots by Dr Marjorie Newton and the influence they exercised on his life and the lives of a wide circle of people were first published in an article 'Shadow without substance' written by the author for *Music Forum*, 2004.[6]

In response to the many requests which followed that article, I have now written a fuller account of this extraordinary man from a different and very personal viewpoint. It is not intended as an exposé, a hagiography, nor to denigrate the memory of a musician who inspired and influenced a generation of Australian musicians and lovers of the arts. It is a memoir of a person who in many ways lived a double life – who engaged in fantasies which heavily influenced his own life and the lives of many around him. One such was a pupil of his, Phillip Wilcher, who, when approached for his recollections, wrote:

> 'Franz Holford taught me about the Arts of mankind. He took me on walks through other worlds that otherwise might not have become such a strength and mainstay in my life. I am who I am because of him and for the best in him, I am the better for it.
> He may not have been a student of Cortot, but he could have been.
> He may not have been a Doctor of Music, but he could have been. He may not have been all he said he was, but he was better at being it than those who were, and somewhere amidst the vast expanse of inventiveness there was another lesson to be learned: that the truly great in their field, although often wise to the wonders of their world, are often frail and that we should allow them their faults and insecurities as we all too readily allow ourselves our own, for who are we to truly judge? I cannot imagine what my life would have been like without him.'

To which – looking back over my own life - I must add: Nor can I.

- Francis Ravel Harvey, Sydney 2024

This house in Gale Street, was the Rectory for St Johns Church of England in the tiny parish of Woolwich, where rehearsals of the Anglican Choir would take place in the 1940s.

Woolwich, 1944

*When music sounds, gone is the earth I know,
and all her lovely things even lovelier grow.*

- DE LA MARE

1

Woolwich is a tiny suburb on a peninsula between the Lane Cove and Parramatta rivers to the north of Sydney which the Aboriginal people called Moocooboolah. The suburb is 'down the road' from the more gentrified Hunters Hill and in the early years of settlement Woolwich was largely defined by a huge dry dock, carved in colonial days out of a cliff face, in which ocean going ships were careened.

There is a small stone church in Woolwich, which took in its first parishioners in 1890, but ultimately fell into disuse and was delisted as an Anglican church in 1988. The building is still there, protected by heritage laws, but these days it is used by local community groups. In 1944, when I was a 14-year-old chorister there, the Anglican parish of St John's was a thriving community, albeit the smallest in Australia, and the old stone church's two Sunday services were always full.

Apart from some wealthy landowners, most Woolwich families and the few shops in the village in those days ultimately derived their income from Woolwich Dock, which during World War II was an especially busy place, servicing warships and troop carriers. The dock's workforce of almost 2,000 men comprised a high percentage of migrants – especially Scandinavian, English and Scotsmen – who worked hard and enjoyed their beer after work at the Woolwich Pier Hotel, overlooking the Dock. Many of my boyhood friends were the children of these migrants, and had surnames such as Einerson, van Gelder and Knutsen.

During the war my brother and I were parentless and were being cared for by an adopted aunt,[7] who lived in Gale Street, Woolwich, a few doors down the road from the Pier Hotel, in a tiny wooden cottage which had been the gardener's house set in the grounds of a splendid stone two-storey mansion. The cottage was so tiny it was referred to by the locals as the 'Doll's House'. The mansion on the other hand – owned by the Edgington Family[8] - occupied a quarter acre block and had its own lawn tennis court and lovely gardens. Another mansion up the same street was used as the Rectory to St John's Anglican Church.

In 1944 the Anglican parish in Woolwich was undergoing something of a resurgence. Anglicanism was by far the dominant religion in both Hunters Hill and Woolwich, and in fact the nearest Catholic Church was several miles away in the adjacent suburb of Gladesville.

The resurgence in St John's parish at this time was due largely to the appointment there of a young cleric with a grandiose vision for the Church of England in Australia. Gordon Smee was a balding, slightly-built clergyman in his late twenties, with a genial smile and a frustrated desire to be a professional musician. A man of immense energy, he had involved himself for many years with Sydney's delinquent youth as Anglican Chaplain of the Children's Court, and was responsible for raising £20,000 to build a new centre for re-training delinquent girls for the Home Missions Society – to be modestly called The Gordon Smee Youth Centre. This project seems never to have eventuated.

Never one to shun publicity, the Rev Smee was an outspoken critic of everyone – from his own church authorities, the federal government and especially parents of Sydney's delinquent youth. His comments as Chaplain of the Children's Court were regularly reported in newspapers all over Australia and made people very uncomfortable. When he recommended that the liquor trade in Australia be nationalised, he went a step too far, especially when he added: '…churchmen who are liquor trade shareholders are equally to blame.'[9]

Gordon Smee was replaced in 1944 – having held the post for five years - and banished to the tiny parish of Woolwich – the smallest Anglican parish in Australia. An excellent pianist and organist, as well as a general handyman, the rector set about restoring the church's ancient harmonium, and quickly established a choir of about thirty voices for the main Sunday services. At rehearsals he would conduct vigorously from the organ and left all the choristers in no doubt as to the lofty plans he had in mind for them.

In fact, it was the unbridled musical ambition which the Reverend Gordon Smee held for his church choir which led to my first encounter with Franz Holford.

******

The Anglican minister had been informed that a mysterious musician of superior qualifications lived in nearby Hunters Hill and Rev Smee unhesitatingly undertook to visit him on his daily round of parishioners, despite the address being outside his Woolwich parish. The following Sunday at the choir's rehearsal after the evening service, the rector was beaming:

'I have some exciting news this evening everyone,' he announced. 'You may have heard me talk of a certain musician residing in Hunters Hill who is quite famous – *and* a doctor of music….Well, as you all know, it is difficult even for *me* to play the organ *and* conduct you at that same time, so this week I visited this gentleman and invited him to come and be our conductor.'

An audible expression of wonder rippled through the choir as the rector continued:

'You will no doubt be as overjoyed as I am to know that he has accepted my invitation and… (consulting his watch) … he should in fact be here at any moment...'

As he was speaking, three people entered the church's front door and walked slowly down the aisle towards the choir stalls. One was a dark-haired young man of Byronic visage, accompanied by an elegant woman in her early forties, and the third was a tall male figure wearing a scarlet-lined black cloak and carrying a silver-topped cane in his gloved right hand. The latter shed his cloak, cane and gloves, handing them to the woman and then with hand outstretched, greeted the vicar warmly, nodding and smiling as the Rev Smee introduced him.

'Ladies and gentlemen, may I introduce *Dr* Franz Holford!'

The newcomer smiled again at the choir, revealing a row of perfectly even white teeth.

'How enjoyable it is to meet people devoted to good music on this insular peninsula,' he responded, in a cultivated voice containing more than a trace of irony. A titter of appreciation ran through the choir.

'Och, a Pommie', muttered one of the basses under his breath. Alec Oliver – to whom no one ever referred as anything else but 'Mister Oliver' - was a Scottish rigger at the Dock. He hated the English.

To Jean Harding – an alto, and wife of the Lord Mayor - the experience of meeting the new conductor was life-changing. She was immediately entranced by the charming newcomer, and likened him to a portrait she had once seen of the German composer Gustav Mahler. The mayor, Alex Harding - another Scotsman – was a cabinet maker to whose house I used to go occasionally on weekdays after school where his wife would feed me boiled fruit cake and ice cream. Later, she would volunteer to do the doctor's laundry twice a week for no fee, which struck me as very strange, since everyone knew that as Lady Mayoress, *she* was important enough to have someone come twice a week to her home to do *her* laundry...

Corona Green, a pretty, chestnut-haired 19-year-old, whose brother Leonard was famous for his paintings of Australian landscapes for the front covers of *The Australian Women's Weekly*, was St John's assistant organist to the Rev Gordon Smee. Everyone called her simply, Rona. The young men of Woolwich adored Rona, who eventually disappointed them all by eloping on the pillion seat of a motorbike driven by a young man from outside the village. On this particular night however, when introduced by the rector to Dr Holford as 'our deputy organist', Rona, whose fair skin blushed a deep scarlet, became speechless with embarrassment – later confiding to her friend Pamela Middleton that she felt she was standing in the presence of greatness.

It would be fair to say that each member of that small choir, especially myself – who knew so little about classical music and the qualities which constituted musical greatness – felt the same attraction to the man who now raised an ivory baton and began to instruct us all in the art of choral singing. In the weeks, months and years which followed, Franz Holford would have a profound influence on the lives of a number of people in the small suburb of Woolwich.

******

When he first visited St John's church in 1944, Franz Holford was thirty-five years of age and lived in a stone house 'Norwood' at No 27 Woolwich Road, Hunters Hill. 'Norwood' was one of those homes which engendered in the proud people who occupied them the use of the phrase: 'We of the Hill'. It is now an historic house and appears on heritage lists. Though not as grand as 'Wybalena' - in whose grounds it was originally set - or some of the other mansions built by Charles Edward Jeanneret in the area, it is still the kind of address sought after by the rich and famous.

Several members of the St John's Choir including myself were invited to 'Norwood' for private lessons with Dr Franz Holford in the late 1940s. Hector White – a future music teacher - was another the same age as myself and the mayor's wife another. Even Mr Oliver eventually compromised his principles and brought his own small children to the great man, hoping that they might distinguish themselves in music and not end up mere dock workers - as he saw himself.

I was fourteen when I received the invitation to have free lessons with Dr Holford. I had a pleasant enough boy soprano's voice – on the verge of breaking – and at that time I was having lessons in singing from an organist named Victor Massey[10], who lived in a charming terrace house opposite Woolwich Public School where I had been a primary student. I also sang in Mr Massey's choir on Sunday mornings at St Mark's Darling Point, where he was resident organist and choirmaster.

What I learned from my early visits to 'Norwood' for singing lessons was that Dr Holford - the elegant teacher and conductor - had very little patience with anything 'Australian'. 'Insular peninsula' was not simply a glib phrase he had let drop on the spur of the moment at his first meeting with the St John's Choir, it was a concept of Australia itself which he embraced wholeheartedly. He was impatient with the Australian musical 'establishment', scorning the idea that Australia could produce anything or anyone of quality in *any* of the fine arts, particularly music. It was only in Europe, according to Dr Holford (from whence *he* had come, he maintained) that one could experience art at its highest level. Yet, I found him to be a relatively poor vocal music teacher when compared with Victor Massey, who had trained so many young boys' voices and knew how to produce those thrilling boy soprano tones, besides being a stickler for musical detail. Even at my young age and lack of musical experience, I could sense a certain authority in Victor Massey's teaching which seemed to be lacking in that of Dr Franz Holford. What Dr Holford possessed in abundance however was charisma, which Victor Massey did not.

The choir of St Mark's Darling Point was infinitely superior to that of St John's Woolwich, by reason of its having trained voices and of being well directed. Nevertheless, such was the power of his personality that when Dr Holford advised me – in the gentlest of fashion – of the aphorism that 'Man cannot serve two masters', I ceased going to Mr Massey's house and instead began visiting 'Norwood' on Sunday mornings for singing lessons.

******

There is a charming description of 'Norwood' in Phillip Wilcher's article written for *Music Teacher Magazine*. Though written in 1974 – some twenty years after my time there, the essential details of the house remain much the same to this day.

> 'Twenty Seven' was an old stone house, secluded by a high stone fence on which had grown a rambling hedge. After unbolting a heavy wooden gate you would approach the house from a gently curving cobbled path, flanked on either side by leaf-shadowed lawns, gingko and cherry trees.[11]

Ah yes, that 'heavy wooden gate' - I remember it well - for I had built it, along with other renovations I carried out at 'Norwood' in the Spring of 1954. Phillip Wilcher's description of 'Norwood' was shared by most people who visited the house, and on my own first visit there in 1944 when I was a choirboy of fourteen, I too had been struck by the very 'English' nature of the house and especially of the garden, which was dominated by flowers such as crocuses, foxgloves, violets and roses.

There were eight rooms in the house, plus a small kitchen, laundry and bathroom at the back, which opened out to a small paved courtyard, lawn and vegetable garden. There was a lane at the rear named Glenview Crescent, and a letterbox on the wooden paling fence, where the mail was delivered. On the walls of the hallway which led to Dr Holford's study were etchings of English cathedrals, paintings of fox hunting and chocolate box illustrations of thatched cottages and landscapes by artists such as John Constable. The study was the epitome of an English gentleman, with walls lined by cedar bookcases filled with rare editions. In the centre of the room was a cedar desk with a green fabric inlay and in the bay window gleamed a black 'boudoir' size Blüthner grand piano.

Adjoining Dr Holford's study was a bedroom, and on the Sunday morning of my first visit, as he led me through the hallway to his study I glimpsed an old lady sitting by the window in a rocking chair, her legs and knees covered by a blanket and with a violet-coloured shawl around her shoulders. She was a little emaciated with old age, but she had an abundance of pure white hair, fastened with a tortoise shell comb, which gleamed in a shaft of morning light streaming through the window. As we passed her door, she called out in a high, querulous tone:

'Who's that, Bill?'

At the sound of the name, Dr Holford paused, and looked at me sharply as I stood awkwardly in the hallway. Then he gestured for me to go into the study. As I did so, I heard the old lady call again.

'Is someone there, Bill?'

He excused himself, and entered the bedroom, where I heard him speak sternly to the old lady, then he returned, closing the study door after him.

'My mother,' he explained. 'Sometimes she calls me Bill as a nickname… silly old possum.'

Being called 'Bill' by his mother was the first of many odd things I was to learn about Dr Franz Holford in the years which followed and his life unfolded.

St John's Anglican Church, Woolwich, built in 1892. It was the centre of the smallest Anglican parish in Australia.

(Above) 'Norwood' in 1947, built by Charles Edward Jeanneret in the 1870s. (Photograph by the author)

The author in the garden at 'Norwood'

Practising on Franz Holford's Blüthner piano. (Photos by John Champ)

Lineage

Though fresh devices come,
Yet is my custom true;
There my vocation is,
That was my cradle too.
Far wave, far heaven, far hill,
I dream of England still.

- DRINKWATER

2

Holford is a very common name in Walsall, Staffordshire, in the midlands of England. In the Pleck District there is even a street named Holford Avenue. Franz Holford's father, William Webster Holford was born in the Pleck in 1861.[12] In the 19th Century, Walsall was a coalmining town and its craftsmen were known for making ironware tools for the mines, and equipment for horses, such as collars, saddles, stirrups, bits and braces.

However, like many 19th century English towns, Walsall was dirty and unsanitary. There were outbreaks of cholera in 1832 and 1849 and a smallpox epidemic in 1872. As a young man in his twenties, William Webster Holford eyed the clean air of Australia and like so many other British workers seeking a better life, decided to emigrate. He arrived in the colony - presumably on assisted passage - around 1882.[13]

Already skilled in the craft of horse collar-making, William Holford apprenticed himself to another migrant, John Perkins[14], a harness maker who lived in the Surry Hills of old Sydney Town. Perkins had come to Australia with his parents and siblings on the *North Britain* in 1839, and married Ellen Elizabeth Smith, the daughter of a convict, in Sydney in

1856.[15] They had two children, Annie Elizabeth (b.1868) and William (b.1872). Although John and Ellen were apparently illiterate, their children were well educated, and Annie was taught dressmaking and to play the piano. William was taught the violin and later in life played the mandolin. The Holford and Perkins families became very close, and indeed remained friends for life.[16] When he was 26, William Webster Holford asked John Perkins for his daughter Annie's hand in marriage. She was just nineteen.

They were married on Christmas Eve, 24 December 1887 under the rites of the Church of England at 244 Devonshire Street Sydney, and between the years 1888-1904 they had six children: Fanny Elinor (1888), Mabel Vera (1892), John George (1894), George W (1896), Frank (1898), and Harry Webster (1904). The family lived at 51 Andreas Street, Petersham, in a house they occupied for the next twenty-four years. On 9th November 1909 William and Annie's eldest daughter Fanny, then 21 – gave birth to an illegitimate child, born at the family home in Andreas Street, Petersham.[17] She named the child Albert, and Fanny was the sole informant of the event. No father's name appeared on the Birth Certificate and the father was never named. Four years later, Fanny left the baby with her parents and went to live in Leichhardt, where she began earning her own living as a dressmaker. A year later in 1914[18] she married Albert Youngs, by whom she had a daughter, whom she named Edna. There were no further children.

Fanny Holford was William ('Franz') Holford's biological mother.

At the time Fanny left the baby Albert with her mother, Annie Elizabeth Holford was 41 years of age. Annie re-named the boy William (though not by Deed Poll), and began raising him as her own child. In this era unwed mothers were usually forced by social pressure to give their children up for adoption, although laws governing adoption did not come into force until 1924. It was quite common for illegitimate children to be reared by grandparents or married relatives as the 'sisters', 'brothers' or 'cousins' of unwed mothers.[19]

The question is: who was William ('Franz') Holford's biological father? If Fanny had named her son after Albert Youngs and *he* was the father – why would they not have reclaimed the child when their marriage was made official? And why would Annie re-name him William, after her own husband's name? Was the real reason to do with incest between William Webster Holford and his own daughter Fanny? Such a dark scenario would indeed provide the motive in later years for William ('Franz') Holford to avoid questions relating to his birth and allow many different myths to develop around his parentage.

In their book *A Franz Holford Miscellany*, the authors Jennifer Hill and Kerry Murphy have noted: 'The picture of him that emerges is one of a man who was in many ways troubled about his past.[20'] This was a major understatement, for Franz Holford was *so* troubled about his past that he carried the secret of his birth to the grave - his last stated wish being 'to avoid all publicity after my death'.[21]

It is most likely that Franz Holford's early piano tuition was given by his adopted mother Annie Elizabeth Holford, and possibly from his birth mother Fanny, for Annie is described on a 1940 Electoral Roll Form as 'Music Teacher'.[22]

Franz Holford of course never acknowledged such humble musical roots – always claiming to have been a prodigy fashioned by the great European masters of the piano such as Cortot, Teichmüller and others. However, it is likely that he was also a protégé of the famous Australian de Cairos-Rego family, who lived in Marrickville – a suburb adjacent to Petersham - where the Holfords lived. This remarkable family consisted of George de Cairos-Rego[23] and his two children Iris and Rex. There seems little doubt that the Holford and de Cairos Rego families were well acquainted at this time.

When approached for piano tuition by the Rev Gordon Smee in the 1940s, Franz Holford referred the rector instead to Rex de Cairos-Rego, intimating that he himself had studied with a member of the de Cairos-Rego family.[24] Whether this was the old man George, or his son Rex is not clear, but evidence of this family's influence on Holford may be seen in the latter's compositions, whose titles bear a remarkable similarity to those of George de Cairos-Rego, and to those of his daughter Iris and son Rex.

NEW SOUTH WALES
BIRTHS, DEATHS AND MARRIAGES REGISTRATION ACT 1995

REGISTRATION NUMBER: 7599/1910

BIRTH CERTIFICATE

1 CHILD	
Family Name	HOLFORD
Christian or Given Name(s)	Albert
Sex	Male
Date of Birth	09 November 1909
Place of Birth	51 Andreas Street, Petersham
2 MOTHER	
Family Name	HOLFORD
Maiden Family Name	HOLFORD
Christian or Given Name(s)	Fanny Elinor
Occupation	-
Age	21 years
Place of Birth	Sydney, NSW
3 FATHER	
Family Name	-
Christian or Given Name(s)	
Occupation	
Age	
Place of Birth	
4 MARRIAGE OF PARENTS	
Date of Marriage	
Place of Marriage	
5 PREVIOUS CHILDREN OF RELATIONSHIP	
6 INFORMANT(S)	
Name	Certified by: Fanny E. Holford
Address	51 Andreas Street, Petersham
	Mother
7 REGISTERING AUTHORITY	
Name	Florence Rossiter, District Registrar
Date	07 January 1910
8 ENDORSEMENT(S)	
Not any	

FRANZ HOLFORD
BIRTH CERTIFICATE

Before accepting copies, sight unaltered original. The original has a coloured background.

REGISTRY OF BIRTHS DEATHS AND MARRIAGES
SYDNEY 28 Nov 2003

I hereby certify that this is a true copy of particulars recorded in a Register in the State of New South Wales, in the Commonwealth of Australia.

Registrar

Franz Holford's Birth Certificate. His mother christened the baby Albert and certified the birth mother as Fanny Elinor Holford. There is no acknowledgment of the father. He was re-named William and raised by Fanny's parents Annie and William Webster Holford.

Franz (William) Holford, at the age of about nine years. (Photograph given to the author by Franz Holford in 1947)

George's composition *Hymn of the Commonwealth* (1901), which he hoped would become the 'Official Hymn of the Commonwealth', bears a striking resemblance to Franz Holford's *An Australian National Anthem*, written in 1954, and to *The Fair Elizabeth*, (1954), also written in 1954, to commemorate the visit of Queen Elizabeth II to Australia, which Holford also hoped would become an official anthem, to be played on ceremonial occasions. However, neither he nor George's hopes for governmental recognition of their anthems were ever realized.

George de Cairos-Rego was also music critic for the *Sydney Daily Telegraph* and wrote significant articles recommending the establishment of a conservatorium of music in Sydney. Franz Holford also would later become a music critic for *The Northern District Times*. There are many echoes of similarity between the life style of members of the de Cairos-Rego family and that which Franz Holford would subsequently adopt. Rex de Cairos-Rego, who gradually dropped 'Cairos' from his name and became known as Rex de Rego, was a good teacher, and had some very talented students at his Sydney studio, playing the big masterpieces of piano literature which Franz Holford also studied. One of these students was Barrie Brettoner[25], who gave a recital in Sydney on 18 February 1930 which included Beethoven's *Appassionata* Sonata, an *Arabesque* by Schultz-Evier and *Etudes Symphoniques* by Schumann.[26]

The Cairos-Rego studio was in Ash Street, behind Paling's music shop, and only a short distance from Breville's, where Franz Holford worked in the glassware department for a period after he left school. It is more than likely that the young Holford took piano lessons in his lunch hour by walking up to the Cairos-Rego studio at Paling's, or after-hours in Petersham.

******

In 1926, at the age of sixty-five, William Webster Holford retired from the harness trade and bought a milk run, which he operated for a few years before full retirement. In 1931, the Holfords, with their unmarried daughter Mabel (1892-1936) and the young William (Franz), moved from Petersham to 34 Rutledge Street Eastwood, where William, after a stint with Brevilles in Sydney and now aged twenty-one, commenced his career as a piano teacher, and was now listed as such on the electoral rolls and in the Sydney telephone directory.

A few years after launching his new career, William engaged in some public debate in the media, following a plea from the renowned Percy Grainger for modern composers to embrace 'free' music. In a letter to the *Sydney Morning Herald*, a certain Ernest Wunderlich[27] deplored Grainger's comments, saying they...'would undermine the very foundations of the art.'[28]

The 25-year-old William Holford agreed with Wunderlich, suggesting in the letters column of the *Sydney Morning Herald* that an application of the ideas proposed by Percy Grainger would be 'nothing less than suicide.'

(Above) Earliest known piano recital in Eastwood, given when Franz was twenty-seven. Calling himself William Holford, the program is dated November 19th, 1936, with associate artist, his student Gordon (Gorden) Day. (Photo by John Champ)

(Right) A photograph taken a few years later, after Franz Holford and his wife Marjorie Cole had moved into the house 'Norwood' at Hunters Hill. (Photo by John Champ)

He went on to write:

> We have a young generation to train, and an environment that is not as helpful as it may seem, from a musical standpoint at least.
> One cannot agree with the views of Mr Grainger the iconoclast as readily as one can with Mr Grainger the classical pianist and with the combined ideas of Schoenberg, Scott, and various others too. I doubt sincerely their ability to write anything worthy to follow Beethoven's immortal nine, both in freedom and melodic invention. I am more inclined to believe the statement made some months ago in Prague by Prokofieff who said that 'revolutionary gestures in

music' had relinquished their grip, and that compositions of a simpler character were the coming new order – let us hope he adopts them.[29]

This initial conservative outlook on the future of music by the young William Holford would later be reflected in the compositions of his doppelgänger Franz Holford, who rarely indulged in dissonant harmonies or complex musical language. Indeed, in later years the Australian composer Larry Sitsky was very dismissive of Franz Holford's *oeuvre*:

> Franz Holford wrote a good deal of oboe/piano music and some clarinet/piano music too. I confess to being bored with it; my harmony professor, Alex Burnard, used to refer to such harmonic progressions as we find here, as 'slops'. Need I say more?'[30]

After a short period settling into the new suburb of Eastwood in 1936, the 27-year-old William Holford gave a piano recital in the Eastwood Masonic Hall, assisted by one of his pupils, Gorden *(sic)* Day. The rare surviving printed program of this concert reveals a demanding list of virtuosic works, such as the Tausig arrangement of a Scarlatti Sonata and Busoni's arrangement of a Bach Toccata.

On the same program he performed a piano sonata by Felix Weingartner, which he described in a program note as '…slightly Beethovian in style'.[31] The latter may well have been an improvised composition of Franz's own, for though the great Austrian conductor was a prolific composer, it appears he never wrote a piano sonata.[32]

Somewhere between 1936-1937 William Holford changed his name and became an established music teacher in Eastwood, where he gave regular recitals with his best pupils and with those selected from the studios of other music teachers in the district.

Some of his students were entered for examinations conducted for the Australian Music Examinations Board (AMEB) by the State Conservatorium of Music. Among these were G Day (Grade II Honours, 1937), and K Knight (Grade V Credit, 1937).[33]

He also included in these recitals students from other studios, including those of a Danish violin teacher Henry Lykke.

Advertisement in Northern District Times, 14 October 1937.

Henry Christian Lykke (1882-1972) was an interesting musician. Awarded a scholarship at the age of twelve by The Australian Musical Association, he went on to become a violin performer and teacher, then turned his hand to violin making. He made just under 100 violins, most of which were sold through A E Smith & Sons, Sydney.[34] Franz (William) Holford was at this time in his late twenties, and he began contributing a regular column on music to the district newspaper *The Northern District Times*.

What set his own subsequent recitals apart from others occurring elsewhere was that his were always followed by a glowing review in this newspaper under the by-line of pseudonyms such as 'Don Giovanni', 'Arioso' or 'Toccata' – and at one time 'Franz' - the same kind of pseudonyms Franz Holford was to use later when writing reviews in his own music magazine *Canon*. Since suburban newspapers of this era seldom employed specialist music review journalists, it is most likely that these reviews were written by Franz Holford himself – possibly at the invitation of the editor, who was himself an amateur flautist.

William Holford used the Christian name Franz publicly for the first time in a duo recital with Henry Lykke at the Masonic Hall, Eastwood, 28th October 1937. It is worth publishing the subsequent review of this concert in its entirety, for if indeed the review was written by Holford himself, using a pen name, it is an astonishing act of self-aggrandisement:

Holford – Lykke Recital
(By 'Toccata')

Last Thursday evening at the Eastwood Masonic Hall, a crowded and enthusiastic audience assembled for the classical recital presented by two well-known local musicians, Franz Holford (pianist) and Henry Lykke (violinist).

The concert must surely have been unique for the district, as regards the programme chosen, the major portion being devoted to comparatively modern composers, and considerable interest was also added by the first public performance of a violin and piano sonata composed by Mr Holford.

The programme opened with the Sonata for violin and piano in D Major, Op 12 No 1 of Beethoven, and both lovers and students of the great master had an invaluable lesson on 'how to play Beethoven'. The artists gave a strictly classical rendering - there were no exaggerated lapses toward the romantic, no rubati that were not logical, and yet it was no austere reading, and the melodic interest was never lacking. Particular mention must be made to the skilful handling of the second movement comprising a set of typically Beethoven variations, and to the sparkling Allegro in 6/8 time which closes the sonata.

Franz Holford was then heard in a bracket of pianoforte items. To the serious musician, modern music in all its forms has provided a wide and comprehensive field for evolving effect, and the pianist provided startling contrasts, firstly an inspiring performance of the Chorale (Cesar Franck), and from the ponderous, quasi-religious nature of the organist composer passed on to a tone picture by Felix Weingartner – "a romantic reflection of old Heidelberg" – revealing rare glimpses of love, laughter and pathos, played with extreme delicacy and expression, and finally Scherzo Fantastique, a forceful and weird study by that much discussed Russian Prokofieff, whose work has excited more controversy than that of any other contemporary composer. Here the pianist displayed a remarkable dexterity in handling the keyboard, and as an encore chose an Etude by Stravinsky.

Music is not the prerogative of the few; it is a thing that has sprung from the very souls of the people themselves. Even in history the down-trodden have been inarticulate in words, through music they have found a truer expression, and the following folk song has been taken by the great masters and developed into a language that transcends word, and it was with the keenest anticipation we awaited Mr Holford's Danish Sonata in G Minor, which the annotations explained was based on a Danish folk song. Following a few soft introductory chords on the piano, the tune is given out by the violin, and this lovely melody dominates the entire work, and Mr Lykke succeeded in maintaining a beautiful tone throughout. This sonata is a delightfully conceived work, with no attempts at artificial effects, full of melody and exciting rhythms.

Rachmaninoff's Sonata in D Minor Op 28 is the first of the two piano sonatas by this composer, and it is an extremely dramatic and difficult work demanding an impeccable technique and intellectual concentration, and Mr Holford gave an amazingly brilliant performance of the whole sonata, and was recalled several times.

The beautiful sonata for violin and piano in A Major by Cesar Franck completed the programme. This work (considered by many to be the most outstanding composition of its type since Beethoven) was written in 1886, and dedicated to the violinist Eugene Ysaye as a wedding gift. It was played with noble simplicity and artistic restraint and the collaboration of the two artists resulted in a sincere and emotional reading, with no straining after technical bravura. At the conclusion of the recital both performers were given a splendid ovation, proving unquestionably that there is the need for artists of the calibre of these two gentlemen to present anything less than first-class music *(sic)*.[36]

The need for William Holford to change his Christian name to Franz may have been influenced by a number of events at this time. For a start, he was beginning to be 'noticed' as a serious musician – as a teacher, solo pianist, and now composer – and people were beginning to ask: 'Who *is* this man? Who was his teacher? Where did he study?'

His growing reputation was enhanced in the year which followed, when on 9th April 1938 he was featured in a recital sponsored by The Churches of Christ Musical and Literary Society at St James's Hall, Sydney. His associate artists were Amy Carey[37] (soprano), Daphne Flood (contralto), Olive Wood (violinist) and his pupil Gorden Day. Under a banner heading: 'Local Artists in City Concert – Fine performances', the concert was again reviewed in the newspaper he wrote for, this time by 'Arioso', who was unstinting in his praise of the principal artist:

> To return to Mr Holford. As he advanced in his programme, so he advanced in command over the huge Steinway, until his playing became something to marvel at, particularly in the great Rachmaninov Sonata. Here, I thought, he displayed his capabilities in such a manner as to positively thrill his hearers. It was a great performance.[38]

The publicity caused people to begin asking him awkward questions about his lineage and his musical pedigree. Those responsible for organizing his recitals quite naturally required such things as a biography to publish in his programs and to use for publicity purposes. Fellow musicians and music teachers were discussing him. Audiences attending his concerts wanted to read about him. Journalists wanted to interview him. Where had he come from? Who were his teachers?

What could he tell them? That he was the illegitimate son of a horse collar and saddle maker, whose principal piano teacher was his mother? Unthinkable. If he was also aware that there was possibly the additional stigma of incest in his background, it represented a terrifying scenario that he would never want to become public knowledge.

Thus, he began to invent stories about his past.

Perhaps his adopted mother Annie may have been a willing accomplice in these fantasies, since the circumstances surrounding his birth must have been gruesome and painful episodes for her as well. In their book *A Franz Holford Miscellany*, the authors state: 'Holford told different tales to different friends' and they document various versions of his lineage: James Murdoch in his obituary in *The Australian* set his place of birth in Heidelberg; Jamie Kassler understood Holford's mother to have been lady-in-waiting to Princess Eugenie; Betty Beath believed that his mother was called Charlotte and was related to the Belgian Court of Leopold II.

Others linked him to the court of Kaiser Wilhelm. Jiri Tancibudek, the Sydney Symphony Orchestra's oboist who recorded Holford's composition *Summer Madrigal* for the ABC, said in an interview that Holford gave out the impression that he was the illegitimate son of the German conductor Felix Weingartner.[39] And so it went on...

Programs presented by him in this period reflect a continuing interest in the piano works of Felix Weingartner, who was very famous in Germany at the time as a conductor. In fact, Franz Holford used every opportunity at this time to identify himself closely with Felix Weingartner, who never visited Australia and whom most Australian music lovers at the time would only have known through gramophone recordings.

The month after his Sydney recital at St James Church he gave similar programs in Casino and Lismore, assisted by the soprano Marjorie Cole and a tenor who presented some of Holford's own songs. Later in the year he briefly replaced Doris Hammond, the regular music columnist for the *Northern District Times*. Hammond was a pupil of Cyril Monk and Frank Hutchens, and left the newspaper to marry its editor, who was a flute teacher in the district.

In the latter half of 1938 something seems to have occurred which caused Franz Holford to panic. Perhaps someone decided to investigate his background and found that it did not equate with the stories he was putting about. He published an open letter in *The Northern District Times*, warning those who were 'defaming his name' that he would take libel action against them if such practice continued.[40] There is no indication as to what people were saying about him, but his solution was to leave the district and to get married.

In December 1939, shortly after the declaration of WWII, he left the family home at Eastwood, and relocated, first to Beecroft and then to Artarmon and on 16th December married the singer Marjorie Doris Cole, whom he had known for several years.[41] She was around the same age, and was enjoying a burgeoning career as a soloist on the ABC. On his Marriage Certificate he signed himself 'Franz W Holford', but soon William was dropped altogether.

Franz Holford was thirty at the time of his marriage. He had always lived with his adopted parents William Webster and Annie Holford, and appears never to have lacked for anything. Finding himself now with a wife to support and his only income deriving from teaching and performing, he decided to return to the financial status quo by inviting William and Annie to share the house with him and his new bride.

As a result of a lifetime of hard work and thrift, William Webster Holford was financially comfortable – being described on his Death Certificate as of 'independent means'.[42]

Together with William Webster and Annie Holford, the newly-married couple moved to Hunters Hill. The house 'Norwood' which the Holford family rented, belonged to the d'Apice family, and for some reason Franz Holford was given the house in perpetuity at the rent of a mere £1 a month, and he became a 'protected tenant'.[43] Under the Landlord and Tenant Act, protected tenants were absolved from rent increases and eviction, and they came to be loathed by landlords. In a curiously ironic twist, the original owner of 'Norwood', the Chevalier Charles d'Apice - who was a genuine Chevalier of the Papal Order of the Golden Spur or the Golden Militia - was also a composer and performer, and was said to have been a professor at the Conservatorium of Naples.

He taught music at Riverview College across the river from Hunters Hill, from the school's opening until his death in 1888. For the next 25 years

'Dr' Franz Holford would live virtually rent-free in one of the loveliest historic houses of one of the wealthiest suburbs in Sydney.

(Left) Chevalier Charles d'Apice (1817-1888), an Italian Professor of Music. (Below) Henry Lykke, Danish violinist and violin maker. A collection of his violins is in the Sydney Powerhouse Museum.

Hunters Hill

*In his imagination rang,
through generations challenging
his peal on simple men.*

- DRINKWATER

3

When he moved to Hunters Hill in the summer of 1940 as a married man of 31, Franz Holford unwittingly acquired another good reason for keeping a low profile (in addition to his lineage). World war II had just commenced, and in substituting the name 'Franz' for William, his newly adopted persona made him vulnerable to accusations of being a German alien, for which citizens in Australia were being detained in internment camps across the nation.[44] It would not have helped that he had also led certain people to believe that he was born and educated in Heidelberg, and that the sounds of German composers such as Bach, Beethoven and Brahms could be heard emanating from a piano somewhere behind the hedges of 'Norwood'.[45]

It was also fortunate for him that as yet he had not told too many people that his father had been a private consultant to Kaiser Wilhelm!

During the war he discontinued public appearances as a pianist, and concentrated on composition - writing mainly songs for his wife Marjorie and a number of well-known tenors such as William Herbert and Ereach Riley. He also tried his hand at writing poetry. All these activities could be carried out in the privacy of his own home and generated little publicity. Perhaps inspired by his brief time as a columnist for *The Northern District Times* he made sporadic forays into the field of publishing, writing three little books of poems, entitled *The building of Goblin Town*[46], *Through the Casement*[47], and *Tone Poems*[48], which he privately published in 1941 through the publisher/printer Deaton and Spencer. One wonders what audience he had in mind for these little books, for the idiosyncratic writing seems too adult for children, yet too naive to be taken seriously by older readers. They didn't sell – perhaps they were never even marketed commercially - and the unsold copies became little tokens of affection which he regularly gave away to friends, or those he was attempting to influence or impress. He also attempted short story writing, without success.[49]

There is nothing to indicate in this period of his life that he was earning a steady income, or indeed *any* income apart from a few piano students – most of whom he taught *gratis*; nor was his wife Marjorie contributing financially to the marriage. One can only assume that apart from any fees earned from his students, the two of them were being supported by William Webster Holford and his wife Annie, who had retired from music teaching.

However, he had chosen well by electing to settle in Hunters Hill. Rich families abounded in this very 'English' of Sydney suburbs, and Franz Holford was about to cultivate some of the best and wealthiest, as he cast about for new students. To equip himself to meet new people he had no compunction in illegally adding 'Dr' to his name when introducing himself, even letting it be known that he was in fact a doctor three times over – of Medicine, Philosophy and of course, Music.[50] Such was his charisma that his personality enabled him to fit any of these profiles quite convincingly. Those professional doctors of medicine whom he later cultivated as personal friends - such as Stuart Scougall, Robert Murphy and Mary Bertram – must have been aware that his claim to be a doctor of medicine was spurious, but such was his personal charm that no one seemed prepared to confront him, nor to question his motives for illegally adopting these honorifics.

There were no children from the Holford marriage, and Marjorie must have learned very quickly that whilst Franz Holford cared very much *about* other people – indeed cultivated them extensively - there was only one person he ever really cared *for*, and that was himself. The circumstances surrounding his birth, parentage and upbringing ensured that he would be indulged and probably greatly spoilt, yet would never know true parental love – especially not the holding and possessive love of a biological mother who had left him, nor from an aloof, adopted, and as he saw it, an uneducated father.

In the only surviving 'family photo' of him at about age eight, which he gave to the author in 1947 (see p.22), he sits in a bentwood chair – legs crossed, arms crossed and with a furrowed brow – staring straight at the camera…an angry boy. His body language says: 'I will take on the whole world…and no one will ever get close to me.'

With a superior attitude to all those around him, it seems that he would never learn *how* to love. When he decided to marry it was more than likely a 'marriage of convenience', since his intended partner was a singer of his songs and someone he could lean upon socially to enhance his own life. It is doubtful that he ever told his wife the truth about his lineage, and there must have been internecine conflict within the Holford family from the very beginning, as Marjorie tried in vain to find out the real facts surrounding her very strange, narcissistic husband.

Two years after moving to 'Norwood', in 1942, William Webster Holford died of asthma, at the age of 81. The death certificate listed five children (one deceased) of his marriage to Annie, but did not list William (Franz). The informant was Franz Holford, who gave his relationship to William Webster as 'son', but did not list himself as a child of the marriage.[51] Whatever remained of William Webster Holford's 'independent means' appears to have been dissipated also, since no property or money was left to his children[52] in the Will.

******

Having secured a patron in the form of the d'Apice Family, who had virtually gifted him a magnificent house at £1 a month in perpetuity, Franz Holford began to look around at other families in Hunters Hill which might provide him with students, or other forms of income which a musician seeking to maintain a low profile but a rich lifestyle might acquire.

Opposite 'Norwood' in Woolwich Road was an inventor, Cecil Harden, who wished to have his daughter Susan taught piano.[53] Cecil claimed to have invented the washing machine and included in his Mitty-like fantasies the anecdote that when he was in America he was such an important figure that if he dropped his hat, three men would bang their heads together to be the first to pick it up. Franz Holford eyed him with a certain scepticism, for although the inventor and his family of three lived in a lovely old two-storied stone cottage, it was badly in need of renovation, and they seemed to have fallen on hard times. Holford could not afford to associate with failures. He took the little girl as a pupil, but kept his distance from the inventor, whose proclivity for fantasy was as rampant as his own. On either side of him were neighbours whom he also chose to avoid, since he became convinced that one of them had reported him to the authorities as a German spy.

(Above) Hancock Pianos in the 1930s, with the staff assembled on the footpath. Franz Holford was a regular visitor here, and acquired his own Blüthner Grand from Harry Hancock. (Photograph by courtesy Donald Newton)

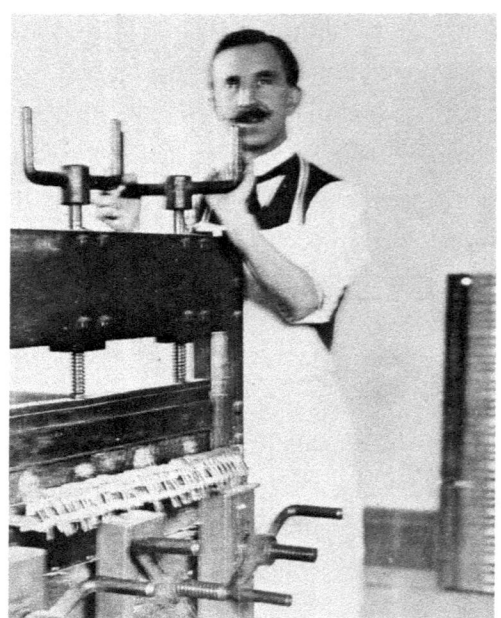 

(Left) Harry Hancock, seen here with his re-felting machine for repairing piano keyboards and hammers. (Right) Reg Newton, who worked at Hancock's as piano tuner. He regularly tuned Franz Holford's pianos over a long period, and his son Donald became one of Holford's most accomplished piano students. (Photographs by courtesy Donald Newton)

His search for a new piano to install in his study at 'Norwood' led him to the western suburbs of Sydney, to Hancock's Pianos where he not only found a superbly suitable Blüthner boudoir grand, but a piano tuner of excellence in the person of Reg Newton, whom Hancock's employed. Reg Newton not only cared for the piano for many years, but also immediately engaged the impressive 'Dr Holford' as a piano teacher for his son Donald.

Hancock's Pianos was on the corner of Constitution Road and New Canterbury Road, Dulwich Hill, a two-storey building where the Hancocks lived upstairs and owned a reasonably sized showroom on the ground floor with entrance to the showroom across the front corner. Despite shortages caused by WWII, they had a good array of upright pianos and a few grands such as the Blüthner, in the 5-foot range.[54]

The workshop for the business was in a building attached to the showroom. Hancock's business was restoring pianos, mainly by re-polishing, and this was carried out downstairs. Other work, such as re-felting the actions, re-covering worn keys or whitening and re-polishing the ivory keys, re-covering hammers, winding the bass strings to replace old and dirty ones etc. was done upstairs. Hancock's had to buy pianos cheaply and carry out all this labour intensive work in order to prepare them for sale.

Part of their business was to cultivate piano teachers, who would come to the shop with parents wishing to buy pianos for their students. This was the way Franz Holford met the Newton family and acquired Reg Newton as his tuner, who stayed loyal to him for many years.

*****

There came a company man

I strut around my stately life
hand in hand with lover and wife
I even own a share or two
in a family firm my father grew

- JULIAN FRANKS

4

A far more important Hunters Hill family with whom Franz Holford became associated early in his musical career was the Champ family. It was an association which would last over fifty years. Reginald Champ was the son of the General Manager of the prominent company John Lysaght and married Gwendolyn Clarke in 1926, so Franz would have been in his early twenties when he first met the family.

At the time of his marriage Reginald was thirty-two, and was thus some fifteen years older than Franz. Gwen Champ's family, the Clarke's[55], lived in Ashfield, which was the next suburb to Petersham, where Franz Holford lived. Gwendolyn – a dark-haired beauty - was nine years older than Franz.

How they met is not clear. Perhaps Gwen Champ sought out Franz, who was already known locally as a musician in the district, as a conveniently placed teacher for her son Reginald John (who dropped his father's Christian name and was thereafter professionally known as John Champ[56]). John was born in 1927 and however it came about, he became a piano pupil of Holford[57] when a small child.

Reg Champ became Franz Holford's unacknowledged benefactor and patron when Franz and his wife Marjorie moved to Hunters Hill, where the Champs had finally settled three years before in 1937. Reg had a deep love of the piano, and as it turned out proved a generous patron of the arts. A brief description of his life is therefore relevant.

******

Reginald Champ's history is impressive. He was the son of Reginald Champ Snr, a 'land owner', who was born in London in 1863.[58] Reginald Snr came to Australia after a failed attempt at establishing the silk trade in London. An imaginative entrepreneur, in 1887 he had visited China to study the raw silk trade, with an eye to establishing a company in London, but when the project failed, he decided to try it in Australia - migrating to Sydney in 1890. In 1891, Sir Henry Parkes, then Colonial Secretary, agreed to the appointment of Reginald Champ Snr as overseer of the first official attempt to establish commercial sericulture in Australia. There appeared to have been encouraging results early, but Champ lacked sufficient knowledge of the local landscape and the scheme gradually failed.[59] A full history of Reginald Champ Snr's attempts to establish a silk industry in Australia is to be found in the Mitchell Library.[60]

Reginald Snr married Hobart-born Alpha Hindes in Port Adelaide in 1891, but by the time their son Reginald Malcolm was born in 1894 the family had moved to Burwood, NSW. He moved his young family early in 1906 to Hunters Hill and lived in Brown Street in a house called 'Medindie'[61] (Brown Street no longer exists on local maps). They moved again, this time to Drummoyne to a house named 'Melton', in order to be closer to the Lysaght factory. By 1937 however, they were back in Hunters Hill.

The family prospered through Reginald Snr's long association with John Lysaght, which became the largest manufacturer of wire in Australia. In 1926 he was finally appointed to the top job of Managing Director, on a salary which would allow him to invest in property, play golf at the Royal Manly Club and indulge his twin passions of tennis and motoring. When Reginald Malcolm Jnr left school, he too joined Lysaght's, and ultimately rose to the same position as his father, by which time the company had expanded enormously, finally joining with the giant ore manufacturing company BHP.

'Threlkeld', the two-storied mansion of the Champ Family in Hunters Hill. The house occupied a quarter acre block, with an orchard and tennis court. (Photo John Champ)

The workbooks of Reginald Malcolm Champ's father - also Reginald - who carried out a long campaign at the highest levels of government in an attempt to establish a silk industry in Australia. (Mitchell Library MLMSS 9473)

Reg's address at the time of his marriage was Drummoyne[62], and his occupation was Assistant Works Manager at Lysaght's.[63] In 1929 he was promoted to Company Manager of Lysaght's, a position which carried a huge salary in the company which joined with BHP and later Billiton, to form BHP Billiton, the biggest minerals manufacturer in the world.

In 1937 Reg moved back to the suburb he had grown up in and bought a two-storey mansion 'Threlkeld' in Woolwich Road, Hunters Hill, situated on a quarter acre block with a tennis court.

Here, he settled down with his wife and two children[64], and it was here he met 'Dr' Franz Holford.

Tailpiece for The Canon

'Threlkeld'

To send light into the darkness of men's hearts –
such is the duty of the artist.

- SCHUMANN

5

It was in Hunters Hill that Franz Holford enjoyed his halcyon years. Having assisted the Champ family in the purchase of two concert size Steinway grands – most likely for a handsome agent's fee - he proceeded to ingratiate himself with Reginald Champ, who was determined to indulge his attractive young wife's passion for the arts.

Gwen Champ was a beautiful, cultivated and intelligent socialite who hosted regular dinner parties for her successful husband and welcomed anyone to their table who could add to their standing in Hunters Hill society. Gwen had made the acquaintance of a Melbourne rare bookseller, Doris Eddey, who ran the Melbourne company N H Seward. On one of Eddey's trips to Sydney to visit the Champs, who had become a valued client of her bookshop, she was introduced to Franz Holford, who then proceeded to usurp her position as the go-between for the Champs with Seward's Bookshop.

He persuaded Doris Eddey to send the selected books first to him, and he would then 'on-sell' the ones he didn't keep for himself to the Champs, and to other newly acquired acquaintances and friends. Many of these volumes were extremely rare and worth hundreds of pounds each, so there was a fair profit to be made.

Franz Holford also benefited from Doris Eddey's extensive knowledge of literature. Though chiefly interested in Australiana, she also had a great understanding of English literature and many of the texts which Franz took for the songs he composed came from volumes of the English poets she recommended, such as John Drinkwater, Shelley, W H Davies, Mary Coleridge, W B Yeats and John Galsworthy.

Gwen Champ and her husband became luminaries of Hunters Hill society. With their magnificent two-storey house and lawn tennis court, Reg was a generous host and an excellent tennis player, who welcomed players from the local tennis club to 'Threlkeld' on Saturday afternoons. Gwen began organizing musical soirees on Saturday nights in her beautiful music room – a perfect setting, with French doors opening out onto a patio overlooking a lovely garden. The large room could comfortably seat twenty or thirty people, and the principal artists at these musical evenings were of course Dr Franz Holford and his wife, the soprano Marjorie Cole. Franz's compositions featured heavily in these programs, and occasionally the Champ children John and Judy added an amusing dimension to the entertainment, as his students.[65]

The Champs bought the very latest radiogram, fitted with two large speakers, and Franz was soon able to introduce to his soiree audiences a device which had just come on the market, called Music Minus One.[66] When the record was played, the solo part was omitted, and could be filled in spontaneously by a live pianist. The solo part was recorded in one channel and the accompaniment in the other channel; the player could use the balance control to listen to the entire performance, just the solo part, or play along with the recorded accompaniment. Many of the titles included a printed copy of the score, liner notes and/or performance suggestions with the score.

Dr Holford would frequently astonish the distinguished gathering of socialites at these Saturday night soirees by playing a major piano concerto such as the Tchaikowsky D Minor, or the Grieg or Schumann concertos on one of the concert Steinways, accompanied by the Music Minus One record on the Radiogram turned up to its highest volume. The effect was quite electrifying. In many ways, Music Minus One was the perfect medium for Franz at this stage of his career, for it allowed him to practice on his own in private, as if he had the full resources of a symphony orchestra at his disposal. Then, when he was ready, he could dazzle a private audience with a performance in which any imperfections by the soloist were not immediately obvious, since the orchestra played its part to perfection!

It took a great deal of skill to synchronize with the phantom orchestras of Music Minus One, but as Stephen Davies has written:

> In conjunction with the privacy of his situation Music-Minus-One provides a perfect prop in the specialized game of make believe. It creates a compelling illusion. If he closes his eyes, it becomes easy (for the pianist) to entertain the thought that the orchestra is in his own living room.[67]

It was also a perfect way for learning new works and building a repertoire.[68]

Another way to make one's compositions known was to create one's own recordings, and Franz Holford at this time began investigating the process for cutting his own records.[69] He did a lot of this work at the recording company EMI, but also at the Champs' house and as a consequence he began spending more and more time there.

At first he visited 'Threlkeld' in order to give lessons to the Champ children, but the allure of the magnificent house, with its gorgeous music room, his experiments with recording, and the fact that he would be picked up each day and driven home again in the Champ's Bentley by the attractive Gwen Champ, was irresistible.

Not to mention that in this setting, such was the charisma he exuded that he was held in the esteem of a potentate presiding over his own fiefdom. Some nights he didn't even bother returning home to 'Norwood', but stayed overnight in a bed at the house which was reserved for his use.

It was inevitable that his own marriage was headed for disaster.

Marjorie Holford left Franz, 'Norwood' and the marriage on 1 August 1947. In a letter to his pupil Don Newton, he mentions the separation briefly and with a touch of disdain:

> Pardon haste. Do not come on Saturday. The wife is leaving and things are very difficult.[70]

On 4th August, she and a friend Jean Gordon embarked on the *Marine Phoenix* and sailed to San Francisco, where on her visa Marjorie described herself as aged 36, a housewife, from Maitland, NSW.[71] How long she stayed is not known, but when she returned, it was to live in Tasmania where, in 1954 she was living in New Town, and working as a sales assistant. Why she went to America is not clear – perhaps it was a last attempt at a full time career as a singer - and why she later chose Tasmania to settle is also unclear – perhaps she wanted to be as far away from Franz as possible while living in Australia.

It appears she took very few possessions with her, as if contemptuous of the style of life in which he kept her and as if to make the statement that she could build a life for herself without him. She passed out of his life entirely, as if the eight years of their marriage was like a ship that passed in the night. There were no children, and apparently very little love. There was no divorce; Marjorie never remarried and died in 1962 at the age of 55.

Franz (William) Holford in the 1950s. (Photograph by John Champ)

Evenings with the rich and famous

*Music, when soft voices die,
vibrates in the memory.*

- SHELLEY

6

Anyone who attended the Saturday night soirees hosted by Gwen Champ and her husband Reg at their home 'Threlkeld' at Hunters Hill in the 1940s and 50s would cherish them as precious memories. The Champs were generous hosts and true patrons of the arts - especially of music.

Their own son John displayed a precocious aptitude for the piano at an early age, and daughter Judith had a good voice and was a talented actress. The parents spared no expense in order to surround their children with the finest artistic and physical environment in which their gifts would flourish.

'Threlkeld' became an artist's crucible, in which Franz Holford played a pivotal role and which he exploited to the full. In this situation, his charisma was tangible.

After a sumptuous dinner on a Friday or Saturday evening, invited guests would adjourn to the music room, to be entertained by Dr Franz Holford and any other musicians he felt disposed to invite for the particular occasion. There were no formal printed programs; he would simply announce what was to be performed, often interspersing the live performances with excerpts from the latest vinyl recordings he had acquired. The guest list included doctors, lawyers, writers, poets, artists, business people and family friends who were music lovers.

With her own dazzling personality, Gwen Champ cultivated a wide circle of friends and admirers whose names would grace any social diary in the world. Perhaps with a touch of cynicism, Reg Champ regularly brought along to the soirees his chief engineer from Lysaght's, a Mr Richardson, and the two men would sit apart from the musical cognoscenti, drinking whisky and marvelling bemusedly at what was taking place. Perhaps Reginald Malcolm Champ may even have reflected wistfully on what his own future might have yielded, had he persisted with his own undoubted musical gifts.

Sir Bernard Heinze was a regular guest, as was Dr Stuart Scougall, an eminent orthopaedic surgeon, whose interests outside medicine included Aboriginal art and literature. Scougall lost his only son in WWII and after the War he created a garden in the young man's memory at his home 'Kepdowrie' in Wahroonga. He enshrined the garden in a self-published book of his own prose and poetry entitled *Consider the Lilies*, illustrated with black and white wood engravings. His sadness about his son's death inspired some memorable lines, written by the gifted medico.

The book also contained an essay 'Reciprocity', contributed by Franz Holford.[72] It may have been edited by Stuart Scougall, who was an excellent writer, but nevertheless it remains one of the best of Franz Holford's literary works. The extraordinary surgeon's association with Holford would be long and fruitful for the latter, who portrayed himself superior to Scougall by at least two fictional doctoral degrees. As a gesture to his friend and in sympathy for the loss of his son, Franz wrote a long poem 'Elegy', which he also self-published through the printer of *Canon*, G W Hall, in a lavish format on fine deckled paper with exquisite uncials hand-drawn by the artist Franklin Bennett.[73] Five hundred signed and numbered copies of 'Elegy' were printed by his *Canon* publisher G W Hall.[74]

The quality of his writing in 'Elegy' was perhaps the closest Franz Holford came to writing significant poetry. He was always caught between the desire to be a composer/pianist and a writer/poet. Yet even here he could not refrain from arrogating another's persona to himself. Just one verse from 'Elegy' reveals his penchant for plagiarism:

> The silence now
> was once a footfall;
> There is stillness near
> where once a form moved;
> And sadness lives
> where once a hope dwelt.
> But tribute now will mark
> a knightly deed:
> The peace of God
> will be the warrior's mead.[75]

Stuart Scougall had already used the very similar first two lines of this poetic imagery in *Consider the Lilies* with the more elegant:

> There is silence now
> where once a footfall stirred my heart.

Dr Robert Murphy was another regular visitor to 'Threlkeld'. An incumbent surgeon at the Mater Misericordiae Hospital (who removed this author's tonsils) he introduced to the soirees Dr Mary Bertram, who yearned to be a poet; Christopher Lodge was another – an English farmer, living in Milton, oboist from the Sydney Symphony Orchestra, Ian Wilson made many visits to 'Norwood' during the period Franz wrote for him his second oboe sonata, and though he was a few years older than this author, we became good friends. Ian had a quirky and cutting sense of humour and was known in the Sydney Symphony Orchestra for his various pranks and practical jokes – including putting 'whoopee cushions' on the chairs of various principals during the interval when the ABC was making direct-to-air broadcasts of the orchestra. Ian Wilson's favourite anecdote concerned the Finnish conductor Georg Schneevoigt, who visited Australia twice for the ABC, in 1937 and 1940 and was known for his 'endearing idiosyncracies'.[76]

During the morning rehearsal for one of his concerts, Schneevoigt was having problems with the brass section. Apparently the orchestra had been to a reception the night before and everyone was a little the worse for wear the following day. During a Wagner work, the Finn stopped the orchestra and made an exaggerated gesture towards his rear end:

'Eh Brass. You play like ze farting pigs. I could do better with zis…!

The rehearsal continued, with the Principal Brass continuing to make false entries, until the conductor flung down his baton in despair. He directed a menacing look at the trombonist.

'Ey you…..I don' 'ave to put up with farting pigs in my orchestra! You get out! You go! NOW!'

Amidst a huge, embarrassed silence, the trombonist packed up his instrument and threaded his way to the exit via the Town Hall organ. Holding onto the 32' Diapason, he slowly and bemusedly turned around to face Schneevoigt. By now he was about one hundred feet from the conductor, who did not have the greatest grasp of the English language. Swaying under the influence of a night's heavy drinking, he surveyed Schneevoigt and said in a loud, sneering voice:

'We…ll, I don't care, you little wop. You can go and get stuffed!' he said. An audible gasp came from the orchestra, upon which Georg Schneevoigt held up an imperious hand:

'No, no, no, no, no….' he replied, shaking his head vigorously. 'It ees useless to apologise!'

******

Many members of the SSO attended Gwen Champ's soirees, including the violist Helen Bainton[77] and her famous father, Sir Edgar, who generously gave me the commission to copy some of the orchestral parts for his D Minor Symphony. Later, when Franz Holford commenced his music journal *Canon* the guest list grew in stature to include such famous overseas celebrities as Karl Rankl, Eugene Goossens, Sir John Barbirolli and his wife the oboist Evelyn Rothwell, Fernando Germani (the Pope's organist) and many others.

The collective wisdom of doctors Scougall, Murphy and Bertram must have made them instantly aware that Franz's claim to be a medico was spurious. One can only assume that after a hard day spent sawing off a patient's leg or removing the smelly adenoids and tonsils of an infected teenager, the exquisite sounds of Ian Wilson's oboe playing the 'slops' music – as Larry Sitsky inelegantly put it – of Holford's *Summer Madrigal* must have seemed like heaven on earth to them. In exchange, how relatively unimportant must a harmless lie about one's qualifications have seemed to these eminent practising professionals!

(Above) Dr Stuart Scougall was a famous orthopaedic surgeon, who regularly attended the soirees at the Champ residence in Hunters Hill. This painting, by Jon Molvig was a finalist in the Archibald Prize of 1962.

(Above right) Bernard (later Sir Bernard) Heinze, was a friend of Franz Holford, who endeavoured without success to obtain an honorary doctorate for Holford at Melbourne University. (Canon photographs)

(Above left) Jiri Tancibudek was a Czechoslovakian oboist who fled to Australia from the communist regime in 1950 and was appointed Principal Oboist to the Sydney Symphony Orchestra on the advice of Sir Eugene Goossens. (Above right) Ian Wilson, who followed Tancibudek, was also a fine oboist in the Sydney Symphony Orchestra. Franz Holford wrote oboe concertos for both these fine soloists, which were recorded and played by the Australian Broadcasting Commission. (Canon photographs)

In addition to the Saturday night soirees, there were also student recitals held at 'Threlkeld' which in 1943-44 featured some of Holford's best students, including John Champ, Peter Miller, Don Newton and John Champ's cousin, Gordon Clarke.

******

I attended my first soiree at 'Threlkeld', along with other members of St John's Woolwich Choir when I was a choirboy of thirteen. It was an evening I will never forget, largely because of the *faux pas* I made. Young as I was, I was conscious of the opulence of the surroundings and aware of the importance of the dozen or so guests.

Dr Holford had chosen to commence the entertainment by playing a new recording he had just acquired of Tchaikovsky's *Symphony* No. 6 in B minor, the *Pathétique*.[78] The lights in the music room were dimmed and I sank into the warm recesses of a velvet lined chair to listen to the first symphony I had ever heard.

The radiogram was at maximum volume, as the first movement of the *Pathétique* opens with a slow bassoon solo, stating a motif that after some time becomes the first theme, accompanied by low strings. A romantic theme occurs 89 bars in, and one is lulled into an almost mesmeric trance, so soft and beguiling is the sound. I quietly dozed in my chair. After some development, the theme fades away in a clarinet passage, which in later life I discovered is marked *pppppp*….in other words as softly as the clarinettist can possibly play. Suddenly there is a violent, crashing chord, followed (at bar 161) by a *tutti fortissimo* and a hugely agitated passage. I sat bolt upright in my chair and let out an audible gasp of astonishment. To my mortification I saw John Champ glance at Dr Holford and smile knowingly. I sank back in the chair, totally humiliated, hoping the music would last forever and that I would not have to face the great man over supper and apologise for my bad manners.

As I sipped on a fruit punch during an interval in the musical program, Dr Scougall sidled up and whispered casually in my ear: 'Caught you napping, did it?' Then he giggled in a high-pitched voice and nudged me playfully. He spoke through lips which hardly moved, and I was conscious of a strange body aroma.[79]

'I made a fool of myself,' I replied, casting about to avoid eye contact with Dr Holford. The famous orthopaedic took me by the arm into a corner of the dining room and regarded me humorously through grey eyes which twinkled from a massive bald head, not unlike the Finnish composer Sibelius.

'Let me tell you about the art of making mistakes, my dear young man…' I gazed into his face, fascinated by the tight, immobile lips. Then he proceeded to tell me about a research project he had carried out on the Aboriginal one-leg stance. He had received a large grant of money to go to Arnhem Land and had spent two years living with, and studying, the Oenpelli tribe.

'Now let me ask you,' he continued, 'Do *you* know why our Aboriginal brothers stand on one leg?'

I shook my head.

'Why, to rest the *other* one of course!' He then burst into an uncontrollable, hissing giggle. 'Oh, they may also use the device to camouflage themselves as a tree. I've also heard that their women also stand on one leg to indicate to others whether or not they have a mate, but mainly it's to rest the other leg! I spent two years of my life trying to find out what should have been obvious in the first place...'

He stabbed his finger at me. 'Now, *that* my boy is how to make a mistake!' He laughed again. 'Compared with *that*, yours doesn't even rate!'

I always endeavoured to sit near Dr Scougall at the Champ soirees, despite the strange odour. Apart from his acknowledged skill as a surgeon, Stuart Scougall was highly cultivated, with an extensive knowledge of the arts, particularly literature, painting and music. Most of all, despite his somewhat severe mien, he was a kindly man and a great raconteur.

Dr Edgar Bainton, with his daughter Helen, who played viola in the Sydney Symphony Orchestra for many years (Canon photograph)

The Warwick Singers

*So leave the road to Mamble
and take another road...*

- DRINKWATER

7

When, in the summer of 1944, the Rev Gordon Smee from the parish of St John's Woolwich discovered Franz Holford and called on him at 'Norwood', it must have been a summit meeting of egos. The confident and energetic Anglican Minister was a largely self-taught pianist and organist, who had been vicar of his tiny parish for the past five years.

Discovering a professional musician on the fringes of his parish was an exciting bonus for the gregarious rector, but Franz was cautious when the Minister began inquiring into his own musical credentials. When Rev Smee asked to be accepted as his student for piano and composition, Franz demurred, referring him instead to Rex de Rego[80], at the latter's teaching studio at Palings. He told the rector that unfortunately he could not take him as a student, as he was about to leave Australia 'for the towering graces of England'. In a spontaneous act of charity – although he embraced no particular religion – Franz Holford wrote a personal letter of recommendation to de Rego, and even paid for the Minister's initial lessons.[81]

Though not wishing to get too close to the ebullient Anglican Minister, Franz Holford was intrigued by the rector's request that he conduct the St John's Choir. Franz was anxious to try out some of his own choral compositions, and this appointment to a small village choir would prove useful in honing some of his own compositional skills without drawing unwelcome attention to himself from the established musical fraternity. Despite the fact that WWII was drawing to a close, anti-German sentiment pervaded the Australian community for generations, and Franz's fanciful stories about his German lineage and education at Heidelberg University, combined with his adoption of a German Christian name would continue to arouse suspicion. And then there was the dark secret surrounding his birth…

The years between 1940 – 1947 were among Franz Holford's most productive as a composer of songs. He was attracted to this form of composition in the same way a writer is to poetry - for they are to a musician what poetry is to a writer – the encapsulation of creative ideas on a small canvas, rather than on a grander and more complicated one. Franz Holford typically turned to the English poets rather than Australian, and he especially enjoyed the works of the poet and playwright John Drinkwater. In this period he set fourteen of Drinkwater's poems for voice and piano, a number of which, such as *The Coming of Spring* (1944), *Mamble* (1944) and *Expectancy* (1977) deserve a place in any singer's repertoire – despite Larry Sitsky's scornful rejection of Holford as a serious composer. The fact is that singers find some of them quite delightful to perform, and they are given credence by the integrity of the poets he chose. Most of these works were given their premieres at the 'Threlkeld' soirees, by singers such as William Herbert, Ereach Riley, Linda Parker, Horace Fuller, Christopher Lodge and of course Franz's wife at the time, Marjorie Cole.

My acquaintance with Franz Holford in the seven years from 1944 to 1951 was mostly limited to that of chorister in the tiny village church of St John's, Woolwich. Singing lessons with him gradually petered out when my voice broke at the age of fourteen, and upon leaving high school I pursued a career in journalism. Singing in the church choir had been a pleasant diversion, as was swimming in the Lane Cove tidal pool at Woolwich, and playing cricket on the common, opposite the primary school where I had been educated. As a consequence, I only saw the great man at choir practice and during performances given by the choir. I would go to choir practice following the 10 am church service on Sunday, or alternatively after the 7.15 pm service on Sunday evening. Occasionally, additional sectional rehearsals would be held at the Rectory in Gale Street Woolwich, presided over by the Rev Gordon Smee, which Franz would rarely attend.

For several years in the 1940s Franz Holford conducted this little village choir in the presentation of harvest festivals, at Easter ceremonies and at Christmas, and every now and then a public concert, or 'Festival of Music' would be given in the church hall to present some of the choral works he had written, such as *Mamble*[82] or the more ambitious *The Stolen Child*[83], to Yeats' text. At Easter the choir typically sang Maunder's *Olivet to Calvary* and Sir John Stainer's *The Crucifixion*; at Christmas it would perform excerpts from Handel's *Messiah*. One of the rector's own compositions, *I love all beauteous things* was also given its premiere by the choir and featured as soloist head choirboy Hector White[84], for whom it was written, at a music festival organized by 'Dr' Holford.

The whole village was inspired by the mysterious musician from nearby Hunters Hill, and the combination of beautiful choral music, and an energetic and charismatic new Anglican Minister caused Sunday congregations at St John's to swell with an influx of newcomers. For someone who appeared to embrace no particular religion, the new choirmaster certainly made his own contribution to expanding the congregations of the Church of England in Australia.

As a choral conductor Franz Holford was charismatic, surprisingly undemonstrative and economic in his beat, which was always assured and confident. Standing in front of the choir he was tall, commanding and always immaculately dressed; he held the choristers' complete attention - most of them paying him the compliment of memorizing the music – even the longer, or newly composed scores. In the main it was uncomplicated music – some, like Sitsky, would even classify it today as mundane, but this in itself revealed the conductor's musical acumen, for he realized that he was dealing with a very fledgling group of village singers with little or no training, and thus chose music largely within their capabilities.

He never conducted the choir during church services, except for one notable occasion. On this particular Sunday evening he happened to arrive an hour early for a choir practice, and found the evening service about to commence. He promptly joined the choir as it processed into the church to sit in the high-backed pews on either side of the nave. He sat between me and the Mayor's wife Jean Harding in the altos, and surprised everyone by getting up and conducting all the hymns and the special anthem we had prepared, a thing he would not normally do. Throughout the sermon by the rector he carried on an amusing, if somewhat undergraduate commentary on religion as he saw it, underneath his breath to those around him and almost engendered full throated laughter when he drew our attention to a wisp of hair on the rector's bald head, which rose and danced in the light of the lectern lamp. It was very funny, but at the same time cruel and childish. When the collection plate was being handed around, I reached under my white surplice and began removing a large button from my cassock, a manouvre which we choirboys carried out occasionally when we had no money for the plate. Dr Holford asked me in a whisper what I was doing, and when I told him, he smiled and unobtrusively slipped a coin into my hand. When I put it in the plate I realized it was a two-shilling piece – a king's ransom for a boy to whom a penny was more than adequate. Born into the Church of England, Dr Holford never spoke about religion, nor would he comment on the religious beliefs of others, preferring instead to use terms such as 'providence', or 'providential' when referring to matters of the spirit. In this he was influenced by the atheism of one of his favourite composers, Frederick Delius, who embraced the teachings of Nietzsche rather than the teachings of Jesus Christ.[85]

At some of the special services in the church's calendar Dr Holford would have his own grand piano installed and tuned the day before the event by Reg Newton.[86] His favourite student John Champ became the choir's regular accompanist. Whether the expenses for installing and tuning the instrument were met by the church is not known. At this time in the mid-1940s he also held casual positions (probably gained for him by Gwen Champ) as a peripatetic music teacher at two colleges: Methodist Ladies College, where Judith Champ went to school and The King's School,

Parramatta, where he organized concerts – often featuring his own music, including *The Stolen Child*. In 1946 he wrote to his student Don Newton:

> I have injured my finger (4th on L.H.) and I may have to stop playing for eight months. Concert will still go on at MLC in case you are worried.[87]

The reason for his involvement as conductor with three separate choirs may have had less to do with selfless devotion to choral music and more to the fact that he wished to establish a choir of his own. In 1946 he did so, forming a group which he called *The Warwick Singers*, choosing a typically English name, which he told some people was dedicated to the county in England where he claimed his family owned a large mansion. Most of the choristers came from the three choirs he conducted, from which he then withdrew his services. John Champ remained as his accompanist, and weekly rehearsals for *The Warwick Singers* commenced in late Summer of 1946 in a small Presbyterian Church hall not far from his house 'Norwood' in Woolwich Road, Hunters Hill.

******

In many ways, the role of conductor was the role which best suited Franz Holford as a musician. A good conductor must first and foremost be a charismatic leader, who knows how to harness the talents of others and meld them into one instrument with which to interpret the creative needs of a composer. For some distinguished soloists, such as Yehudi Menuhin, Daniel Barenboim or Vladimir Ashkenazy, conducting came as the apogee of their attainments, allowing them to continue to pursue music at the highest level, and grow old gracefully as a performer. For Franz Holford, conducting was a way to meet and impress new people and garner their support for him both musically and financially for his way of life and for his compositions.

My brother and I joined *The Warwick Singers* in the summer of 1946, when I had just turned sixteen, along with the Mayor's wife Jean Harding and her sister Florence, an excellent soprano. The new choir numbered thirty singers, with John Champ as the accompanist. Unlike the choir of St John's

Church, Woolwich, The Warwick Singers served no special function, and for some time was content to remain a kind of sophisticated village glee club. It performed publicly several times at 'Threlkeld', but even the Champs' capacious music room was too confined to accommodate a thirty-voice choir, two large grand pianos *and* an audience. Thus, late in 1949 Franz Holford began grooming his singers for a somewhat bolder public appearance and he booked the Hunters Hill Town Hall for an 'authentic' performance of *Messiah* to be held in December 1950.

This was a period in the history of music in Australia when even well-known works such as *Messiah* were not considered particularly hackneyed, nor had they suffered from over-exposure; Handel's famous oratorio attracted audiences whenever and wherever it was presented, but complete and especially *authentic* performances of it in Sydney were still comparatively rare; performances in the suburbs were rarer still and usually confined to churches, consisting mainly of popular excerpts from the work.

Therefore, when Franz Holford booked the Hunters Hill Town Hall for a complete performance of *Messiah* prior to Christmas 1950 it sent a buzz of anticipation along the whole peninsula. Unabashed by the unseasoned voices which comprised *The Warwick Singers* Franz invited the famous Australian Handel scholar Dr Robert Dalley-Scarlett[88] to a rehearsal, and this chain-smoking recipient of the coveted Hallé Medal contributed a testimonial, which appeared in the printed program:

> Quite recently I heard a rehearsal of the work by a little group of folk who, unhampered by prejudices, approached it in a simple, unaffected manner. Despite the imperfections inevitably due to the human factor, they realised so much of what I believe to have been Handel's intentions that the work sounded – for this country at any rate – something quite new.[89]

Vastly impressed by the Holford persona, Dalley-Scarlett also gave the conductor some invaluable advice in constructing an authentic instrumental ensemble, consisting of three first and four second violins, two violas, a cello and harpsichord. It was a minimal orchestral force, and lacked a solo trumpet for 'The trumpet shall sound'[90], but the balance was excellent between the instruments, the thirty-voice choir and soloists. The four soloists were Linda Parker (soprano), Jacqueline Talbert (contralto), Christopher Lodge (tenor) and Frank Lisle (bass) and John Champ played a harpsichord obtained on loan from the Music Department of Sydney University.

Every ticket to the single performance was pre-sold and profits went to the Drummoyne Music Club, which Gwen Champ had organized as sponsor.[91] Dozens of late comers stood along both interior walls and crowded into the foyer of the Town Hall, spilling out into the street from the attractive old stone 19th century building.

The evening was a spectacular success, and members of *The Warwick Singers* and the orchestra were invited afterwards to the house of Reg and Gwen Champ, where they were treated to a lavish supper and entertained by Dr Holford, performing the Tchaikovsky B Flat Minor Piano Concerto, accompanied by a 'Music minus One' recording.

The performance of *Messiah* was the only public performance ever given by *The Warwick Singers*. It was a performance talked about in the district for years, but shortly after, and to the amazement of all the choristers who had sung for him for almost four years, the choir was suddenly disbanded. Its very success, which should have catapulted Franz Holford into the forefront of professional conducting in Sydney, was its failure. After briefly taking centre stage, the conductor chose to step back into the wings and avoid too much publicity – good *or* bad.

No explanation was ever given for the choir's demise.

Shortly after forming *The Warwick Singers* Franz Holford also launched his music journal *The Canon*.[92] The address given for the secretary of the journal was number 18 Woolwich Road – 'Threlkeld' - not Franz's house 'Norwood'. The secretary was John Champ, and the journal was undoubtedly funded by his father, the steel tycoon Reginald Champ. It commenced life as an unpretentious little octavo size magazine of two dozen pages, with its name in Old English typography, printed on a simple coloured cardboard cover. If its founder aspired to a lofty musical

(Top left) Linda Parker, a soprano famous in her day, performed many of Franz's songs. (Top right) Ereach Riley, an Australian tenor and one-time principal at Sadlers Wells, also performed and recorded dozens of Franz Holford's songs, from 1943 to 1945. (Below) Dr Robert Dalley-Scarlett, internationally renowned Handel scholar, championed Holford's music in Queensland and wrote many articles for the magazine Canon. (Linda Parker photo by courtesy Arts Centre Melbourne, others from Canon).

or academic ideal such as Schumann's *Neue Zeitschrift für Musik*, this initial step into musical journalism was somewhat conservative.

However, the magazine at that time occupied a somewhat unexploited niche in Australian literature known as vanity publishing, in which works of little commercial value find a private press and patron. In a rodomontade editorial aptly titled 'The Overture', its editor Dr Franz Holford seemed almost to eschew responsibility for its publication. He protested his reluctance at 'bowing to the wishes of friends' who it appears had almost coerced him into launching the venture - promising their support for the magazine. He eventually acceded to their pleas and wrote: 'I at last have consented to produce a music review for their delight.' This modest explication was followed by an agglomeration of musical essays and reviews with the promise of an editorial integrity which would embody 'sincerity without weakness and candour without malice.'[93]

Undoubtedly the little magazine, which averaged 24-28 pages each issue of its first year and sold for 1/6d a copy[94], was to provide a forum for a rich vein of classical music activity in this period of Australia's history. One of its most valuable services was to record the visit to Australia of a passing parade of eminent overseas and local musicians beginning with such international celebrities as Claudio Arrau, Eileen Joyce, Igor Hmelnitsky, Valda Aveling, Father Sydney MacEwan, and of course the famous Boyd Neel String Orchestra.

Whilst the standard of criticism may have suffered from the lack of an experienced critic such as Neville Cardus, the writing was lively and often very engaging, and eventually musicologists and music critics such as Ernest Briggs, Wolfgang Wagner, Kenneth Hince, Roger Covell and Andrew McCredie began their successful careers following contributions made to *The Canon*.

When it first appeared, copies of the magazine would be displayed by Dr Holford at rehearsals of *The Warwick Singers* and members of the choir would be urged to subscribe and to recommend the publication to their friends. It began to be reviewed by newspapers all around Australia –

all of which were encouraging[95], yet despite this, the magazine never achieved a very wide readership - at the height of its popularity *The Canon* peaked at a circulation of just over 2,000.[96]

John Champ (Centre) Franz Holford's pupil and associate editor of Canon. He is seen here with Rowena Crowley (Left) and Rita Streich. John toured Australia as accompanist to Victoria de los Angeles for the ABC, and became well known to radio listeners for his series 'The Way of Music'.
(Photo: John Champ)

During a break in rehearsal one evening the conductor called me over to the elite group set apart from the choir, which generally consisted of Gwen Champ, Judith her daughter, John Champ and one or two observers. Knowing that I was at that time working for an advertising agency as a copy writer/layout artist, the conductor asked me if I would contribute some musical designs in the form of tailpieces to articles, or 'dinkuses' as they were referred to by printers. I nervously accepted the commission, and arranged a date to take some samples to him at 'Norwood'.

This was to be the first occasion that I would meet the great man informally. I had just turned twenty.

******

Amanuensis

Duty is what one expects from others.

- OSCAR WILDE

8

The wooden veranda posts at 'Norwood' were heavily laden with white and purple wisteria in full spring blossom when I arrived for my meeting with Dr Franz Holford in September 1950. I had timed my arrival to precisely the appointed hour, 10 am, on a Sunday morning and as I rang the doorbell, it chimed deeply inside the house. After a few moments the curtains moved slightly in one of the bay windows and following a short delay the door was opened by the mysterious musician, wearing a long silk dressing gown.

'Ah my dear, come in, come in…' came his unexpectedly affectionate greeting, and taking me by the arm he ushered me down the hallway and into his study.

'I heard your middle name is Ravel.' He gave a flashing smile. 'Not the composer chappie though, eh? He was a….well, let's just say he did not have any children, did he?' In later years I was to learn that Maurice Ravel was gay.

'No, it's my mother's name…my grandfather was French.'

'Please sit down and make yourself comfortable,' he continued, offering me a chair, and gesturing at several bookcases containing a huge collection of books. 'Read a book if you like. I had a concert last night and have only just woken up. I'll take a bath and be with you shortly.'

He reappeared fifteen minutes later, wearing a fashionable cream safari jacket, starched white collar and a blue bow tie with white polka dots.

Then he sat behind the elegant writing desk and folded his long white hands on the leather-cornered blotting pad. 'Now, let's see what you've done for me…'

'They're not very good,' I mumbled, pushing the folder across the desk.

'On the contrary, they are just beautiful,' he responded, examining each of the half-dozen drawings carefully. 'What an interesting technique you've used…'

'It's called scraperboard. They're the first dinkuses I've done.'

'Dinkuses?'

'It's a word publishers use for little tailpieces,' I said with modest authority. 'The scraperboard is meant to imitate woodcuts.' I explained the technique of laying down Indian ink on the chalky white surface of a board and scraping images in white relief, using a variety of etching pens.

'Well, they are perfect for my needs.' He sat back in the black leather chair, hands placed fingertip to fingertip beneath his chin and regarded me steadily – a faintly ironic smile playing around his lips. 'You know young man, from those early singing lessons I once gave you, and hearing your voice in my choir, then seeing these works of art… you are obviously very talented. What is it you want to become?'

'I don't really know. I like painting – I'm studying painting and calligraphy at art school. But I love music too, and writing. I would love to learn the piano, but I don't have a piano.'

'Do you have a family which supports you in these endeavours?'

'Only my sisters and my brother…who sings in the choir.'

'Of course, Welsman. What a strange name. No mother or father?'

'No. My mother died when I was three, and my father was killed in Port Moresby during the war.'

'I'm so sorry.'

I shrugged stoically. 'We survived. Mainly because of my sisters.'

'They must be wonderful. Tell me, are you happy in your present job?'

'Yes, it's great.' This was a strange question, and noting my puzzled look, he smiled mysteriously. 'Why?'

'Well, it so happens that I have a need for an amanuensis. Do you know what that is?' I shook my head.

'It's like a personal assistant.'

'A secretary?'

He shook his head and laughed cajolingly. 'Much more than that. It's someone who can do a whole range of things. Take down notes, typing, catalogue my books, do music copying, assist in the preparation and production of my music magazine – even help look after my mother a bit.'

'I see.'

'You have such a wide range of skills already. I think you would be a perfect amanuensis.'

My head began reeling. This was the first time I had ever been 'head hunted' for a job. In fact, it was the first time I had ever been complimented for my work…by *anyone*…it was all very flattering.

'What…what did you have in mind?'

'Well, this is a large house. I could offer you a room to work in and you would have the run of the house and gardens to use as you please. You could even come to live here if you wanted to, and as an added bonus, I would be very honoured to teach you the piano.'

Honoured, indeed! I was speechless, and as I groped for the right words to respond, Dr Holford was smiling again understandingly.

'How would I *live*?' I stammered.

He laughed. 'You mean financially? I would provide you with all the material things you need, and whatever money you require.' I just stared at him, lost for words. This all seemed just too good to be possible.

He went on: 'Look, it's not the kind of decision you have to make immediately. Go home and talk it over with your brother and sisters, umm?'

'Thank you. It's a…a big decision…I mean…'

'I *know* what you mean. Oh, and by the way, I have something for you, for doing that lovely artwork.' He went to a cupboard beneath one of the cedar bookcases and took out several 12" x 78 rpm records in paper sleeves and handed them to me. 'It is a recording I made a long time ago of the Tchaikowsky piano concerto. I noticed how you enjoyed it at the Champs soiree.'

I looked at the records and noticed that the identifying names for the soloist and the orchestra had all been scratched from the label, and glanced up at him with a puzzled expression.

'The labels?' He laughed. 'Don't worry about those – it was a test recording and they just stuck any old label on them. The important thing is that it's *me* playing.[97]'

I believed him. Why would I not believe him?

******

My three sisters and especially my brother were not happy about me leaving the family to live at 'Norwood'. Despite having no parents, we were a close-knit family, and my eldest sister Barbara had fought for many years to prevent what was left of her siblings breaking apart. She was also suspicious of Franz Holford's motives. She hinted darkly at what could be seen as a homosexual relationship – a subject about which I was entirely naïve.[98] When I conveyed her reservations to Dr Holford he immediately invited her to come and talk to him about his offer.

I was embarrassed about my sister's meeting with such an eminent musician, and sat outside on the veranda while she was closeted with him. When the interview was over, and my sister came out to the front porch where I was waiting, she had a beaming smile on her face and as we walked slowly back to Woolwich she could talk of nothing else but the man she had just met.

'What a charmer,' she said. 'He's offered to buy me a piano and give me free piano lessons!'

Franz Holford in the 1950s. (Photograph by courtesy Australian Music Centre)

Isolation

*'Come away, O human child,
to the waters and the wild,
for the world's more full of weeping
than you can understand.'*

- YEATS

9

When I arrived at 'Norwood', just after Christmas 1950, carrying a small suitcase containing just a few clothes and some toiletries, I was given no specific duties.

In the Public Service the situation would have been the equivalent to writing one's own job description, since there were so many obvious tasks to undertake, and so many avenues of my own which I wished to pursue. There was one task however which I made it clear from the outset that I was not equipped to handle, that of caring for the conductor's mother.

'Of course not,' came the instant response. 'Nor would I expect you to. No, I am making arrangements for a housekeeper to come in daily and see to my mother's needs.'

A housekeeper called Mrs Cooper did indeed commence duties shortly after I arrived. She had been working at the Champ household several hundred metres down Woolwich Road and was sent by Gwen Champ to spend three days a week caring for the needs of the conductor and his adopted mother Annie Holford - another act of generosity from Franz's benefactor Reginald Champ, who paid Mrs Cooper's wages.

She travelled by train from Kulnura on the Central coast, arriving each morning at 'Norwood' at 9 o'clock precisely, invariably carrying a large basket of groceries or household goods. With his penchant for giving those around him rather bizarre nicknames, Franz immediately dubbed her 'Cooee'[99], which became the only name I ever knew her by. She was a kindly, down to earth country soul, and she and I got on well, although occasionally I fancied that she looked at me askance and thought: 'What is a young man like *you* doing in a household like *this*?' She remained housekeeper at 'Norwood' for several years until she fell ill and Dr Holford dispensed with her services.[100]

Another person who came to the house twice a week, on the days Mrs Cooper had off, was the mayor's wife Jean Harding, who volunteered her services to do the conductor's laundry and to cook meals for us.

In my schooldays Mrs Harding was like a second mother to me and I used to call at her house in Elgin Street for afternoon tea, on my way home from Woolwich Public School. She missed her own son dearly when, in the early days of WWII Robbie Harding's Lancaster Bomber in which he was a navigator was shot down on its first mission over Germany and he died at the age of eighteen.

The room allotted to me at 'Norwood' was not large, but it had a fireplace, a window overlooking a garden in the house's side passage, and enough space for a drawing board and bookshelves. It became the centre of my world and each day I stole there as if called by Yeats' mystic poetry.

Some words of the Irish poet which had been set to music by the conductor might have described the phasis which seemed to have fashioned my destiny: 'Come away O human child, to the waters and the wild, for the world's more full of weeping than you can understand.'[101] I had indeed come away from the world as I knew it, and this room for almost ten years would 'sing peace into my breast'.

I had not read much poetry and when Dr Holford began giving me books of verse I often searched the poems for a meaningful phrase which would relate to my actions in shutting myself off from the world.

One such was by Gerard Manley Hopkins:

> Heaven Haven
> *I have desired to go*
> *Where springs not fail;*
> *To fields where flies no sharp and sided hail*
> *And a few lilies blow.*
>
> *And I have asked to be*
> *Where no storms come;*
> *Where the green swell is in the havens dumb*
> *And out of the swing of the sea.*

I was certainly 'out of the swing of the sea' and saw my situation as similar to that of a nun taking the veil, and the room as my cell. But at the same time I made this room my own little art studio and music room - a study my father never had, in which to express his heart's desire - the special place to which I retreated and where I could be alone, but not necessarily lonely. As the conductor promised, I *did* have the run of the entire house and garden, but this room was to be the special place to which I clove - to sleep in, to work in and in which to dream.

As the world around me changed, I too began to undergo a strange kind of metamorphosis in which my normally extravert nature became gradually more and more introverted, as if what was taking place within me was the reverse process of a butterfly emerging from its chrysalis. The world beyond the stone wall fringed by its hawthorn hedge began to recede, and came to resemble the river Tamar my English father often spoke about, which divided the people of Cornwall from the rest of England. Each time I went out the front gate of 'Norwood' it felt like a crossing of the River Tamar.

******

I had received ample warnings as to Franz Holford's possible sexual proclivities before taking up residence at his house. Everyone, including the friends I had made at the advertising agency Goldberg's in George Street Sydney where I worked, and my own family had taxed me with the inevitabilities of what I was undertaking and warned me of the dire concatenation of evil which would be the result of such a liaison – be it for business or personal reasons. Homosexual relations between adults was a jailable offence in Australia in the 1950s. It came as something of a shock therefore to discover very early in our association that the conductor had been married nine years before.

'I might as well tell you this now,' he said one morning as we took breakfast on the front veranda, while nearby a group of tiny silvereyes feasted on crataegus berries.

'I married some years ago. A dreadful mistake. She was a singer. She appeared one night recently as I was giving a dinner party…stark naked. Very embarrassing, and it might give you an idea as to her nature. If she should turn up again…..' He cut the conversation short when he could see the expression on my face, and concluded: 'Well, I don't think she will….she has moved to Melbourne, I think.' I discovered later that they had been separated for several years and that she was in fact living in Tasmania.[102]

The question of any homosexual relationship between Franz Holford and myself was settled very early in my stay at 'Norwood'. He had a habit of putting his arm around the shoulders of anyone who stood near him, patting arms and knees, and filling his letters with gushing sentiments which bordered on the sexual, but I made it quite clear to him from the outset that our relationship was going to be totally platonic – even though I regarded him with great affection. What his relationship was with other young men in his circle – such as John Champ, Gordon Clarke and Donald Newton[103] – and whether or not it went beyond deep friendship, I never discovered. He once described himself to me as bi-sexual, and whilst I found him many times in compromising situations with the very desirable Gwen Champ[104], there never appeared on the scene any particular male friend with whom one could say he partnered – perhaps with the exception of his pupil John Champ[105]; to my knowledge he never brought anyone – male or female back to 'Norwood' for any other reason than would be classified as 'usual'. Gwen Champ was the one exception.

******

If I had chosen a seminary, or a closed order of monks working within a cloistered monastery, I could not have so effectively entered into exile from those who had known me for twenty years.

As well as giving up my job in the city at the Goldberg art studio, I gave up all my sporting activities - even swimming, and my visits to the Lane Cove River to fish as I frequently did after school, ceased altogether. I began seeing less and less of my brother, who was extremely hurt by our separation, and finally I gave up seeing him at all. There was no reason now for me to commute to the city, as I had done for several years, and I rarely went shopping. When the choral group *The Warwick Singers* was abruptly terminated early in 1951, my social contacts dried up almost overnight. Everyone in my life seemed to view with scepticism the decision to quit my 'real' job and commence another with such strange dimensions, and this caused me to retreat from contact with people, as I entered a totally unknown space and way of life.

The musician to whom I would serve as amanuensis for almost ten years was in his early forties when I arrived at 'Norwood' and to most people including myself he was a total mystery. He was not listed in telephone directories and never wrote a cheque from a bank account, and even though everyone acknowledged him as 'doctor', no certificate verifying such status hung on the walls of his book-lined study. He never kept a diary and appeared not to embrace any religion; when he visited St John's Anglican Church it was apparent that he was unfamiliar with its liturgy, and despite his self-proclaimed Germanic background he never followed Martin Luther's practice when he rose in the morning, of making the sign of the cross and praying: 'God the Father, Son and Holy Spirit watch over me. Amen.' Yet he never avowed himself an atheist. His large library contained neither bible nor catholic missal. The fact is, religion of any sort was of little or no interest to him, since most religions involve the act of giving, and Franz Holford's whole *raison d'etre* was predicated on the act of receiving.

An example of how he had withdrawn from normal society occurred during the 1949 Census, before I went to live and work at 'Norwood'.

I happened to be visiting the house when an electoral officer called. Peering through the lace curtains of a bay window at the front of the house, Dr Holford seemed to divine the purpose of the visitor's mission and with his finger to his lips he instructed me not to answer the door. We both stood still in the hallway without speaking, until the census reporter eventually gave up and went away.

'I'm not giving anyone access to *my* personal details,' he said angrily, by way of explanation. As I was ineligible to vote at that time anyway, it mattered little to me. But he made it very clear from the outset that unannounced visitors were to be avoided.

I discovered that nowhere in the extensive collection of music manuscripts in his possession were there early editions or piano methods indicating with whom he studied, or at what institutions. No school class or graduation photographs stood upon mantelpieces and none taken of family members hung on the walls of 'Norwood'. Though he claimed to have been taught by some eminent European masters, nowhere were there letters, music manuscripts, workbooks or certificates from them indicating the progress he made. Dr Holford did not own a car and possessed no driver's licence, being driven everywhere at that time by members of the Champ family. I was totally nonplussed one morning when he casually suggested that I get my driver's licence, and do some research on what model of new vehicle I would care to drive as his personal chauffeur. To a young man who had never owned a car before this was a hugely exciting project and I quickly arrived at a decision on what would be an ideal vehicle – a Sunbeam Talbot. However, to my great disappointment no such vehicle eventuated and after a few desultory reminders, the idea came to nought. Nor did I ever arrive at any accurate assessment of his financial status. To my knowledge he never filed an income tax return, even during the nineteen years or so his *Canon* music magazine was conducted as a business. The journal was registered in the name of the Champ family, who took care of business matters concerning it under the aegis of their own taxation requirements.[106] When the printer had to be paid it was usually with a cheque signed by Reginald or Gwendolyn Champ.

******

Before arriving at 'Norwood', the possibility had entered my mind that Franz Holford might be a German spy, following a hearsay suggestion from a girlfriend of mine who sang in *The Warwick Singers*. It was a period when there was great hatred in Australia for Germans, Italians and Japanese, or for anyone who was seen to be a security risk. People of known German descent were often arrested immediately without trial and placed in jails and internment camps - many of them being incarcerated upon mere suspicion or gossip. Under the Aliens Registration Act of 1939 thousands of resident Germans, Italians and Japanese were sent to specially constructed internment camps all around Australia, not to be released until the end of hostilities. German and Italian internees could sometimes be released if they were able to convince a Tribunal Board of Enquiry that they were not a threat to Australia's security, but this was a difficult and demanding procedure. It was largely the fact that to acknowledge one's German background in those times meant instant internment, combined with my inability to convince myself that Dr Franz Holford was engaged in espionage, which ultimately led me to doubt his claims of German descent. If he was ever investigated by the authorities as a security risk, he never disclosed the fact to friends or business acquaintances.

The mystery surrounding him when I arrived was exacerbated by the presence in his house of the frail, aged lady – ostensibly his mother - who always called him 'Bill'. She was seldom seen, and appeared to be largely confined to her bed in a central room of the cottage, tended weekly by a nurse and a doctor who visited occasionally to check her physical status. I was not permitted to enter this room, but from the small hallway it opened upon one could tell that it was sparsely furnished, with a single bed, a rocking chair by the window, a dressing table and wardrobe, and a small radio on the bedside table, which was seldom played. On rare occasions the conductor sat her upon her rocking chair in the kitchen while he made her a bowl of soup, and I would sometimes brush the old lady's fine white hair and tie it in a bun.

'Why do you call him Bill?' I asked her on several such occasions when the conductor was not around. But she would never answer the question and instead she would cackle a laugh in her shrill old voice and admonish me for attempting to learn her secret, waving a bony finger under my chin.

Established in the latter half of 1947[107], a number of editions of the magazine *Canon* had already appeared before I arrived. In fact it was in its third year of publication and another was in progress, since it was a monthly publication. Even to my inexperienced eye it seemed an amateurishly produced magazine, falling far short of what was obviously intended as a replication of Schumann's erudite 19th century music journal *Neue Zeitschrift für Musik*.

I quickly found that one of its inherent problems was its name. A canon is a musical 'round' and Franz Holford's pun *The Canon*, was meant to symbolize the cyclical nature of the journal, coming 'round' to its readers each month. The name often confused people who failed to recognize the intended pun, including on one occasion an artist who was invited to prepare a 'logo' for its cover. One day, on a desk in the tiny office in the centre of the house from which the magazine was produced, I found one of this artist's sketches for a design, which depicted a cannon with a musical note hanging out the end of its barrel. Fortunately, this was rejected and thereafter I grew to despise the use of the pun in journalism.

The choice of names is very important, whether of objects or people. Names chosen by parents are often selected very cavalierly when compared with the considered conservatism of a corporation when choosing a company name. Naming such an object as a magazine can have an important effect on its future, just as the naming of a child can affect the pattern of its personality and intellectual development. From the outset I was keen to add the words Australian Music Journal to *Canon* in order to establish for it a more recognizable and professional identity. This suggestion did not at first meet with a favourable response from the Editor, and was one of many early lessons I was to receive on the wisdom of overstepping the bounds of authority. There was also the question of my *own* name.

'I don't much care for "Frank" as a name…or even "Francis", do *you* my boy?' the conductor said over breakfast one morning. 'I've been giving it some thought, and I'd like to christen you "Bruno", what do you think?'

When I looked startled, he continued: 'After a dear friend of mine…the German conductor Bruno Walter.' (he had never met Bruno Walter)

It was not the first time I had felt a sense of dissatisfaction with my name in its abbreviated form. On my birth certificate my mother had insisted on the name appearing as Francis, but it was invariably reduced to Frank, which indeed I did not care for. To receive the entirely new appellation of Bruno however seemed utterly pretentious, but at the time I made no objection, thinking he may not have been serious. Some time later when reading an analysis of my name by someone versed in Kabalarian Philosophy they referred to the fact that when 'Franks' were required to express themselves in matters requiring finesse and diplomacy they became awkward and embarrassed. As time went by I realized that the conductor *was* serious about re-naming me 'Bruno', and that there was a serious intent behind the change of name. It was part of an overall strategy to encourage me to shed my past, identify more closely with him and to begin a new life.

'What should I call *you* then?' I asked.

'Well, I could say "Uncle Franz", but that might sound a little coy for someone your age I suppose.' He paused for a moment: 'Just call me Franz.'

******

Some of the artists reviewed in the early days of Canon (Top left) Claudio Arrau (Top right) Eileen Joyce (Below left) Igor Hmelnitsky, seated, with composer/teacher Raymond Hanson. (Below right) Boyd Neel, English conductor who brought the Boyd Neel Orchestra to Australia. Dr Neel was generous in his praise of The Canon when interviewed by the Australian media. (Canon Photographs)

The Doppelgänger

The greatest deception men suffer is from their own opinions.

- LEONARDO DA VINCI

10

Changing my given name represented a point of no return. I could never go back to my siblings or my friends, nor to the job I once occupied in the art studio of Goldberg Advertising Agency with such an ill-fitting name as Bruno even if I wanted to, so I now began to avoid meeting friends and past acquaintances for fear of how they would greet me. I came to understand why film stars had their names changed by agents and agencies – 'Groucho' instead of Julius Marx or 'Rock' Hudson instead of Roy Scherer. It not only made them more marketable, it created a whole new persona. This was certainly the case with the great pianist Solomon, who dropped his surname Cutner and was only ever known to audiences as plain Solomon. In my own case the embarrassment of this new name only succeeded in increasing my introversion, which was most likely part of the whole scenario.

With the question of caring for the old lady resolved, it was time to establish a routine, and in the summer of 1950 I commenced compiling a list of the projects it was my intention to work upon in the years ahead, which included music, writing and painting, in addition to producing the music journal; I also prepared a timetable for my week's immediate activities, one of which included practising the piano for several hours a day. When I showed the schedule to the conductor he read it and smiled: 'Just take your time to settle in. When you are ready, you might take a look at my library, which is in dire need of a catalogue. Oh, and the front hedge needs clipping, I think.'

In those early days at 'Norwood' I saw little of the great man. He attended soirees, performed at private parties and regularly ate dinner at the house of his principal benefactors Reginald and Gwen Champ at 18 Woolwich Road, often in the company of distinguished guests, for whom he would play in the subdued lighting of their magnificent music room. When attending dinner at the Champ's house he frequently stayed the night, took breakfast there and would arrive back at 'Norwood' around 10 am the following morning. He would then spend an hour or two in his study, reading mail, answering letters and perhaps playing his grand piano, following which someone would arrive by car – usually his student John Champ, or John's younger sister Judith – and he would leave to have lunch with them or with friends, arriving back at the cocktail hour to dress formally and go out again for dinner, unless he had a pupil or two to fit in before leaving. I was rarely invited to accompany him on these occasions, and since I rose early to practice and went to bed early after often working right through the day at various projects without a break, a week could go by during which the conductor and I might have exchanged only a few words.

The books he asked me to catalogue covered almost every square inch of wall space in the study, and spilled over into a large room at the back of the house which contained some choice pieces of antique furniture and a large open fireplace. Most of the rooms had fireplaces, including my own, and were frequently visited by ringtail possums, some of whom had taken up residence in the ceiling. I spent one very pleasant summer day encouraging a family of possums to quit their residence at 'Norwood' and look for accommodation elsewhere. I found that several of the purple slate tiles on the roof of the house had become dislodged and a hole was the possums' entry point. When I could hear they were all at home, I took a ladder and restored the tiles, sealing the hole. Then, downstairs I removed the ceiling trapdoor and inserted a long pole into the cavity and waited. When evening fell, the anxious little faces of four possums appeared, and one by one they climbed nervously down the pole and bounded out of the house through doors I had left open. I never saw them again and I missed them.

******

The conductor bought a large leather-bound indexed ledger in which to record his books, requiring me to cross-reference them under title and author and then assign them a place on numbered shelves. It was a painstaking task for one who was not a skilled librarian, but the sheer joy of holding the volumes he received and occasionally settling down on a sofa to read excerpts from them more than compensated for any tedium involved.

Time almost ceased to exist, and days passed in silence as I trawled through each bookcase and discovered treasures, such as 19th century first editions of Thackeray rubbing dust jackets with the hand-illustrated *Journeys in Spain* bound in the purple-streaked testicles of a bull. I marvelled at the broad ranging taste of this musician who had swept into the lives of so many ordinary Woolwich people and had given them a glimpse of the glories inherent in all the arts, but in particular music and poetry. He had turned many peoples' lives upside down and ignited in many including myself a desire to raise themselves above mediocrity and aspire to some measure of what they felt he himself had achieved.

Every so often – sometimes weekly, sometimes monthly – a large parcel of books would arrive, postmarked 'Melbourne'. It was not my prerogative to open such parcels, but their contents would eventually be handed to me to be added to certain shelves, with a written instruction to remove other books in order to create a space for the new arrivals. The displaced items would be given away as gifts to the conductor's friends on occasions such as Easter, Christmas, birthdays and anniversaries.

On other occasions, large parcels of books concerned with music would arrive from publishers for review in the magazine *Canon*. These were scanned by the editor and given perfunctory reviews, or on other occasions a significant volume might be sent to a musician he wished to curry favour with for a *pro bono* review, on the understanding that the volume be returned to the editor.

Being the person responsible for cataloguing them, it was the steady stream of books which arrived from Melbourne which most intrigued me. Someone with extremely good taste in literature was responsible for their selection, and it came as no great surprise to open the door at

'Norwood' one morning and find a stout, perspiring lady with a bundle of books under her arm, enquiring after Dr Franz Holford.

'The name is Eddey,' she said. 'Doris Eddey. And you're Bruno, aren't you? Franz has told me all about you. Is he in?'

Doris Eddey was the chief buyer and sales representative for the Melbourne firm of booksellers N H Seward Pty Ltd. I ushered her into his study, where she filled a large armchair, put the parcel of books on her lap and fanned herself vigorously with a handkerchief. When I offered to relieve her of the parcel she waved me away.

'No…thank you Bruno, I'll wait till he gets here. These are some rare editions for the Champs' library, and I'd prefer not to let them out of my sight. Could I have a glass of water, please?'

As she drank, she regarded me steadily and then waved her hand in the direction of the bookshelves: 'So, what do you make of all this, young Bruno?'

When I was at a loss to respond she continued: 'There's a small fortune in this room you know. On that shelf behind you is a copy of Rondelet's *Libri de piscibus marinus* published in 1554 – it's one of the oldest printed books in the world – there aren't too many of *those* lying around let me tell you…'

She crossed the room and reached behind me to take a book from the shelf: 'And this one, by Lycosthenes…' She read the spine in a very Australian accent: '*Prodigiorum ac ostentorum* published three years after Rondelet's. Any idea what it's worth?'

I shrugged: 'What's it about?'

'Oh, you think I haven't read it, eh? Know the price of everything and the value of nothing, umm?'

'I only wondered…'

'Fair enough…fair enough young Bruno. Well, it's a book of strange events, from the story of the Garden of Eden onwards, foretelling comets, floods, fires and monsters. A really weird read.'

She went to another part of the shelves and pointed: 'That's the Verdi edition of *The Great Operas,* signed by him. Only fifty copies printed. Worth thousands of pounds, that book.' She picked out another, smaller volume: 'Here's another little gem. Ever heard of a writer called Ernest Hemingway? He wrote this eight years ago and signed a few copies. *For Whom the Bell Tolls.* That book would bring five thousand American dollars.'

She pointed out a large collection of the works of Robert Schuman, which had once been in the library of Cipriani Potter,[108] whose name was embossed on their bindings. Another rare musical item was a first edition of Wagner's famous essay 'Artwork of the Future'.

This fat lady from Melbourne seemed to know the background of every book in the Holford library. She talked almost non-stop for an hour in a bright, bubbly voice, occasionally stopping to daub the perspiration on her face with a cambric handkerchief. During the course of the conversation she told me that one of the most pleasurable aspects of her job was to supply rare books to the private libraries of the rich and famous, and hinted that in the case of Dr Franz Holford she not only supplied all his books, but gave him volumes for Reginald Champ's library at a special rate, which the conductor 'on-sold' to the steel tycoon. As we awaited the conductor's return she gave me a crash course in cataloguing, which enhanced my standing with him in my new-found role of amanuensis.

******

Doris Eddey was a regular visitor to 'Norwood', but chose not to mix with Franz Holford's inner circle of friends, such as the Champ family, nor with members of the choir. She had known Franz since 1938, when he dedicated a song *Night is fallen* to her.[109] From its very beginning she had supported the magazine *Canon* by placing a full page advertisement for her Melbourne bookshop in each edition (sometimes two or three pages) and acting as a representative for both subscriptions and sales of the magazine and advertisements from Victorian music institutions and publishers, without charging any commission. She adored the magazine's elegant editor, for whom she harboured hopes of more than a business relationship, and being single and wealthy she regularly gave him money with no expectation of it being repaid. He accepted her patronage as if it was his due, but privately he despised her – on one occasion describing her to me as 'that disgusting woman', when on one occasion she attempted to kiss him passionately.

Although most of the books in the Holford library were in perfect condition, some of them had gathered dust, and I kept by me a soft cloth with which I wiped both the book and the shelf before cataloguing and replacing it. I seldom indexed a book without at least riffling through it, for it was surprising what some of them contained in the way of pressed flowers, bookmarks of one kind or another and sometimes notes, photographs and letters.

Some contained postcards from Europe, which appeared to have been sent to Franz from famous musicians, which he altered so that the messages gave the impression that he had once lived and studied abroad.

One day as I thumbed through a rare London edition of *Little Dorrit*, a small press cutting fell from the volume and fluttered to the floor. It was an extract from an Australian suburban newspaper containing a brief letter to the editor bearing no date, but carrying the message: 'This is to warn those who are slandering my name that unless they desist I will be forced to take legal action.' The letter was signed 'Franz Holford, Beecroft'.

I hastily put the cutting back inside the book and placed the volume in its position on the shelf, reflecting on what aspect of his life people could use to slander such an eminent man.

******

The office from which the magazine *Canon* was published was no larger than 10' x 8' and occupied a room in the middle of the house, opening onto a small hallway which led out past a breakfast room on the left to the back garden. The office contained little furniture besides a 4-door filing cabinet, an oak desk on which stood the telephone and a portable electric typewriter. There was a hard-backed chair and wall shelves bulging with office supplies, manuscripts and printer's galley proofs.

Since my main mission was to help produce the magazine, I was given immediate entrée to this room, and on my first day working there I discovered the reason I had been approached by Franz Holford. Amongst the mass of correspondence awaiting filing was a letter from the English musician Eric Fenby[110] in North Riding, Yorkshire, and it was a reply to a request from Dr Holford asking Fenby to contribute an article to *Canon* describing the years from 1928-1934 when he had acted as amanuensis to the great composer Frederick Delius.

In accepting the invitation, Fenby congratulated Holford on acquiring an amanuensis of his own, and extended the sincere wish that the association would be as fruitful and happy as that which he had experienced with Delius at Grez-sur-Loing in France. I realized with a shock that the amanuensis Fenby was referring to was myself.

Did Franz Holford see himself then in the same category of genius as Frederick Delius? Was I expected to be his Eric Fenby?

******

Among the myriad of smaller duties for which I became responsible, my new employer informed me that the standard procedure for answering the front door was first to ascertain who the visitor was, by peeking through the lace curtains in the bay window fronting the veranda. There were certain people, he said, to whom he would not open his door… including his separated wife.

One Sunday morning in response to the front doorbell, I peered through the lace curtains and saw to my utter amazement that the visitor was none other than a girlfriend I had made in the choir. The curtain fell from my fingers and I turned from the window and froze. I had never mentioned my relationship with her to him. As I turned, Franz Holford stood hovering in the hallway, his lips framing the silent question: 'Who?' As I stood with my mouth agape, he looked through the window, and then without exchanging a word, we waited until she rang again, then after a few moments she gave up, and turning, walked out through the front gate.

The Doppelgänger

(Above) Franz Holford and Evelyn Rothwell, wife of Sir John Barbirolli, prior to recording Holford's Sonata for Oboe and Piano at the ABC Studios in Sydney, 1951. Holford wrote four oboe sonatas, including one each for Ian Wilson and Jiri Tancibudek. (Below) Eric Fenby, amanuensis to Frederick Delius, with Yehudi Menuhin. Franz Holford conducted a long correspondence with Fenby, who never visited Australia. (Photographs from Canon)

He looked at me, waving a forefinger from side to side.

'I understand, Bruno', he said finally, with a malicious smile. 'Don't let it worry you, all women are bitches.' I felt ashamed at my cowardice, and wondered vaguely if I would ever see her, or indeed any of my boyhood friends again. She did not deserve to be called a bitch and we had always had a warm and amiable relationship. I found myself wondering if my new employer was a misogynist.

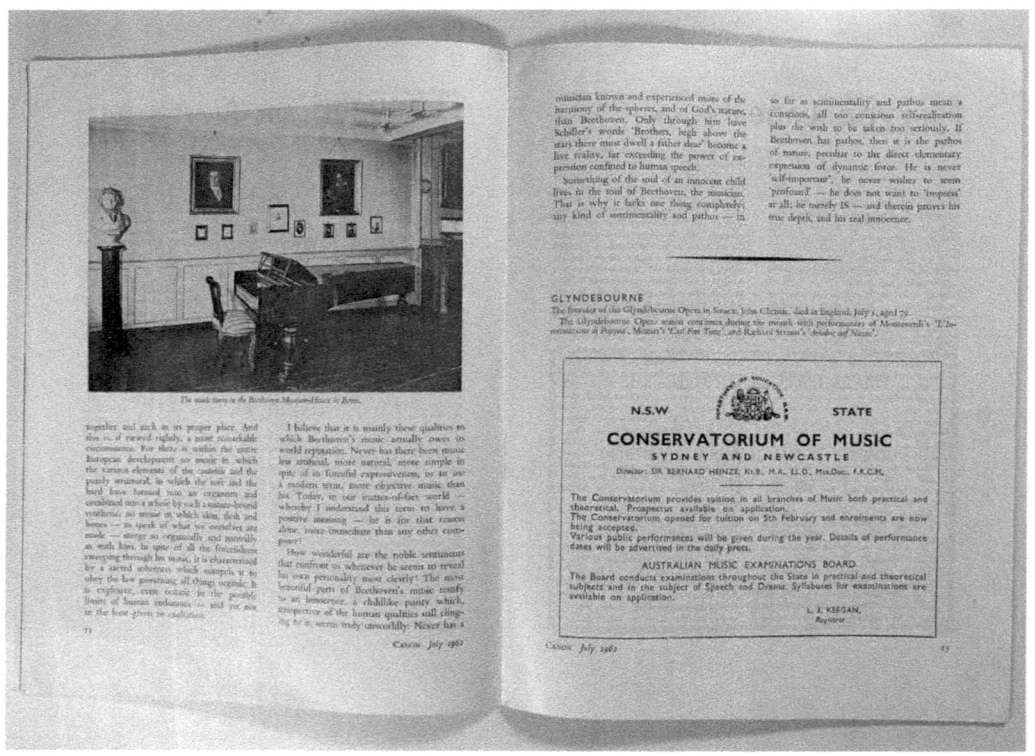

Inside pages from the Musica Viva edition of Canon, produced when the magazine was in its sixteenth year of publication.

The Apocalypse

What thou seest, write in a book...

- REVELATION OF ST JOHN

11

Gradually I evolved a schedule which embraced practising the piano, producing the magazine *Canon*, doing artwork for the journal and trying to paint in oils; writing and editing articles, tending 'Norwood' and its garden, and acquiring a new skill - the art of music copying. I gradually learned music copying by attempting compositions of my own, and also copying those of the conductor.

Whenever I had time to stop and evaluate my life I considered I was living in a space as close to utopia as it might be possible to attain.

Whatever project I was working upon, there was never a shortage of money, and even though I never received a regular income, my financial needs would always be met, for whatever purpose...always in cash. Every now and then I would be taken out shopping for new clothes – often in the expert company of Gwen Champ, who treated me as if I was her own son – which seemed to please the conductor. I made scarcely any monetary demands for personal reasons, having few material needs, but very early in our association it was deemed necessary for me to have a piano of my own to practice upon, instead of inconveniencing the conductor by monopolizing his beautiful soft-voiced Blüthner grand.

One morning a Paling's pantechnicon arrived at 'Norwood' and its workmen installed an upright Belling piano in my room. Belling was a competent German piano manufacturer working in Queensland, whom Dr Holford claimed to know, who imported the necessary components for his pianos from Germany and put them into cases made from Australian timbers. My Belling was a heavy, square, converted pianola, and though it was a drab brown hen beside the blue wren of the conductor's Blüthner, it gave good service for nearly a decade, and when it was serviced, the ever-loyal Reg Newton imparted a velvety touch to its keyboard, which made it a joy to play.

Initially I had no idea where the money came from for costly items such as this piano, assuming it to be from fees the conductor was paid for his performances, from teaching, sales of his music and from revenue produced by the magazine. On certain occasions friends close to him told me that Dr Holford was a man 'of independent means', but at that time I had little understanding of what that phrase meant, nor did I consider it my place to enquire.

As I grew more and more interested in restoring the beautiful sandstone cottage 'Norwood' however, the costs for materials began to escalate as I grew in confidence as a handyman.

At first pleased with my interest in restoring the house and gardens, I began to sense a certain reluctance on the conductor's part when it came to meeting the expenses for renovations such as repairing the stone footings which were wicking ground water, resulting in damp interior walls. According to the home repair manual - which became my bible for renovation work - unless dampness was eliminated, the beautiful wallpapers I was contemplating using would gather mould and eventually peel off the walls.

It was when I insisted on the urgency of this particular repair Franz informed me for the first time that in fact he did not *own* the house as I had imagined, but that he occupied it as a 'protected tenant' - paying the incredibly low rental of only £1 per month. It appeared that his occupancy of the house was a gift during his lifetime from a benefactor who admired his piano playing. Whilst this disappointing news did not diminish my ardour for restoring 'Norwood', it did ring alarm bells in my mind for the first time as to the true financial status of Dr Franz Holford.

******

In all the years I spent at 'Norwood', I cannot recall having more than a handful of formal piano lessons. This was due in part to the assumption ultimately arrived at by both Dr Holford and myself, that amidst the welter of my artistic aspirations, playing the piano was never going to take pride of place, for I had commenced learning so comparatively late in life that I would never reach the standard required to perform in public.

Nevertheless, he provided me with certain books containing pianoforte 'methods', including the volume of sixty-three studies by Friedrich Wieck – Clara Schumann's father – and the pianoforte exercises of Hanon. Another fortunate source for me was all the latest manuals and modern piano pieces being published which came to the magazine *Canon* for a review, many of which I struggled to master.

I gradually discovered, with a deepening sense of disillusionment, that Franz Holford was not a great teacher – some would have said not even a very competent teacher – of the piano, and he never attempted to pass on what he may have known about the theory of music. The very first time I heard him play was the performance he gave of the Tchaikowsky piano concerto at the Champ's house, in which his technique and general appreciation of the music seemed utterly dazzling, but the closer my association with him grew the more I realized how little I had known about music or even music appreciation at that time. As I slowly acquired a more mature musical acumen I realized how lacking he was in finesse, musical insight and sometimes of even basic piano technique.

I began to doubt also his claims of having been taught by the great French pianist Alfred Cortot, and others such as Vladimir de Pachmann and Teichmüller, for as I began to collect Cortot's records and played them over and over again, there was virtually no homothetic relationship between the two pianists' interpretations or styles. Cortot's poetic, delicately immaculate technique would have almost certainly led him to disapprove of Franz Holford's flashy and often waywardly improvisatorial and unimaginative embellishments of most scores he played, including Chopin's most famous works.

It was almost as if the conductor had learned to play the piano 'by ear' – the outward architecture being pleasant enough, but the structure seemed to lack a keystone. When he occasionally played light classics or jazz his touch at the keyboard was delightful, but for music requiring greater depth of technique it became superficial, and he resorted to improvisatory flashes of scales and arpeggios to cover the more complex passages in some of the difficult music he attempted to present.

I never heard him practice technique, such as Dohnányi's notoriously difficult piano studies, which are considered a cornerstone to a pianist's technique, nor did he spend time with scales, arpeggios, double thirds and fourths, double octaves and all the accepted armory of *gradus ad parnassum*. Perhaps he himself recognised this weakness in his technique, for he frequently quoted the words of the great German pianist Walter Gieseking, who maintained he never practised piano technique - having left scales behind where he considered they belonged - in the conservatorium.

******

It was not *what* Franz Holford played so much as *how* he presented his music which endeared him to many people. Without doubt his most lustrous attribute was the charm with which he related to those he met – not 'menials' in the form of tradespeople, whom he tended to dismiss with a wave of his hand - but anyone who displayed an interest in the arts, particularly music. It came as no surprise when he casually announced one day that the famous British musician Eugene Goossens was coming to lunch at the Champ's residence, to give Franz Holford the editor details about Goossens' appointment as director to the Conservatorium of Music in Sydney, a review of which was later to be published in *Canon*.[111]

'I might bring him back here afterwards, Bruno,' he added graciously.

True to his word, the black Bentley belonging to the Champ family pulled up outside 'Norwood' at 5pm and I was introduced to the great British conductor when I opened the door. After being closeted with Dr Holford in the study drinking whisky for a time, I was then summoned to talk briefly with the two musicians. A tallish man of thickset build, Eugene Goossens' presence was intimidating and he had a flair for extremely fashionable clothes - often capping his ensemble with a cloak and broad-brimmed soft felt hat. His face was full, with fine taut white skin and high forehead, peaked eyebrows and steel-blue eyes heavily lidded; a long nose ended bluntly above sensuous lips, around which a faintly ironic smile often hovered.

'I have shown Gene some of your music copying,' Dr Holford said, beaming. 'He would like you to do some for a work he is writing.'

(Left) Eugene Goossens examines a copy of Canon devoted to his life in music (Volume 2 No 5). He said of the journal: 'There are certain amenities of our musical life we mustn't lose. The Canon is one of the most important.'

(Below) The world premiere performance of The Apocalypse, 22 November 1954 in the Sydney Town Hall. Goossens' magnificent oratorio for mixed voices and orchestra was one of the most significant concerts ever given in Australia. (Photos by the author)

In his expansive, cultivated voice Goossens described an oratorio he was planning, set to a text taken from The Apocalypse of St John the Divine. It was a large choral and symphonic work he said, which he had been working on for almost ten years.[112] It was nearing completion, and there would be a great deal of music copying required for orchestral and choral parts, which in those days was done painstakingly by hand.

Although most of it would be done by the ABC copyists he said, he would be pleased if I would handle the copying of a specific group, such as the flutes. No one asked a question as to my ability to cope with such a commission – no inquiry as to what work I had done in this field in the past, nor a request for samples of my copying. I would be responsible for the flute parts – that was that. I learned later that this was typical of Goossens' assessment of people.

Eugene Goossens' main reason for coming to Australia was to fill the post of resident conductor of the Sydney Symphony Orchestra. The orchestra rehearsed in the Sydney Town Hall, and with his typically autocratic generosity the new director said to me: 'My dear, if you're free during the day, come any time you wish and sit in the hall and listen – there's no better musical education.'

Franz Holford bit his lip, but I resolved to take up an offer far too good to refuse. To be called 'dear' by this amazing musician was something I had never experienced before.

Sometime after this initial meeting, Franz began bringing home extracts from the score of Eugene Goossens' massive oratorio *The Apocalypse*. Scored for the resources of two symphony orchestras, brass band, augmented choirs, soloists and the huge Town Hall grand organ, the process of copying the parts for its premiere strained the Australian Broadcasting Corporation's music copying department to the limit, and individual sections were out-sourced to private copiers, of whom I was lucky to be one. My task was to copy parts for the woodwind section – mainly the flutes - and this was a large enough commission to keep me busy for many weeks.

As I worked, I became familiar with the often enchanting melodic lines occupied by the flutes in Goossens' mighty work. I used to whistle them to myself as I worked and one day when I knew the composer was closeted with Franz in his study, I took a toilet break and walked through the house, unashamably whistling the flute line I was copying. As he was leaving, Eugene Goossens thrust his head around my half-open door.

'So you like those flute lines then?' he asked with a broad smile.

'I really do,' I replied. 'It's.....'

He didn't wait to hear my evaluation of *The Apocalypse*, but as he left, I heard him say to Franz with typical immodesty: 'The boy's got taste.'

******

The performance of *The Apocalypse* on 22nd November 1954 was, in this author's opinion - one of the most significant concerts in Australia's musical history.

The Sydney Town Hall was packed to overflowing, both in the body of the hall and on its large stage. A 400-voice choir consisted of the combined Hurlstone Choral Society, the Royal Philharmonic Society, the Sydney Male Voice Choir and the Conservatorium Select Choir, in which my future wife sang. There was also a consort of recorders from the Sydney Conservatorium and the Sydney Symphony Orchestra was augmented by players from two Sydney brass bands. The whole fabric was underpinned by the massive Sydney Town Hall Grand Organ.

Before the concert Franz went backstage to assist his friend Goossens, but such was the crowd I had to find a standing-room-only position under one of the galleries. The thrill of hearing the music I had a hand in copying more than made up for the fatigue of standing through the long performance, especially as the opening theme enters with the stratospheric flutes, and as Franz later put it in an excellent review in *Canon*: 'This germ, with its immense possibilities, becomes the binding element of the whole work.'[113]

Goossens led the gigantic work through all its majestic choruses, solos and symphonic permutations with mesmeric conducting, only being slightly let down at the conclusion of Part One by a 32 ft Diapason on the organ which refused to shut down, carrying its booming note throughout the hall for several seconds longer than it should have. There was no such aberration in the second half, when the organ cut off crisply on the final mighty chord. With his inimitable sense of humour, Goossens blew the organist a kiss as the audience erupted into prolonged applause.

The Apocalypse had taken Eugene Goossens ten years to write. Remarkably it had only that one performance in 1954, until it was revived almost thirty years later at the Sydney Opera House with a performance by the conductor Myer Fredman and the Sydney Symphony Orchestra 13th November 1982.

A little over a year after presenting his choral masterpiece, Eugene Goossens would be confronted with his own apocalyptic moment which would ultimately ruin him.

******

On Friday 9 March 1956, Sir Eugene Goossens stepped off a plane at 8am in Sydney after a holiday conducting tour of England and the Continent and was immediately detained by Customs officers. The Vice Squad was called to examine various items found in his luggage. Led by Detective-Inspector R Walden, the detectives questioned Goossens for four hours in the doctor's room in the Custom's section of the overseas terminal; at midday Sir Eugene went with detectives to the Criminal Investigation Branch, where detectives again questioned him until 3 pm. A week later he was charged by the Federal Court under the Customs Act for bringing 1,100 indecent pictures, a number of books, rubber masks and several films into the country. He was fined £100, but because of his position escaped a gaol sentence.

Amidst the glare of publicity, all Goossens' friends deserted him – Head of the ABC Charles Moses being the only one to speak on his behalf. Terrified of what the media scrutiny might reveal about *himself*, Franz Holford also remained silent, but subsequently published a paean of praise to his friend in an 'Overture' devoted to the incident in the April edition of *Canon*, which we had been preparing at the time. It concluded thus:

> The core of this matter is, again, Sir Eugene's musicianship: with the agony of his Faustian pathology we are not concerned.[114]

Goossens went into exile in England for six years. He became ill on a visit to Switzerland in 1962 and returned to London, where he died shortly after in Hillingdon Middlesex Hospital. He was only 69.

Extract from The Sydney Morning Herald, 3 January 1993

Cut down to size

It's hard to hate someone once you understand them.

- LUCY CHRISTOPHER

12

The time I spent at Goldberg Advertising Agency had taught me that any publication which was published independently of financial assistance from governments, commercial organizations, benefactors or some form of philanthropy, required advertising for its survival – even if it boasted a wide base of subscribers. *The Canon* unfortunately had a very narrow subscription base, which rarely rose above 2,000 and thus its need for financial support from another source was obvious.

Unfortunately the idea of soliciting advertising for a magazine whose message was esoteric and whose apotheosis utopian was unfortunately anathema to *Canon's* editor. It became clear that if advertising was deemed to be necessary or desirable, the process of obtaining it would fall to someone else.

Despite Dr Holford's protest that I should not concern myself with financial matters, I became increasingly driven by guilt feelings that my role as amanuensis produced no tangible revenue, and that to be true to myself I needed to earn my financial keep. Even though it was obvious that the financial benefactor behind *Canon* was the generous Reginald Champ, I became possessed of the idea of making the magazine more professional looking, with the ultimate aim of its becoming economically viable. Thus a great deal of my time began to be spent seeking out music stores, publishers and advertisers who were attempting to reach readers such as those who bought *Canon*.

The soliciting of advertising became a subject which generally annoyed the conductor and he tolerated my efforts rather than encouraged them, for since the magazine was being underwritten by Reg Champ anyway, he felt no obligation to make it pay for itself. At the time I understood this attitude, for like others, I tended to place him above such worldly considerations as selling advertising space; but to my relief and great internal satisfaction I found a surprising number of firms which when approached were instantly positive, and I began to collect a number of regular advertisers.

One of the regular advertisers who had supported the magazine almost since its inception was the firm of A E Smith who had offices at Hunter Street in the city and who manufactured and sold stringed instruments. I came to enjoy my visits to Arthur Smith's shop - to watch the 68-year-old English luthier at work, making his sought after violins. Working in a very restricted Australian market he gave opportunities to many young violin makers, and took advertising space in *Canon* more to support an ideal than to advance his business.

It was in his shop that I met one of his most gifted employees, Lloyd Adams. Adams was thirty-eight at the time - a tall, elegant and urbane man with finely chiselled features and a mass of dark hair which he brushed back without parting. He resembled the Canadian actor Christopher Plummer. Adams had learned his craft with Arthur Smith in the 1920s and after practising in Western Australia for a time, moved back to Sydney to join A E Smith in Hunter Street. When I met him he was contemplating moving again to start his own business, which he ultimately did, setting up a repair and violin making shop in Castlereagh Street in the city.

One of the large commissions Lloyd Adams took with him when he left A E Smith was the restoration of a Cremonese viola belonging to the leader of the violas in the Sydney Symphony Orchestra at that time, Robert Pikler. The instrument was of aristocratic Italian origin, bearing an authentic label by Giovanni Grancino of Milan dated 1685, but tragically the viola had been cut down to the size of a freakishly small violin, probably because its owner had small hands and found it difficult to hold for long periods.

Purchased in 1930 in Vienna by Richard Goldner, the founder of Musica Viva in Australia, Adams' seemingly impossible task was to restore the valuable instrument to its original size, by putting back what had been cut away. Visiting his bohemian style workshop overlooking Castlereagh Street, I became fascinated with this project, and commenced documenting it with photographs and extensive notes, for publication in *Canon*. Over a period of two years Adams patiently added ¾" all round the edge of this instrument - matching the ancient wood, fibre for fibre and splicing in the magnificent varnish from a recipe he succeeded in blending with the original – then almost three hundred years old. When the restoration was complete it was almost impossible to trace where the join occurred on the instrument.

Lloyd Adams was delighted with the success of the quite miraculous feat he had accomplished – the most difficult in the whole repertoire of violin making – and when the long, illustrated article appeared in *Canon* for which this author acted as his 'ghost writer', his fame spread and demand for his services came from several overseas countries in addition to Australia. One day as he was completing repairs on a double bass owned by a prominent American jazz player, he asked me if I had ever contemplated learning a stringed instrument. I shook my head, but added that I would like to try.

'Then since you have been so kind to *me*, let me do *you* a favour.' He disappeared into his workshop for a moment and returned holding a cello. 'Maybe this will serve as the incentive you need. I bought it from a deceased estate for £90. It's worth at least a thousand – probably much more. It's yours.'

He explained that it was a German-made instrument, and even though it had no label, it was extremely finely made. 'It is of such high quality it will last you all your life, should you decide to learn.' I ultimately paid the £90 which it had cost him, upon which he 'threw in' a felt-lined carrying bag. Later he sold me a Hill bow for £100, which after a few years was also valued at many thousands of pounds.

When I arrived back at 'Norwood' with the cello I showed it to Dr Holford excitedly, but his reaction was immediately sour. He resented me having friends or even business acquaintances outside the immediate circle of his influence, and lately my work selling advertising on the magazine had begun to take me back into the 'real world'.

(Above) Australian luthier Lloyd Adams undertook the almost impossible task of restoring a valuable Cremonese viola, which had been cut down to the size of a violin, by adding ¾" all round its edge. The complete story appeared in the March 1955 edition of Canon. (Below) Principal Violist with the Sydney Symphony Orchestra Robert Pikler (left), paid tribute to Adams' feat. (Photos by the Author)

The fact that someone else would think enough of my work to reward me in such a handsome fashion annoyed him. He remained aloof for several days, but one morning as I was struggling to tune the instrument, his head appeared around my doorway and he said cheerfully: 'If you're determined to play that hideous thing, I have a teacher for you.'

He gave me a letter of introduction to a Hungarian cellist newly arrived in Australia whom Eugene Goossens had appointed to the Sydney Symphony Orchestra. Hans Gyors lived at Bondi, where I began to travel once a week for lessons. A small, rotund man of swarthy complexion, Hans Gyors – who quickly adopted the more anglicized surname George – was a refugee from the communist invasion of Hungary. In appearance he resembled a European gnome, but he had a near perfect technique on the cello, and immediately attracted a number of excellent students who went on to become professional performers.

******

Selling advertising for the music magazine forced me out of my reclusive existence, and I began travelling to the city again in search of advertising clients for the magazine, and in between spending hours at a time sitting in the Town Hall listening to rehearsals of the Sydney Symphony Orchestra, after I had done my rounds. Staff of the Town Hall became quite used to seeing me sitting in a not too prominent position, either at the back of the hall or off to the side under the east or west balconies and I was never challenged as to why I was there. Whether the English maestro spoke to someone on my behalf I never knew, but over the months of sitting in at rehearsals of this famous orchestra under its resident conductor and the many visiting conductors from overseas, my general knowledge and appreciation of music certainly increased, as the great man had assured me it would.

Occasionally I would sit in the balcony where I could see the conductor's face, and as Eugene Goossens walked briskly on stage for a rehearsal – usually accompanied by an enthusiastic fanfare from the brass section of the orchestra – he would sometimes see me and nod approvingly. Now that I had taken up the cello, to sit in that august company of musicians became my desideratum.

Eugene goossens became a regular visitor to the Champ mansion 'Threlkeld', as did a gathering galaxy of distinguished international musicians, such as Robert Dalley-Scarlett, who won the Hallé Medal for his brilliant work on Handel; Georg Schneevoigt, the Finnish conductor who was a personal friend of Sibelius; Dr Edgar Bainton; Sir John Barbirolli and his famous oboist wife Evelyn Rothwell; the Pope's organist Fernando Germani and many others.

Sometimes Dr Holford would bring them back to 'Norwood' for an additional whisky or two if he thought it safe to reveal his workplace, but 'Threlkeld' was a far grander arena and I gradually began to realize why the house and its incumbents was so important to him. The Champs by reason of their position in society gathered around them a circle of the powerful and moneyed elite, who delighted in the almost Lisztian atmosphere engendered by good food and wine, luxurious surroundings and music presented in an incomparable soiree setting. Doctors of medicine, bankers, publishers, corporate directors, industrialists and their wives all trekked to Hunters Hill to be entertained by the Champ family and its star attraction, Dr Franz Holford. Nothing so meretricious or plebeian as a fee or donation was ever requested of the audience, but many gave generously in support of Dr Holford and in particular his idealistic venture *Canon*, now carrying its sub-title: Australian Music Journal.

******

Idealism was a theme he constantly stressed when referring to his editorship of *The Canon*. In a letter to his pupil Don Newton[115] he once wrote:

> No one seems to even sense the radient *(sic)* yet nameless
> ideal I strive for…

In his beautiful copperplate hand, the conductor would write to overseas musicians whose forthcoming tours to Australia would be revealed to him by his friend Bernard Heinze in the Australian Broadcasting Commission - the monopolist entrepreneur – and he would offer them hospitality upon their arrival. This would frequently be coupled with a request for them to contribute an article or interview for *Canon* readers when they arrived.

He was seldom refused, since a performer's vanity and the prospect of sympathetic press notices were powerful motivators. The strategy was masterful, for the visitors did not stay long enough to investigate in detail Franz Holford's background, nor his actual role in the Australian musical scene, yet they added lustre to his burgeoning *curriculum vitae*, and to the scholarship of his journal, to which they frequently contributed articles gratis and gave financial support.

It became clear to me over the years that whilst he lived and conducted his musical life through *The Canon* as a kind of reclusive patron of Australian music, Franz Holford actually despised Australia and Australian musicians generally. He constantly yearned to be identified with England or Europe.

The house and magnificent gardens of 'Threlkeld' could have been transplanted to Hunters Hill from a county such as Surrey in England, and the invariable comment drawn from visitors to both 'Threlkeld' and 'Norwood' was: 'How *English* looking!' When closeted with a famous overseas celebrity, Dr Holford would proceed to damn with faint praise Australia's position in the world musical scene and lament his own isolation from the hub and heartbeat of the great centres he had supposedly left behind – England and Germany.

An example of the regard in which he held Australian music was his estimation of John Antill, composer of the famous ballet *Corroboree*, who lived in another area of Hunters Hill. I visited Antill on several occasions at the ABC on music copying matters, as well as to interview him for an article in *Canon*[116], when he was experimenting with a new device for writing musical scores, called the Music Writer[117], a kind of musical typewriter. On one of these visits, following his birthday, he scratched his head and said in a genuinely mystified voice:

'Why would Franz send me a book called *Poisonous Fungi of Australia* as a birthday present?'

It was one of the many books I had displaced during my cataloguing of the Holford library and was one of Franz's ironic gestures to an Australian composer with whose works he had little in common.

******

The role of conductor is almost designed to transform an ordinary human being into a narcissist. Some few may escape the temptation to fall in love with the image of their other self which they create via that incredible organ of pooled talent the symphony orchestra, but to most, narcissism becomes and remains their *arrière-pensée*. Like a general leading an army of individuals, the role of conductor produces few Alexanders, Marlboroughs, Wellingtons or Napoleons whose names endure throughout the pages of music history, but some do, and such a one in Australia was undoubtedly Eugene Goossens. However, he wore his narcissism as lightly as he wore his cloak, and the faintly ironic smile which constantly played about his full and rounded lips told the world: 'There, I am aware of my genius, but I can laugh at it!' Thus when the brass section played a signatory fanfare as he walked on stage at rehearsals, or as in Spain, members of the orchestra once bestrewed an indoor swimming pool with pink and white frangipani flowers for the great man to swim among, he deemed it to be no more than his due and no less than he expected. His autocratic presence alone lent verisimilitude to such occasions.

Goossens created enemies from the moment of his arrival in Australia, from lesser musicians who saw him as arrogant – a word which brings with it the kiss of death in this country – especially when he removed from his orchestra some players whose time had obviously come, and replaced them with rising young stars and with imports from war-ravaged countries such as Hungary. He insisted on the highest standards, from the back desk of his violins to the soloist who might be performing with him, and I observed this at close range during a particular concert at the Sydney Town Hall in June 1948.

During the rehearsal there was obvious tension between the female soloist and Goossens concerning a passage in the third movement of the Grieg Piano Concerto, for which the pianist had not had sufficient rehearsal time. That evening I was privileged to be in the Green Room with Franz Holford at the invitation of the resident conductor and was assigned the task of rubbing some brandy into the lower part of Goossens' back, since he suffered disc problems in his spine. As he was finishing dressing, the door opened and the soloist appeared.

'I cannot go on, Gene,' she said in a distressed voice, 'The third movement…I haven't got it.' Goossens stared at her in disbelief, and with total lack of sympathy said: 'Nonsense. It will be fine.'

To everyone's consternation the famous pianist threw herself into a complete tantrum and began screaming and sobbing hysterically as she begged Goossens to have an announcer tell the audience that she was unwell and could not play. Goossens looked at her contemptuously for a moment and then began pushing her out through the door.

'You may do as you please at your own recitals my dear,' he said waspishly, 'But you'll not ruin *mine*. Now, let's go.' He pushed the pianist along the corridor and up to the steps, giving her a final shove out onto the stage, where she immediately regained her composure and smiled and waved graciously to the enthusiastic audience as she made her way to the piano at centre stage. Dr Holford went to a seat in the southern gallery with a group of friends and I sat in a favourite position in the crowded organ gallery, from where I could see the conductor's face, and follow the music in a miniature score.

The first two movements of the concerto passed beautifully and without incident, but when the fatal passage in the third movement arrived, the pianist had the massive memory lapse she knew was going to occur and leaped forward about three pages in the score.

Marvellous players that they were, the leaders of the various sections of the orchestra somehow managed to keep the music going as Goossens searched furiously in his conductor's score and found the spot at which the pianist had arrived. Quickly he hissed out the number which corresponded with that in the orchestral parts, and gradually the whole orchestra became unified again and 'caught up' with its illustrious soloist. It was one of the finest examples of musicianship I ever witnessed and as Goossens gave an appreciative nod to all members of the orchestra at its conclusion, the audience gave rapturous applause to the soloist, whose face reflected the enormous relief she must have felt.

Science replaces a cottage industry. Australian composer John Antill, who was in charge of music copying at the ABC, imported this 'Music Writer' from America, which went a long way to eradicating errors made when copying scores by hand. It was gradually replaced by computing software programs. (Photos from Canon)

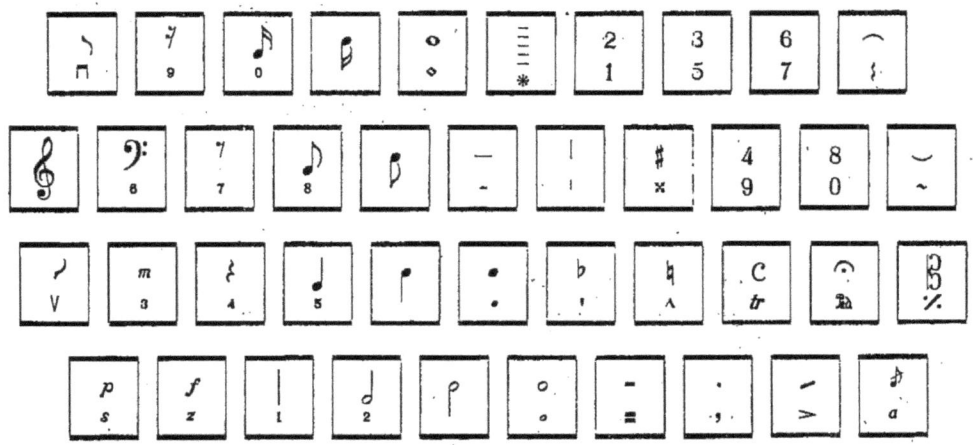

(Above) Keyboard of the 'Music Writer'

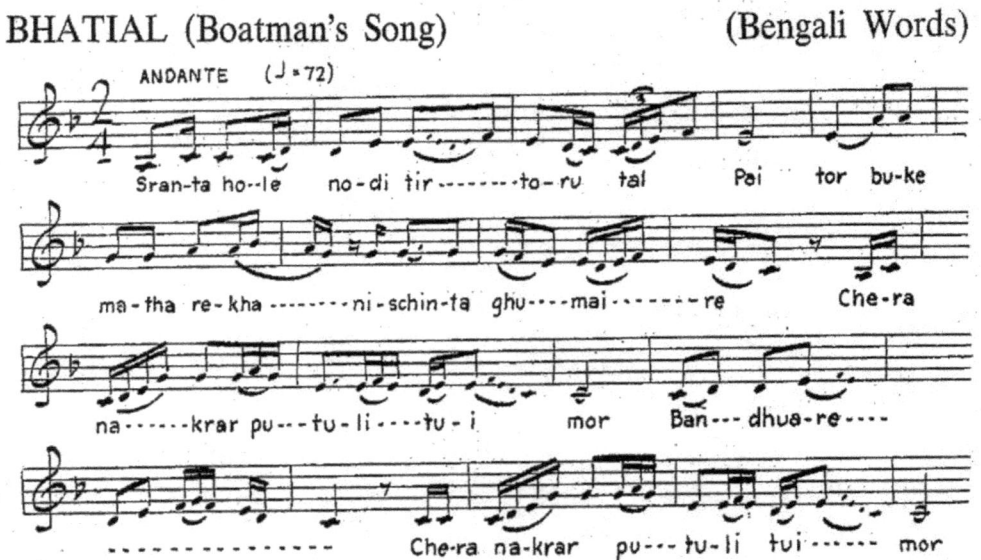

(Above) Sample of the author's musical handwriting

In the press critique which followed, the enormous gaffe passed unnoticed, and confirmed my own suspicions about the musical acumen of some of Sydney's music critics.

******

One of the legacies of my yeoman ancestry was to be blessed with rude good health, and this had undoubtedly played a part in pulling me through a coma following a cricketing accident when I was fifteen, when I was struck a vicious blow on the right temple by a cricket ball. The doctor informed me later that it should have killed me. Therefore when at twenty one my tonsils became infected and the glands in my neck swelled painfully, I knew I needed professional treatment. Since visits to a doctor were not encouraged, because of the necessity of filling in forms which gave away information, the conductor arranged for one of the doctors who was a regular visitor to the Champ's soirees to examine me after a Saturday night concert.

Dr Robert Murphy needed only the most cursory examination of my throat, before declaring: 'Tonsillectomy. Immediately. I'll book you into the Mater Hospital, where I operate.'

The operation was a standard procedure and there were no complications. Lying in a shared public ward after reviving from the anaesthetic, I became conscious of a man in a bed opposite mine, whose face seemed vaguely familiar. He was watching me intently and he had a sketch pad in his hand. When he saw that I was awake, he tore off a sheet with a craggy smile and leaned across to lay it on my bed. 'Portrait of a young man on drugs,' he said, and the smile broadened. 'Keep it if you like, the name's Bill.' With a shock I realized it was William Dobell, the artist who that year had won the Archibald Prize with his portrait of Margaret Olley.

Photograph from the ABC Weekly of 2 June 1951 which advertised the 42 year-old Franz Holford, playing his own Piano Sonata in B Minor in 'Afternoon Classics' on Radio 2SM.

No one came to visit me in hospital. I did not inform my family about the operation, and I would not have expected a visit from Dr Holford. However, when Dr Murphy came by on his daily rounds, he said: 'You'll be fine, young fella. Lots of jelly and ice cream. Oh, and you're lucky… Gwen Champ said you can stay at her house for a week until you're quite well again.'

Later I learned that Gwen Champ's offer was the result of the conductor confiding in her that he had no idea how he was going to cope with a sick amanuensis on his hands for an indefinite period.

This period of convalescence at 'Threlkeld' was to provide me with a firsthand glimpse into Reginald Champ's household, and of the special relationship Dr Franz Holford enjoyed with this affluent family.

******

The narcissist

*Expect nothing. Live frugally
on surprise.*

- ALICE WALKER

13

The address given for the early editions of *The Canon* was number 18 Woolwich Road, where I now lay recovering from my tonsillectomy in an upstairs bedroom overlooking the entrance to the house. Prostrate and with a furnace raging in my throat, I awoke to hear voices at play outside the window and the dull thwack of a tennis ball. As I sat up to listen more carefully, Gwen Champ's head suddenly appeared round the door.

'Hullo Bruno,' she said in a deep and slightly husky tone. 'How are you feeling?' It was quite a shock to hear her call me by my new name, but not unpleasant. It dawned on me that the conductor must have told her that I was no longer 'Frank'. I wondered who else he had told besides her and Doris Eddey.

I could not speak and waved my arms in a gesture of frustration.

'I understand, don't try to talk.' She pointed to a button on the wall beside the bed. 'Do you see that button? If you need anything…like a glass of water, or some fresh jelly, just press it.'

I stared curiously at this beautiful middle-aged woman who had so generously taken me into her home, and whom I had only ever seen from a distance at choir rehearsals. Still possessed of an elegant figure after two children, she was of medium build, with wonderfully thick, jet-black hair graying slightly at the temples, framing a face with high cheekbones and an arched nose. She had a nervous tic in her eyes which caused her on occasions to blink rapidly several times and raise her eyebrows at the same time, a characteristic which often disconcerted people. When I looked at the cigarette she held between the first and second fingers of her right hand, she seemed to become embarrassed, and waving the smoke away, she left just as suddenly as she had appeared.

I got out of bed and groggily made my way across a hallway to a larger bedroom which overlooked the tennis court and peered out the curtained windows. Reg Champ, tall and lean, with a cadaverous face not unlike Abraham Lincoln, was playing tennis with his daughter Judith, and both appeared to be excellent players. After watching them for a few moments, I began looking around the room I was in, which appeared to be John Champ's bedroom. In pride of place over a large single bed was a framed studio portrait of Franz Holford, wearing a dinner suit and spotted bow tie, his dark hair neatly cut and brushed straight back, showing side levers of gray; he wore a pair of heavy, horn-rimmed glasses. The photo bore an inscription in white ink on its dark background and I kneeled on the bed to read it: 'To dearest John. Affectionately, Franz'. Soon I became giddy and weak again and staggered back across the hall and flopped into bed, my eyes alighting on the wall button. Instinctively I leaned across and pressed it, and heard the tinkle of a bell downstairs towards the rear of the house. A few moments later a thin woman wearing an apron appeared at the door.

'Hello luv,' she said in a kindly voice, 'Can I get you anythink?'

I made a gesture with my hand indicating I would like a drink, and she nodded briefly and disappeared. As I waited for her I dozed off again and when I awoke, to my surprise Judith Champ in her tennis dress was sitting on the end of the bed, holding a glass of water and smiling.

'I'm Judy…from the choir, remember?' She passed me the glass. 'Thought I'd bring this to you and have a bit of a chat.'

'Thanks,' I muttered hoarsely, with daggers stabbing at my throat.

'You're the new amanuensis, aren't you?', She said. 'Mum says you'll be staying with us for a week or so?'

The narcissist

I nodded and with difficulty drank some water from the glass. Judith watched me closely as if trying to understand what I was doing in her parents' house. She was an attractive girl, not much older than myself - tall, with naturally curly black hair which gleamed with health and she smiled easily with her grey eyes.

'You might find us a strange family,' she continued. 'We entertain a lot. Tonight we're having a séance. Have you ever been to a séance?' I shook my head. 'Eugene Goossens is coming – the conductor, you know?' then she added almost petulantly 'Oh, but you've met him, haven't you…he's coming after his concert. You can come and watch, if you like.'

She studied me thoughtfully for a moment. 'We all love Franz, you know…' Again I nodded assent. 'Especially my mother. What do you know about him?'

'Know about him…? Not very much,' I croaked. 'Why?'

'Well, you'll get to know a lot about him, living in his house. Look, he means a lot to this family, particularly to my mother', upon which she gave me a meaningful glance. I wondered vaguely how this was possible, since Gwen Champ was already married to the steel tycoon, but I let it pass. She continued.

'Has his mother ever said anything to you? You know…about his life or anything?'

I now had the feeling I was being given the third degree and that the questioning contained more than a touch of urgency. It was becoming hostile. Still, I thought Judith might know the answer to the puzzle of his name, so I forced myself to answer.

'What about? I haven't spoken much to his mother…all I know is that she sometimes calls him Bill. Why do *you* think she calls him Bill?' I asked hoarsely.

She reacted sharply and again eyed me closely. 'It's supposed to be a nickname. Do you believe that? I started doing his family tree, but ran into all kinds of dead-ends. Did you ever hear him called Albert?'

I shook my head, whereupon she continued: 'Bruno, if she ever says anything…you know…significant, about him…his mother I mean…about his past…I want you to tell *me* first, understand?'

There it was again…more than a touch of hostility. She *too* called me Bruno, as if I had always had the name. I was becoming a little annoyed at the peremptory nature of her questions, but I nodded weakly. She was obviously a person used to getting her own way.

******

It was a saturday evening and after sleeping all afternoon I awoke to a beautifully still, purple-coloured twilight, with the remaining rays of a golden sunset streaming through the casement windows - a perfect Australian summer's day. On the end of the bed was a woollen dressing gown and a pair of felt slippers, which I dressed in and groped my way unsteadily down the polished wooden staircase towards the entrance foyer. The stairs had a Persian carpet runner held in place by bright brass rods and my feet made no sound. Pausing outside the music room I noticed that one of the two 9' Steinway grand pianos had its keyboard open, and overcome with curiosity and awe I entered the room and sat down on its piano stool. I struck several chords upon its ivory keys, and almost immediately John Champ appeared in the doorway.

'Please don't play that,' he cried angrily. 'It's just been tuned for tonight's concert.'

Startled, I got to my feet, but almost before I had time to respond to the command, his mood changed and he smiled disarmingly.

'Oh, I *am* sorry Bruno, I didn't mean to be rude…it's just that they go out of tune so quickly for those of us that have perfect pitch.'

If his tone of voice was condescending, it was intentional, for his whole demeanour left no doubt he felt he was dealing with someone clearly beneath him in social status. It came as a source of satisfaction when years later I learned that few musicians actually possess 'perfect pitch' and what John Champ possessed was not *perfect* pitch, but excellent *relative* pitch, and there was quite a difference between the two.

(Above) Judith Champ, with Franz Holford's piano student Donald Newton in the 1940s. Judith pursued a career in acting in Australia and England and had a lifelong interest in the psychic and spirituality. She published a book on the subject in 2002 containing interviews with ten acknowledged experts in the field. (Photos by courtesy Donald Newton)

(Below) Franz Holford at the keyboard of his Blüthner piano in the 1950s.

After dinner, guests began arriving for the Saturday night soirée. The séance I learned was to be held late in the evening, after most guests had departed and when the famous Eugene Goossens would be present, following his concert at the Sydney Town Hall.

A successful séance, Judith Champ informed everyone, could only be held among a small group – usually no more than three or four – as it was unwieldy for more than this number to operate the planchette on the Ouija Board. No amount of persuasion could inveigle Dr Holford to be part of this group, even though Judith tried her utmost to entice him to take part. He was obviously uneasy about the whole process and tried in vain to dissuade her from holding the séance. However, he was forced to go along with the wishes of his hosts, and it was finally agreed that the group would comprise Judith Champ, Goossens – who was always anxious to participate – the orthopaedic surgeon Dr Stuart Scougall, and Judith's brother John. Several others, including myself, would be permitted to be present, but seated well back from the table and in semi-darkness.

There was an element of danger and excitement about holding a séance at this time, for it was for many years considered an illegal activity. During the Second World War, the Scottish Medium Helen Duncan was jailed in a London women's prison and died an early death, for the 'appalling crime' of holding physical phenomena séances. Shortly after WWII, Eugene Goossens became interested in the idea of talking to spirits who had passed over, when he heard about the English Medium Leslie Flint's claim that he spoke regularly to Frederic Chopin and took down musical notation from the famous Polish composer.[118]

It became clear that Judith Champ's motive in trying to involve Franz Holford in the séance was to discover more about his past, and I soon realized that, even though this family were numbered among his closest confidantes, the doctor had revealed little or nothing to them of his personal history.

I returned to the bedroom above the stairs when the guests began to arrive, since it was considered unwise for me to sit through what was always a fairly lengthy musical program before the séance commenced.

On this particular evening a new tenor whom Dr Holford had met was to sing through a number of songs the conductor had written especially for him. The tenor was Christopher Lodge, an English farmer who owned a valuable 250 acre sheep property named 'Rosewick' at Millthorpe in southwest New South Wales, but he had also recorded for the BBC and had an impressive tenor voice. He was prosperous and anxious to use some of his hard earned wealth to fund the recording of some Franz Holford songs, sung by himself. I went back to sleep in the upstairs room as I awaited being called to attend the séance, to the sounds of him singing one of Dr Holford's most pleasant songs, *The coming of Spring*.

Sometime later I was awakened to the sounds of someone moving in the bedroom and through half-closed eyes I observed Franz Holford with his back to me looking at his own image in a full-length mirror. It was this chance observation more than any other which confirmed my view of him as a narcissist, for it was not so much that he spent a long time gazing at his own image, but from the manner in which he did so it appeared that he found it to be the most satisfying of pursuits.

Dr Holford's narcissism found expression in any number of personal idiosyncrasies, as well as in the more overt gestures of conductor and pianist. His personal vanities included eliciting assistance from those closest to him to take a 'barrel' type key and press it into the gnarled skin of his neck in order to remove blackheads. He was obsessed with the possibility that blackheads and pimples might be lurking out of sight at the back of his neck which could not be revealed by a mirror Body hair also repelled him and he would regularly remove the thick black hair which grew on his long fingers by covering them with an evil smelling, sulphorous white paste, which he would scrape off a few minutes later, removing hair and all, using a slender wooden spatula. He regularly smoked Benson and Hedges cigarettes, which he held as gracefully as a conductor's baton, but one had the feeling that they were an accessory rather than the result of a nicotine habit; it was very fashionable to smoke in those days. He could do little about the warts on his face, so he would grumble vaguely about them as he gazed in a mirror, or if he was in someone else's company and they were remarked upon, he would attribute them to the genetics of his German lineage, or he might console himself and others by comparing his warts to those revealed in photographs of the great Franz Liszt.

The most outward expression of his narcissism was the care with which he dressed – seldom appearing without a starched collar and tie, and he *never* dressed in shorts, sandals, or the normal casual clothes others wore, even in the height of an Australian summer. The only concession he ever made to the heat was in the form of a linen safari jacket, but even under this was to be seen a starched shirt and a spotted bow, or full-length tie.

Referring to the generally low standard of dress in Australia he once criticized a famous pianist for appearing in public badly dressed, and wrote about her in *Canon*[119]: 'To catch a glimpse of Lili Kraus[120] flitting about the streets of the city in slacks is a case in point. Can you imagine anything more ridiculous than Goossens in a seersucker and a top hat, or for that matter Beecham conducting *The Fair Maid of Perth* in a French bathing suit?' These fatuous published comments must have hurt Lili Kraus, who arrived in Australia after the war with nothing but the clothes she wore, following her liberation by the Americans from the Japanese prisoner-of-war camp where she had spent several bitter years.

When he saw that I was awake, Dr Holford turned from the mirror and smiled.

'Ah my dear, you are awake at last. I have come to take you down to the séance – it will be starting any minute.'

Leslie Flint, an English spiritualist of the 1930s, famous for claiming to contact the spirits of dead celebrities, including the composer Frederic Chopin. He would often record his sessions. (Canon photo)

The Séance

Our reasons are not prophets,
When oft our fancies are.

- SHAKESPEARE

14

The first person I saw upon entering the living room for the séance was the doctor who had operated on me, Dr Robert Murphy. He was talking animatedly to his friend and colleague Dr Stuart Scougall. As well as being a leading orthopaedic surgeon, Dr Scougall was a man of fine artistic sensibilities, an excellent writer and sometime poet, with a particular interest in Aboriginal art. I always tried to sit next to him at the few social functions to which I was invited at the Champ's house, for he was a kindly man, with the bedside manner of a general practitioner, even though he was such a highly regarded surgeon. Like Dr Bob Murphy, he was a fund of amusing anecdotes, and he was always seemed interested in what others had to say.

One of his favourite stories concerned a prostitute who on one occasion accosted him as he left his Macquarie Street rooms late one night. With his customary courtesy he declined the prostitute's offer, saying that it was 'too late', upon which the young woman consulted her watch.

'It's only eleven thirty, love,' she said.

'My dear, it's thirty *years* too late,' came Scougall's genial response.

On this particular evening the idea of a séance was an attractive diversion after a long day of surgery at the Royal North Shore Hospital. As I sat beside him, clad still in my pyjamas and dressing gown, he confided that he held slender hopes that by means of this séance he might make spiritual contact with his only son, killed in World War II. He was attracted to the phenomena which was occurring in Great Britain, where thousands of people were flocking to spiritualists such as Helen Duncan and Leslie Flint, in a desperate effort to contact loved ones killed during the world conflict.

A circular card table was set in the midst of the living room, with several candles and a Ouija Board on its green felt surface. Six bentwood chairs were in place around the table, and the remaining few guests stood chatting quietly as they awaited the arrival of Eugene Goossens.

When the famous conductor arrived, accompanied by two members of the Sydney Symphony Orchestra, he handed his cloak and hat to the butler in the hallway and I heard him ask in a loud voice: 'Where's the Medium?'

However, because of the risk of detection and prosecution for conducting a séance – especially in the house of such a prominent businessman as Reginald Champ - it had been decided not to seek out a known Medium, but to use Judith Champ in this capacity, especially since the séance was her idea. She had a genuine flair for drama, and the spiritual, and appeared to relish the prospect – later in life producing a book on the subject.[121]

It was all intended as a diverting game, although some did believe in the power of a séance. Amidst some good natured, but somewhat apprehensive banter, the six participants were seated around the séance table, whilst the onlookers, including Franz and myself, were banished to an outer circle of lounges and chairs in semi-darkness on the fringes surrounding the table. Judy Champ sat with the rectangular Ouija Board and its heart-shaped planchette directly in front of her. Eugene Goossens was on her right and Dr Scougall on her left; the others comprised Dr Murphy and the two orchestral musicians.

Judith explained that the rules were simple. Everyone was to hold their neighbour's hands until a circle was formed, culminating in the Medium, who with her right hand would operate the moveable planchette, which she explained would point to various letters of the alphabet and gradually spell out any messages received from 'beyond'. A notepad and pencil were placed nearby on which to record them. Amidst a hushed silence all did as they were bid, heads bowed forward in concentration, as the onlookers settled back to watch in silent fascination.

As I focused my attention on the Ouija board I gradually became aware that the temperature in the room seemed to be dropping. It had been a pleasantly warm evening after a sunny day in Sydney, but there was no mistaking the change which was now occurring. I began shivering and drew the woollen dressing gown more closely around me, but it made no difference – the room was growing colder and colder. I was about to slip away noiselessly through an open door to seek warmth in the dining room when I saw the planchette on the table in front of Judy Champ begin to move. It began spinning – slowly at first, and then gathering momentum. Everyone was mesmerized, when it stopped suddenly, pointing to the letter A on the board. Judy wrote down the letter on the pad, and the planchette resumed its spinning, this time coming to rest on the letter L. It performed the same action six times, until it had formed the name ALBERT, then it stopped. As everyone craned forward to read the name in the notepad Judy's eyes closed and her head began to tilt slowly upwards. The colour was draining from her face, until it became deathly white. Then she spoke, in unearthly sepulchral tones which no one could recognize.

'Albert…'

The small audience was totally awestruck, until Eugene Goossens broke the silence and addressed a question to the medium in a whisper: 'Who is Albert?'

'Albert my son…'

Franz Holford suddenly stood up, knocking over a small side table on which his whisky glass had been standing. His normal congenial manner had vanished and his face was contorted with fury.

'This is ridiculous and has to stop!' he exclaimed loudly, and striding across the room he switched on the main lights. The effect was shocking - everyone including the medium snapping back into reality.

'Christ, Franz!' Goossens shouted in frustration, 'what the hell did you do *that* for?'

'I've had enough of this voodoo!' Holford responded angrily. 'I'm going home.' And he left the room, followed by a bewildered but solicitous Gwen Champ.

The guests, including Goossens, were so amazed by the sequence of events, they began reaching for their coats, and after muttering self-conscious farewells to the Champ family they too melted away. Like everyone else, I was dumbstruck and began to feel quite ill, so I slipped away to the guestroom I was occupying and fell into bed. Some hours later I awoke to the sound of the telephone ringing downstairs and rose to investigate. Halfway down the stairs I could see and hear John Champ talking and as I approached, he put down the receiver and looked at me strangely.

'That was Franz,' he said in a sombre voice, 'His mother has just had a stroke and he is bringing her down here.'

******

The old lady was looked after for several days by a nurse together with Gwen Champ, and Franz stayed at 'Threlkeld' with her. She died shortly after and was cremated at the North Ryde Crematorium. I did not attend the funeral, but as my short stay with the Champs had come to an end, and being fully recovered from my operation, I returned to 'Norwood', just a short walk up the road.

It was a Sunday morning when I arrived, to find the house deserted.

I meandered from room to room, admiring some of the recent renovations I had carried out, largely by painting and wallpapering, and on an impulse went into the room previously occupied by Franz Holford's mother. It was dilapidated and empty, apart from the bed, upon which was the rolled-up mattress. There were no portraits or paintings on the walls and the few furnishings such as dressing table, wardrobe and chair had been removed. The walls contained fungus from rising damp and a smell of decay was in the air. I drew back the curtains and opened the windows with difficulty, since they were stuck with old paint, then quitting the room quickly, I made my way out onto the veranda to sit in the sun.

I fell asleep and was quietly dozing in a wicker chair, when the front gate opened and the doctor attending Franz's mother walked up the driveway. He greeted me cheerfully and handed me a letter.

'Give this to Franz for me will you young fella?' Then he left.

I took the letter and settled back in the chair again, intending to soak up a little more sun before going into the house to start work on *Canon*. I dozed for a while, and when I awoke the letter was still in my hand. The envelope was blank, unsealed and with no address or name. I twirled it in my fingers for a moment, and then on an impulse opened it. It was the Death Certificate for Annie Holford, which the doctor had intended handing personally to Franz, but gave to me. Idly I scanned the document, not really taking in the cold formality of its contents until some of the names which had been entered in the various columns caused me to sit up and scrutinize it more closely. In view of the mystery which surrounded Franz Holford, I was astounded by what I read.

According to the certificate, Anne Elizabeth Holford was eighty-six at the time of her recent death from arterio sclerosis. The death was witnessed by her 'son' William Franz Holford, aged forty-eight, who according to the 'Children of the Marriage' column had a sister Fanny and three brothers, John, George and Harry still living. It appeared that all had been born in Australia, as had their mother. Their father was listed as William Webster Holford, a maker of saddles and horse collars, who had been 'In the Colony' since his early twenties. Nowhere in the document was there any reference to Franz Holford being the offspring of German royalty, nor was there any link to the famous conductor Felix Weingartner.

I put the certificate down and stared vacantly into space. So he was *not* a doctor of music, nor of philosophy, nor of medicine. So his name was *not* Franz, but William. So he was the son of an Australian saddle maker. Why then had he allowed such stories about him to circulate, when glaring evidence to the contrary existed on this official registration form? And why had he hidden his mother away from the world and not acknowledged William Webster Holford as his father?

Then my mind went back to the séance, and the conductor's violent reaction to what the Medium was saying. What *was* the meaning of the name 'Albert', spelt out by the planchette, and why had he reacted so violently? Did Judith Champ know more about him than any of us realized?

Tailpiece for Canon

'Glorious John'...and others

*What a man thinks of himself, that it is which determines,
or rather indicates, his fate.*

- THOREAU

15

As the years passed, there were many times when I wanted to leave 'Norwood' and lead what any rational person would have considered a normal life. Then I would reflect on how much I had come to love the house - whose walls I had papered, whose verandas I had mended, whose hedges I had trimmed and whose gardens I had tended, even the front gate which I had built; I would reflect on my lifestyle and especially the people whom, through Franz Holford, I had been privileged to meet. By inviting me to live and work at his house, Franz may have believed he was acquiring an unpaid labourer, but he may also have believed that in doing so he was also offering some young person with his whole life ahead of him complete freedom to develop in an artistic environment. Unfortunately, through an inevitable lack of direction at this early stage of my life, and with the demands on my time producing *The Canon*, and a myriad other ventures, I managed to turn that freedom into a prison from which ultimately there seemed no escape.

There was no doubt that by mixing with the passing panoply of people inhabiting the pages of *The Canon* I was provided with an opportunity given to few others in their lifetime. Among the most interesting of these famous personages was the great Italian/English conductor Sir John Barbirolli[122] and his oboist wife Evelyn Rothwell, who visited Australia in 1950.

Following his usual practice, Franz had written to John Barbirolli in advance and offered him hospitality and space in his magazine, which the Barbirolli's accepted with alacrity. Evelyn Rothwell replied that there was a window of opportunity following Sir John's Sydney concert on 29th December 1949, and it was agreed that the pair would have supper at the Champ's residence following the great conductor's performance with the Sydney Symphony Orchestra. Barbirolli was renowned for his work ethic of getting through a day with an average of four hours sleep and one meal a day, so meeting people after his concerts was an opportunity for him to socialise. It was a meal he would invariably cook himself for his friends and colleagues, following the evening concert and thus it was arranged for him to do the same at 'Threlkeld', where he promised to indulge his host and guests with his favourite dish - a dessert of *zabaglione* from his own grandmother's recipe.

Three great overseas conductors whose concerts were extensively covered in The Canon over the years: (Above left) Eugene Goossens (Above right) John Barbirolli. (Canon photos)

The third was Karl Rankl. Each of these three conductors contributed fine articles to The Canon, including Goossens on his masterpiece Apocalypse and Barbirolli on The Art of Conducting.

We all attended Barbirolli's opening concert at the Sydney Town Hall, which almost turned out to be a disaster.

As I headed towards my favourite spot in the organ gallery at 7.45 pm there was unrest in the 2000-seat hall and an ABC official was at the microphone, about to make an announcement. He was ashen-faced, and nervously told the capacity crowd that the sheet music and scores for the evening's concert had been stolen. An audible gasp among patrons could be heard as the official informed them of what had taken place, but he added that a concert *would* be given, and alternative music was being sought. This would take a little time he said and he implored the audience's patience.

Eugene Goossens - who was resident conductor of the SSO at this time - immediately leapt into action and led a small party to the Sydney Conservatorium (where Goossens was also Director), broke into the darkened building and raided the library, searching for replacement, or substitute scores which the orchestra might play without a rehearsal.

While this was happening, back at the Town Hall John Barbirolli was making a calm and relaxed speech from the conductor's podium. He told his audience that this was not the first time someone had played this kind of a prank - it had happened before to him in Seattle, when someone stole his conductor's score and he was forced to conduct the evening's performance from memory. Referring to an item listed on the present program he continued: 'I don't think tonight's action can be blamed on the Thieving Magpie Overture. If it was, Churchill might say about it, "Some thief! Some magpie!"' A ripple of laughter ran through the audience and everyone relaxed.

The ensuing concert, which commenced at 9pm and lasted less than an hour, was a huge success, with Barbirolli taking at least six curtain calls. When the guests – which included Sir Eugene Goossens – arrived back at 'Threlkeld' for supper, the air was thick with conspiracy theories about who was responsible for the musical outrage. Goossens was convinced that it had been a disgruntled member of the orchestra, or even someone from the Musicians' Union. He had been in trouble with both the orchestra and the union from the very beginning of his tenure as Director, since he had tried in vain to sack various orchestral members who were past their prime and replace them with professional musicians from overseas.[123]

At this supper, I was lucky enough to be seated alongside Sir John, and helped him bring from the kitchen to the Champ's long dining table the various dishes he prepared – to the constant amazement of Gwendolyn Champ, who hovered constantly in the background. Seated opposite was Eugene Goossens, who held forth eloquently on the recent events at the Town Hall.

Goossens reiterated his theory that the prank had been cooked up between an orchestral member and someone from the Union. The union, he said, had a policy which refused membership to musical 'aliens'[124], even if they were superior players. It was an ongoing problem which beset Australian orchestras for many years, because Australian musicians and other workers were fearful of their jobs being taken by foreign immigrants.

John Barbirolli was unfazed by all the commotion this spectacular musical incident caused and declined to be involved, even in the police investigation which followed. At the Champ's table he genially dismissed the prank, making an interesting comment on the subject of his own technique as a conductor. He told his rapt hosts that he only ever conducted from memory those works which if necessary he could actually sit down and write out from memory in their entirety.

I fancied that the look of scorn flitting across the face of Eugene Goossens turned to wonderment as the little Italian-turned-cockney conductor spoke. He was about to press Glorious John on the subject when Barbirolli pulled a white handkerchief out of his top pocket which sent a set of extra false teeth stored there flying in the air, to land underneath the table. Everyone made a mad scramble to locate the errant molars, which amidst great hilarity were finally restored to the maestro's dinner jacket.

On the flip side of the coin to Barbirolli's supreme genius as a musician lay a man of simple tastes, who enjoyed cooking and cricket in about the same measure as he enjoyed his own musical gifts.[125]

Following the supper at around 2am, Sir John expressed the desire to visit Franz's house for a final whisky. It was a warm summer's night as he, Lady Barbirolli, Franz and myself walked the few hundred metres up Woolwich Road to 'Norwood'. As we entered the hallway Barbirolli noticed my cello, which I had inadvertently left standing in a corner, out of its protective case. With an exclamation of joy, he pounced on the instrument and after testing its strings for tuning he sat down on a hallway chair and began playing an excerpt from a Bach suite. It was a magical moment, from a musician who, many initially thought, could have become as famous a cellist as Pablo Casals.

******

Aware of his love for cricket, I hinted to Sir John that I might be distantly related to Neil Harvey – the great Australian batsman and integral member of Don Bradman's 'Invincibles' team of 1948. At my age I did resemble Neil Harvey a little and we were almost exactly the same height, which is not tall. Barbirolli was uncomfortable with tall men and women – the exception being Lady Barbirolli, but even with her, he would never permit a photo of them be taken together unless both were seated.

To my amazement – and as if it was the most natural thing in the world – Sir John invited me to go with him and Lady Barbirolli to Adelaide in February 1951 to watch the fourth cricket test between England and Australia, upon which Franz immediately frowned and said: 'Oh, I think not John…we have an important special edition coming up shortly and Bruno is my right hand man.'

Looking back on this incident, it may not have turned out as enjoyable as it first promised, since Sir John was devoted to the English cricket team, and on this occasion they were well and truly thrashed by the Australians!

Barbirolli was at times a very lonely man. On one occasion during his stay in Sydney I came upon him sitting outside the recording studio of the ABC at Chatswood, waiting for his wife Evelyn to finish a recording of Franz's Oboe Sonata. How long he had been there I never knew, but it must have been a considerable time; it was not an isolated incident either, as he told me he was often wont to wait for Evelyn after concerts, rehearsals or other special events.

For her part, Evelyn Rothwell did Franz an enormous favour by agreeing to give performances of his works – including this sonata which he had written as a Christmas gift to her in 1951. She substantially edited his compositions and was constantly irritated by the fact that he would never complete the piano scores of his works, preferring instead to simply improvise them, as he did so often with his songs. This was a major barrier to having them published, which Lady Rothwell discovered when she attempted to persuade a leading music publishing house to take an interest in his compositions. In addition, the ABC had a strong policy concerning original compositions - that they must be accompanied by a completed score before they would proceed with either recording, or on-air performances.

On studying the large list of recordings made by Franz and associate artists as 'Processed' Columbia Records at the end of this book, it is astonishing how many have non-existent or incomplete manuscripts. Works for solo piano such as *Delian Phantasy, Variations on a theme of Paganini*, the ballads, scherzos and sonatas were often recorded largely as extemporisations by Franz with a few scraps of manuscript paper as memory joggers. The faithful John Champ took many of these recordings to the ABC in an attempt to have them broadcast, but apart from one or two exceptions, which they sent out to regional stations, the ABC refused to put them to air, and most were simply given away to musical friends and have slipped into obscurity.

Some of his compositions were performed by artists such as Evelyn Rothwell, Ian Wilson, and Jiri Tancibudek and his charming *Summer Madrigal* for oboe and piano is still occasionally played on the ABC. But they are rare exceptions in such a large output of his music.

******

Fernando Germani was obsessed with the organ. When I interviewed him in 1956 for *Canon* he said that when he was at home in Rome he would sometimes practise 'all the weekend'. This seemed a reasonable amount of preparation for a concert, until he revealed that by 'all the weekend' he meant literally *all the weekend*, commencing on Friday evening, he would not leave the organ until Monday morning. The housekeeper of the apartment he occupied at the Vatican would bring trays of food up to the organ loft and leave them outside the entrance door. Often they would be there untouched when she came on her rounds again on Monday morning. When he was so exhausted he had to sleep, Germani would rest a board at the end of his bed and practice foot pedal exercises prior to nodding off and immediately upon waking.

It was his astonishing technique which left an audience spellbound. At his Sydney recital in 1956 I sat in the South Gallery of the Sydney Town Hall and watched mesmerised as he played on its magnificent grand organ – at that time the largest in the Southern Hemisphere. It was an all Bach recital, which concluded with the mighty *Fugue in D Major BWV 532*, which has extensive work for the foot pedals.[126] When it finished – to a roar of approval from the large audience, Germani complimented them by following it with an encore…the amazing *Pedal Exercitium BWV*, which employs *only* the foot pedals. The Italian's feet flashed over the wooden pedals in a blur as he executed one of the most difficult studies in the organ's repertoire. At its conclusion there was simply a stunned silence in the audience before an explosion of applause, which went on for minutes.

Fernando Germani complimented me on my role in producing *The Canon* by sending a postcard the year following his visit. He invited me to visit Rome for a musical holiday and to stay with him at the Vatican, but I was a little doubtful as to his motives, so I offered a polite refusal, to which he cheerfully replied: 'Oh well never mind then. But if you ever want me to visit Australia again, just whistle!' A very curious man, but a highly accomplished artist.

The Pope's organist, Fernando Germani visited Australia in 1956, giving a number of solo recitals in various State capital cities, and contributing articles to The Canon. His visit sparked a revival in solo organ recitals in Australia, which Canon covered extensively.

Robert Cuckson (left) and Malcolm Catt. Cuckson was a finalist in an ABC Concerto and Vocal Competition, and in the 50's he went on to forge a brilliant career in America as a composer and academic.

Martin Mather was an English pianist and composer in his late twenties who 'jumped ship' in Sydney in 1956 when he was touring as repetiteur for a group of Spanish dancers from England, under the auspices of the Glyndebourne Opera Company. We met when Martin joined the Elizabethan Opera Company as repetiteur in 1958, and he became a regular visitor to 'Norwood', seeking publicity for his compositions through *Canon*. Martin and I became close friends, although he was three years my senior, and later after I finally left 'Norwood' we shared a house with my brother for some years.

Mather began studying piano with Eunice Gardner at the Sydney Conservatorium, and came to Franz Holford seeking lessons in composition. He was working on a song cycle of fourteen poems by German poets such as Goethe, Hölderlin, Rilke, Binding, Dehmel and Hofmannsthal, for Baritone, Horn and Piano, which he brought with him to 'Norwood'. Franz took one look at his manuscripts and knew instantly that there was nothing he could teach the ardent young composer.

Martin's songs were heavily influenced by Hugo Wolf - who wrote about 300 - many of which were published posthumously. He found Wolf's songs highly original, in the finest tradition of the German lied. They ranged from tender love lyrics to satirical humour to deeply felt spiritual suffering, and the piano accompaniments were densely configured, representing a challenge to any accompanist. Mather's song cycle was cast in a similar mould, but though they were influenced by the great German composer, they were by no means derivative. He spoke with an authentic voice.

The difference between Martin Mather's songs, and those of Franz Holford could not have been starker – the choice of poets alone being indicative. Martin's compositions were – as with Hugo Wolf – written in complex keys, often comprising up to five or six sharps and flats, the accompaniments being of equal importance to the melodic line, whilst the accompaniments by Franz (when he bothered to write them) were totally simple - for most he would simply extemporise the piano part.

As Martin and I became friends, Franz did not encourage his visits to 'Norwood'. Pointedly, he never invited Mather to the Saturday night soirees, nor performed his music there, although he did invite the young Englishman to write an article for *Canon*[127] - which produced a rambling discourse as complex as his compositions, on the 'new absolutism' of the 20th Century, that 'music can express nothing'.

When Martin visited 'Norwood', he and I spent many an hour together, mainly listening to his latest compositions, which I enjoyed immensely. I soon became aware of the reason for Franz's antipathy towards him, for the Englishman was curious about Franz's background and had asked leading questions of him. As a graduate from King's College London, Mather naturally wanted to find out more about Holford's period of study at Oxford, which of course Franz could not answer because he had never been there.

Through Dorothy Helmrich of the Arts Council of Australia a concert was arranged of Martin Mather's *Liederbook*: a cycle of fourteen songs for Baritone, Horn and Piano. Helmrich - a former Covent Garden soprano - engaged the well-known soprano Patricia Moore and equally well known baritone Stewart Harvey to sing them. For other songs on the program in addition to the pianist Henri Penn, she engaged Peter Richardson (Flute) and a young French horn player Graham Mackenzie.[128] The concert was held in the Anzac Auditorium in Sydney in September 1957 and despite receiving the traditional critics' complimentary tickets, Franz showed no desire to attend. When it was suggested that we should review the concert for *Canon*, he replied sourly: 'Go if you must then…'

This concert launched Mather's career in Sydney as a composer, and the critics – though a little puzzled by the complexity and density of his compositions - were generally very encouraging about his musical future. A review of this concert appeared in the October edition of *Canon* and he acknowledged it as a spur to an outpouring of compositions which followed.[129] Martin Mather went on to write the *Last Voyage of Matthew Flinders* (1964), a cantata for choir and orchestra, for the 150th anniversary of Flinders' death. It was recorded in 1965 by the Sydney Symphony Orchestra conducted by Joseph Post.[130] Mather's other large-scale work for choir and orchestra, *ANZAC Requiem* (1967) had to wait nine years for its premiere, being first performed by the Adelaide Symphony Orchestra on Remembrance Day 1976 and broadcast nationally by ABC radio on Anzac Day the following year. This piece was principally inspired by John Manifold's poem *The Tomb of Lt John Learmonth, AIF* and by the notion that a new image for Anzacs had been long overdue. It too awaits a revival.

Martin once sent me a letter, full of his effusive musical rhetoric and a cartoon which he had drawn in black biro (he was, amongst all his other achievements, a talented artist). The cartoon depicted me as an angel, piloting an aeroplane, on the sides of which was its name '*The Canon*'. The caption read: 'When are you going to fly a plane of your own…?'

Martin Mather died, relatively unrecognised as a composer, in 2002. Like many other Australian composers, his music – especially the highly interesting *Liederbook* – though technically difficult, deserves to be revived and given a place in the permanent repertoire of classical music.

******

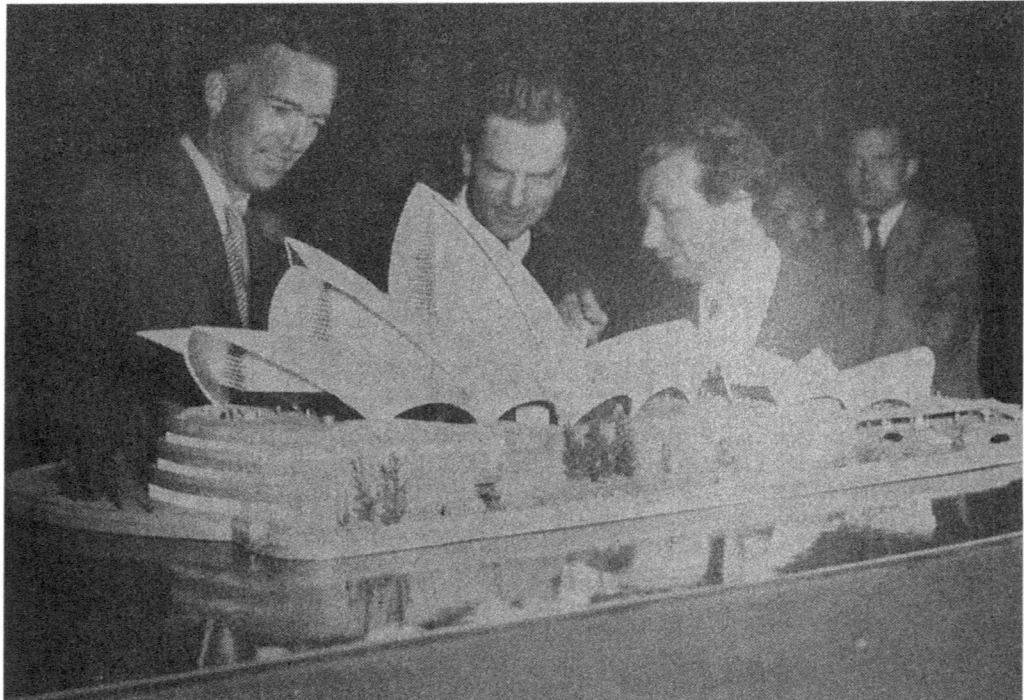

(Top left) Martin Mather, an English composer who settled in Australia in the 1950s. (Top right) The English poet John Drinkwater, many of whose poems Franz Holford set to music. (Below) Jorn Utzon (left) with Professor Robert Quentin (centre) and Swedish architect Erik Andersson, inspecting the first model of the Sydney Opera House, constructed from Utzon's prize-winning sketches.

Caught Out

*Rather fail with honour
than succeed with fraud.*

- SOPHOCLES

16

Each year I scanned with great eagerness the press notices coming regularly to *The Canon* from the ABC, announcing the celebrities who would be visiting Australia, for I knew that through the magazine I would eventually meet and interview some of them. They would invariably be invited by the editor to contribute to *Canon* and to participate in the musical soirees held at the Champs' residence 'Threlkeld'.

One of these ABC visiting artists was a relatively unknown German pianist Gerhard Willner, then living in New Zealand, who had made a particular study of the music of Beethoven and who was said to be a pupil of the great Artur Schnabel. An advance press release issued by the ABC stated that Willner had committed most of the great German composer's entire piano *oeuvre* to memory, and could play flawlessly upon request any excerpt from Beethoven's thirty-two piano sonatas. When he and his opera singer wife Dora arrived in Sydney he was introduced to the Australian composer John Antill – who worked in the ABC as composer and arranger of music – who suggested he call upon Franz Holford - whom, Antill told Willner '…had a German background'.

Something made me ignore the rule of not admitting strangers one morning when the doorbell rang, and I opened the front door to find Gerhard Willner had arrived unannounced, looking for Doctor Holford. He was of medium height, thickset and unprepossessing in appearance, wearing a brown raincoat and carrying a sheaf of music under his arm. He had been driven out to Hunters Hill by an ABC official, who waited for him in a black hire car in the street outside the house.

'Bitter, könnte ich Doktor Franz Holford sehen?' ('Please, could I see Dr Franz Holford?') asked Willner.

Hovering behind me in the background and hearing his name, Dr Holford stepped forward with outstretched hand: 'I am Doctor Franz Holford,' he said, with his customary genial smile. Willner seized his hand enthusiastically, and began pumping it up and down.

'Ach, mein lieber Doktor, wie schön sie zu treffen! ich hesse Gerhard Willner - ein student der musik des großen Ludwig van Beethoven, und ich demütig seine musik nach Australien bringen'. ('Ah, my dear doctor, how wonderful to meet you! My name is Gerhard Willner - a student of the music of the great Ludwig van Beethoven - and I humbly bring his music to Australia.')

Dr Holford was totally bemused. He did not understood a word Willner had said. The German pianist looked at him keenly.

'Speak...German?' He said in English.

'Jah ... jah,' Holford responded unconvincingly.

Willner continued with renewed energy: 'Ah dann, ich sagte ihnen anscheinend Deutsch sind. Sind Sie Deutsch? Sprichst du Deutsch?' ('Ah then, I was told you are apparently German. Are you German? Do you speak German?')

'Jah...jah,' came the reply.

This was not the response the German pianist was expecting. Willner was rapidly becoming exasperated and downcast: 'Dann warum sprechen sie nicht mit mir?' ('Then, why will you not speak with me?') he asked, somewhat forlornly.

'Jah...jah,' Franz repeated. Then, sensing the situation was never going to be resolved, he looked at his watch and said: 'Look, I'm sorry old boy, but I have to go...'

The German looked nonplussed, so Holford pointed again at his watch. 'I...have an...appointment...do you understand? Jah? Must...leave...

now.' He shook Willner's hand briefly and strode off down the gravel path and out the front gate, heading in the direction of the Champ's house.

When he had gone, the puzzled visitor turned to me and said in perfect English: 'Why would he not speak to me?'

I was dumbstruck. 'You… speak English *yourself* then?'

'Of course,' Willner responded.

'Then…why didn't you talk to Dr Holford in English?' I stammered.

'Because I was told by your broadcasting company that he was German. *Is* he German?'

I was totally confused and muttered weakly: 'I…he's….he has German lineage, I believe…'

As the pianist stood on the veranda regarding me in mutual embarrassment, a man in black wearing a valet's cap appeared around the hawthorn hedge. It was the ABC official. I explained that there had been literally a 'breakdown in communication' and that Dr Holford had to leave urgently for a prior engagement. He was very understanding and quite relaxed about the incident, even offering an apology for not making an official appointment, and explaining that he was Gerhard Willner's driver. Then he turned to his distinguished visitor.

'I'll take you back to the ABC then, sir?'

Willner frowned in annoyance: 'Well, I came all the way out here to play for the editor of *The Canon*…and I have an article for the magazine…'

'Oh, then I suppose…look, I…work for the magazine,' I said tentatively, 'I am Dr Holford's …assistant.'

The pianist's mood changed immediately and he said genially: 'Ah then, I should like to play for *you*.'

There passed the most agreeable morning of piano music I was to enjoy for many years. Seated at Franz Holford's Blüthner, without bothering to remove his raincoat, Willner invited me to name any excerpts I liked from Beethoven's thirty-two piano sonatas, and when I did so, he would play them superbly from memory, without a moment's hesitation. When he finished each excerpt I applauded warmly, after which the German would say 'Nächtes?' ('Next?') and I would ask for another movement from a different work. At the end of the recital he arose from the piano and fossicked amongst the papers he was carrying and drew forth some typewritten sheets, which he proceeded to hand to me.

Gerhard and Dora Willner. (Photo from Canon)

'This is for publication in your excellent journal,' he said.

It was a beautifully written article on Schnabel by Willner, entitled 'Monumentalis', which we reproduced in a following edition.[131]

He gave a very formal goodbye, and shaking my hand gravely extended an invitation for me to attend his Beethoven recitals for the ABC at the Sydney Town Hall. I explained with some embarrassment that I rarely went out in the evenings, whereupon he and his minder left.[132]

Caught Out

That evening Franz returned late. He was not pleased that I had been entertained by the German pianist.

'The nerve of that little twerp to embarrass me like that, turning up unannounced,' he said.

He was not in the least disturbed at having been caught out pretending to speak German when he obviously could not, and the incident was not even raised in the days which followed. It passed as one of his little 'eccentricities', but it was also an unspoken message that he preferred me not to mix with his distinguished visitors unless it suited him that I do so.

Being caught out took on many forms over the years of my stay at 'Norwood', when Dr Holford was every now and then tripped up by the fantasies of his own creation.

On one occasion as I was feeding the yellow budgerigar 'Mozart' on the front veranda I heard an almighty crash from the roadway outside the house. A few moments later a middle-aged woman came running up the gravelled driveway and screamed at me: 'There's been a terrible accident and my son is badly hurt', she cried in distress.

'What....what can I do?' I stammered.

"Is the doctor in…?' she yelled. I was completely taken aback and could only stare at her. Suddenly Franz appeared at the front door and froze.

'Somebody said a doctor lives here,' the poor woman sobbed. Then she saw Franz standing in the doorway. 'Is that *you*…?' she continued. Whereupon, Franz slipped quickly inside and closed the door in her face. She looked at me in a bewildered fashion.

'He is….he's a doctor of music, you see,' I said lamely. 'Not…er…'

She looked at me, and then at the house for a moment, then turn and ran towards the gate. As she opened it, I heard her scream 'Shiiiit!'

******

Love in the afternoon

One is never too old to yearn.

- ITALIAN PROVERB

17

It was apparent that as I grew in confidence and experience in producing the music journal *Canon* Dr Holford became more and more anxious to confine my duties to purely production and practical skills in preparing it for the printer each month. I was not encouraged to write major articles or reviews, although I did so anyway when we were short of material, and on many occasions it suited him to send me out to interview visitors whom he considered of minor importance, if he was too preoccupied.

One such visitor was Karl Rankl (1898-1968) - a British conductor and composer and a pupil of the composers Schoenberg and Webern. Rankl conducted at opera houses in Austria, Germany and Czechoslovakia until fleeing from the Nazis and taking refuge in England in 1939, where he was interned on the Isle of Man for the duration of WWII. Following a 20-year career conducting leading British orchestras and opera companies, he was appointed to the newly formed Elizabethan Opera Company in Australia in May 1958.[133]

I interviewed Karl Rankl in the downstairs restaurant The Brasserie in Martin Place shortly after he arrived in Australia. He had been persuaded to come to Sydney as director of the Elizabethan Opera by the Executive Director of the Trust, Hugh Hunt - Founding Professor of Drama at Manchester University.

Rankl was a very undervalued conductor, who refused to engage in the posturing of musical superiority which characterised most leading conductors of his time. A simple man who had known hard times, he conducted without a baton and mostly wore plain clothes when relaxing, usually topped by a grey cardigan. His second wife Christine, who came to Australia with him, made all his shirts – of which he possessed over fifty – since he was forced to change so often during long rehearsals. He had recently resigned as Musical Director of Covent Garden after five years of controversy, largely inspired by Sir Thomas Beecham, who had derided Rankl's appointment there in 1946, describing it as 'incredible'. Referring to the appointment of an 'Austrian refugee' so soon after the conclusion of WWII, Beecham ranted at the Covent Garden Board, calling them: 'A hapless set of ignoramuses and nitwits (who) conspired to bring this disaster'.[135] No doubt the great Beecham was furious that *he* had been overlooked for the post.

In the dim recesses of The Brasserie, Rankl opened up to me about his reasons for coming to Australia. He was genuinely curious to discover how Australia managed to produce so many great singers. He had recently given an all-Wagner concert in London, featuring the Australian soprano Rosina Raisbeck, whom the critic Neville Cardus had lauded. Cardus said:

> Why does Australasia continue to discover excellent voices? To tell the truth, they usually need some polishing and rounding off aesthetically when they come to London; but the quality is unmistakenly there, and the quickness to learn. The Australian is notably sedulous and something of an actor in the way he and she can acquire a style and diction not at all Australian. In fact, some Australians I know in London are more English than Kensington Gore, more Oxford than Boar's Hill.[136]

When Sir Thomas Beecham was casting about for the most suitable soloist for his definitive recording of *The Mass of Life* by Delius, he approached Neville Cardus and asked him to recommend the best vocalist. Cardus suggested Eleanor Houston (who was trained in Sydney), but after much consideration Beecham preferred Rosina Raisbeck, also from Sydney.

Some critics put the plethora of great Australian voices down to the climate – likening this country to Italy, whilst others – such as the great baritone Peter Dawson, assigned a more practical reason:

> 'Australian singers in London have more push than others. "They are up and doing, and get work from theatrical agents before English singers are out of bed," said the well-known Australian baritone, Mr. Peter Dawson'.[137]

Some of the Australian singers who sang under Karl Rankl at Covent Garden came to Australia to sing for him. Kenneth Neate came out to sing Pinkerton and Tamino and Sylvia Fischer sang in *Fidelio* with great success; Joan Hammond was another of course, and she sang 'Salome' with Rankl at a matinee at the Adelaide Festival.

In a refutation of Sir Thomas Beecham's famous statement to a gathering of musicians in the 1950s that '…there is no future for opera or opera singers in Britain', and later that 'Britain (and by implication Australia) could not produce the type of voice necessary for a dramatic soprano or a robust tenor'[138], a certain journalist known only as HTH (perhaps to protect himself from legal action) put together a list of Australian contemporary classical musicians of the day for Beecham's edification.

It is worth including this list here in its entirety. Among conductors: Constant Lambert (son of the Australian painter George Lambert), Aylmer Buesst (Covent Garden, BBC), Frank St Leger (Chicago Civic Opera). In opera: Florence Austral, John Brownlee, Harold Williams, Lionello Cecil, Dorothy Helmrich, Frances Alda, Evelyn Scotney, Horace Stevens, Rowena Ronald, Maxwell Oldacre, Rita Miller, Wilma Berkeley, Browning Mummery, Tom Minogue, Fred Collier, Elsie Treweek, Eda Bennie, Gertrude Johnson. Among composers, instrumentalists and teachers: Arthur Benjamin, John Amadio, Percy Grainger, Roy Agnew, Peter Dawson, Daisy Kennedy, May Brahe, Antone Winn, Allan Priora, Dudley Glass, Gertrude Concannon, Jessie King, Anne Williams, Cecil Berry, Gladys Cole, Madame Masson, Dorothy Canberra, Wilfred Thomas, Daphne Harpur, Eileen Joyce, Norma Gadsden, Francesca Duret, Helene Esserman, Nancy Marley, Elise Steele, Margaret Pitman, May Craven,

Greta Callow, Margaret Jewell, Geraldine Calca, Neryl Thurston, Ethel Osborne, Essie Ackland, Malcolm McEachern, Alma Moody and Clara Serena.[139]

******

It was through Karl Rankl that I met Hugh Hunt. He was at a meeting with the conductor when I arrived with page proofs of my article to check with the amiable Austrian. A reserved and quietly spoken Englishman, Hunt spoke of his plans for opera and drama in Australia, and especially the establishment of a truly Australian theatre, which would include a training school, later to be known as The National Institute of Dramatic Art (NIDA).

The Elizabethan Theatre Trust had just appointed Robert Quentin[140] to head the new drama school, and Hunt gave me a ticket to their first production, the play *Our Town* by Thornton Wilder, which was staged in the Physics Lecture Theatre at the University of New South Wales. Sometime later productions were moved to an old tin shed called The Totalisator, which ultimately became The Old Tote Theatre. I did an interview for *Canon* with Hugh Hunt[141] and he asked me if I would be interested to edit a yearbook of the Trust's activities. He also pointed out that Australia at that time lacked a magazine devoted entirely to the live theatre and recommended it as a potential niche publication.

Hunt's suggestion came at a time when I was feeling disillusioned with *The Canon* and my relationship with Franz Holford. As things stood, I had no real authority with *Canon*. Franz rarely credited my efforts by publishing my name inside the magazine, unless it was a by-line to an article I had written, but even then he might insist on my changing this to some trite *nom de plume*.

One important task which constantly fell to my lot however, was liaising with the printer – a bluff and generous man named Hall. I quickly discovered that despite Reg Champ's patronage, several editions of the magazine had not been paid for, and the printer G W Hall was carrying a mounting debt against his own small printery, simply because Mr Hall could not bring himself to confront the editor and demand payment.

As I was leaving the printery one day after checking some page proofs, Mr Hall said tentatively: 'Er, d'you think you could tell Franz (he used the vowel 'an', rather than 'ahn') that a cheque would be handy?'

When I relayed the message and asked if the magazine was in trouble financially, the rejoinder was swift and sharp: 'Bruno, you need not concern yourself with such matters – I will deal with that Neanderthal.'

But it became increasingly awkward visiting the printery, parrying questions from its worried manager as the size of the debt grew, so I worked harder at trying to attract paying advertisers to the magazine – some of whom were not always directly in the musical field.

One of these was a company in Penrith named 'Rondo Zippers', run by a Czechoslovakian migrant who had come to Australia via Wales with a group of workers in 1949. I noticed that this company advertised in other arts organisations programs, including the ABC, so I designed the company an advertisement with a play on words featuring the Rondo from the third movement of Beethoven's first piano concerto, and managed to get an interview with the manager, Eric Cuckson, who lived and worked in Penrith.

A lover of classical music who had a prodigiously gifted son, this shrewd migrant was delighted with the advertisement and expressed the wish to visit 'Norwood' with his teenage pianist son Robert[142], in order to meet the editor personally.

When they finally arrived one Saturday afternoon, Franz instructed me to 'look after the boy', as he closeted himself in the study with the company's owner, to work upon him as a source of finance (later it proved that the editor also took credit for my design of the words and artwork for the Rondo advertisement). I took the 'boy' Robert, who was thirteen years younger than me, into my room for a talk and his eyes immediately lighted on my piano. Rummaging in a satchel he was wearing over one shoulder, he withdrew a sheaf of manuscripts and thrust them at me.

'These are some of my compositions,' he said nonchalantly.

There were several small pieces written for piano solo, and a larger work for a trio of violin, cello and piano. Even at first glance I could see that the trio was the work of a mature musical mind. It was Beethoven who once said to a student: 'If a composition *looks* good in manuscript, it will generally *sound* good too.' This manuscript looked very good.

'Have you heard it performed yet?' I asked.

'Of course not,' he replied sharply, 'How would I *do* that?'

'Well, I'd begin by getting each part copied out, then get your father to find the players you need to perform it.'

'I could do that easily,' he replied. 'My father puts on concerts in his factory at Penrith and lots of people come there to play. Would you like to hear my piano sonata?'

Without waiting for a reply he sat down and began playing with intense concentration and technical expertise. I learned later that Robert had been the youngest finalist at that time in the ABC Concerto and Vocal Competition[143], playing the third Bartok Piano Concerto and had been featured in the *Women's Weekly* magazine. His composition was wonderfully modern, if somewhat idiosyncratic and as he played he would look up occasionally, noting with satisfaction my look of awe.

'Listen! Listen!' he cried as the music rose to a furious crescendo, finishing with six loud, staccato chords.

'Pistol shots,' he yelled, smashing the keys with his left hand and making the sign of a pistol with his right hand – pointing it in the direction of the room in which his father was closeted with the editor of *Canon*.

When the conductor and the businessman had finished talking in the study, they came out looking for Robert. As soon as Eric Cuckson's head appeared around my door his son pointed at me and said to him excitedly: 'You have to get him to copy my trio and get some musicians to perform it!'

'I would be very happy to pay you to copy the parts, young man,' the father murmured graciously, as if he was resigned to meeting every demand his gifted son placed upon him.

I wondered what kind of a relationship the young prodigy enjoyed with his indulgent father, for whom no sacrifice seemed too great to further his son's career as a musician. As I grew older, I saw this pattern of parental indulgence replicated in so many families, in which parents poured time and money into the musical education of their children in the hopes of producing a child prodigy. It rarely ended well - the Cucksons being an exception.

In a generous act of philanthropy, Eric Cuckson allowed advertisements for Rondo Zippers to run from Volume 10 Number 7 (February 1957) until the magazine's final edition in April 1966. How much additional money he gave Franz for himself and the magazine is not known.[144] The pair visited 'Norwood' many times – usually on a Saturday morning, when Franz would give the boy a lesson. Eric Cuckson confided to me on one occasion that he would like Robert and I to become 'good friends', but unfortunately it was not to be. As Franz Holford began to apply emotional pressure on the shrewd industrialist to support him more and more financially, their visits became less and less frequent, until they ceased altogether.

******

Hans Gyors was an excellent performer and teacher and I became good friends with two of his students – Brian Strong and Gregory Elmaloglu. Short, thickset and swarthy, with a dark moustache, Gyors seemed to resemble a Hungarian gnome, but he played with great power and beauty of tone. Where other teachers taught vibrato from the wrist, he produced the tone from his short, steely fingers, and the thumb of his left hand was splayed flat like a miniature cutlet and ridged from constantly being pressed hard across the four strings of his cello.

Like so many migrants of that period, he soon anglicized his surname to George. To me, Gyors seemed a far more desirable name for an artist than George and in later years I felt sorry for those migrants who came to Australia and yielded to the pressure of ignoramuses to change their names (and sometimes appearances) in order to 'fit in'. Gregory Elmaloglu was an extremely handsome young man with a shock of black hair and a fine Grecian nose, which I used to envy because my own was so 'snub'. To everyone's dismay he had an operation to change his nose's shape, and though still very handsome, it was to my mind far less becoming of the great artist he became.

Eric Cuckson and his wife Marie emigrated to Australia in 1949 and relocated their zipper factory to St Mary's, where he introduced revolutionary ideas to the workplace, including concerts and other cultural events. He supported The Canon with his company's advertising for many years. (Photograph from Canon)

The Rondo company advertised in every edition of Canon, from the early 50s until the last editions in 1963, more to support the arts than to acquire business.

Another migrant mentioned in a newspaper column soon after the end of WWII was named Adolf Schidt, who was informed by his workmates that he would never 'get on' in Australia with such a name. Thinking it was his affinity with the Great Dictator which was causing the problem, the migrant changed his name by deed poll – but only the first part, which he altered to Bill. The Schidt remained.

Hans Gyors had a number of outstanding pupils who went regularly for private lessons to his home studio in Bondi. Among them was an attractive teenager named Juliette, whose lesson followed mine. She was often waiting on the balcony at the front of the house and as I was leaving we would smile at each other and exchange brief greetings. Noting this one day, Gyors chuckled and at my next lesson said: 'Juliette, lenugoz, ugye?' ('Juliette's stunning, isn't she?') Then in English he added: 'She ask me that you should play in the youth orchestra with her.'

'I'm twenty-six,' I replied. 'And I'm not good enough yet to play in an orchestra, am I?'

He beamed and gestured with his hands: 'Bruno…you are…how to say it…megfeleló…adekvat?'

'Adequate?'

'Igen! Igen! Adekvat!'

Next lesson, as I was packing up my cello, Juliette appeared at the doorway of Hans Gyors' studio. I thanked her for asking me to join the Youth Orchestra, but again demurred, citing my age and inexperience.

'Fiddlededee!' she exclaimed. 'There are some members who are *much* older than you. Even some *teachers* play at concerts when we're short of players. Do come along!'

She was very persuasive and her hazel eyes flashed. It had been so long since I had enjoyed female companionship and here was the prospect of seeing Hans Gyors' beautiful pupil on a more regular basis, even though I knew in my heart that the difference in our ages would inevitably preclude anything more than a platonic relationship. So I began attending weekly rehearsals with the National Youth Orchestra.

Cellist Gregory Elmaloglu. (Photo by George Lindstrom)

As it happened, the National Youth Orchestra[145] at this time was in its early development; it was founded and conducted by Gorden Day, who was Franz Holford's student during the latter's years at Eastwood. Gorden Day, who went on to study at the Trinity School of Music In London and returned to Australia in 1954 to found the youth orchestra, said he was very pleased to have me in his orchestra, and spoke to me frequently about Franz and *The Canon* during breaks in rehearsal, which caused the other orchestral members – including Juliette – to look at me with a certain curiosity.

******

Juliette lived with her single mother in a quaint house in Vaucluse, not far from the city and from the music store Paling's, where the orchestra rehearsed, and I began taking the young cellist home each week.

Her mother – a handsome woman in her early forties – would always be waiting at the front gate for her daughter, and one afternoon she invited me inside for a cup of tea. I braced myself for an interrogation as to my intentions towards her teenage daughter, but soon discovered she was quite happy for me to walk her Juliette home each week, and was only curious to learn how a young man could manage to attend rehearsals of a student orchestra in the afternoon, instead of having a nine till five job.

Without going into details, I told her that I was a freelance journalist and that I helped produce a music journal. That seemed to satisfy her curiosity and it pleased her that her daughter had chosen to associate with someone who was interested in music. Thus I continued to take my place beside Juliette in the cello section of the National Youth Orchestra, and to walk her home after rehearsals.

Juliette talked incessantly – of her love of art and poetry, and especially music. She was clever, interested in what I said and very beguiling. I mostly just looked at her with a half smile as she prattled on – basking in the radiance of her beauty.

I was entranced by the young girl's musical prowess, and watched in fascination as she played the often quite difficult orchestral scores with such grace and power. Juliette was one of the first young musicians to receive a scholarship from the orchestra to study cello with Hans Gyors. She was an angel. She called me, simply, 'Bear', for she noticed how uncomfortable I appeared to be with the name Bruno, which Franz Holford had bestowed upon me. Of course I couldn't bring myself to tell her my real name, nor the circumstances which surrounded my association with the conductor.

As we paused at her front gate one afternoon, she took one of my hands in hers: 'You know you are my boyfriend now, don't you Bear?'

My heart sank. I thought of my situation at 'Norwood' and realized that I was really acting quite fraudulently, for I had nothing to offer her – or anyone, for that matter. Then I thought of how furious Franz would be if he suspected that I was having an affair.

'What would your mother say to that?' I replied, parrying her question.

'Oh, she loves you already,' she laughed. 'In fact, I'll have to be careful of *her*...I think she's keen on you too!' She fondled my hand and regarded me seriously for a moment: 'I want you to meet some of my friends...'

'I told you I don't go out much in the evenings,' I returned.

'No, no,' she quickly replied. 'In the afternoon - about this time...say next week. We don't have a rehearsal, remember? Will you come for afternoon tea?'

Against my better judgment I agreed, and went to her house the following week at four o'clock. As I walked up the path to the front door I fancied I saw several faces peering out through the lace curtains of a front window, but they quickly disappeared.

I was ushered into a dining room in the middle of the house by Juliette, to find it full of wide-eyed teenage girls, who regarded me in critical silence for a moment, then burst out in vigorous conversation with each other as I was introduced to them. I realized with a shock of embarrassment that I was apparently Juliette's first boyfriend, and she had assembled all her teenage girlfriends to meet me and put me on display. It also dawned upon me for the first time that I was becoming seriously involved with a girl eleven years my junior.

As I looked at them all I began vaguely wondering what were the legal ramifications of becoming emotionally involved with a possibly under-age teenager. The girls all began introducing themselves, whilst talking non-stop and climbing all over me in the process. Each one proudly nominated herself to be Juliette's best friend, then one of them tugged my forelock playfully, and said: 'Is your hair starting to go thin?'

******

The relationship did not last long. Beautiful and talented as she was, the gap between our ages was too great, and the task of remaining close friends – let alone lovers – was beyond me. I began disassociating myself from Juliette, and finally left the orchestra. But the brief liaison had broken the long drought in close friendships I had experienced now over several years – particularly with the opposite sex – and I found myself yearning for more female companionship.

The mischievous Hans Gyors was sympathetic, even though he considered me crazy for not wanting to nurture the relationship with his gorgeous young pupil.

'Plenty older men marry younger girls, Bruno! You lucky she like you...'

However, at my request he changed my lesson time and suggested that to gain experience in ensemble playing I place a message on the notice board of the Sydney Conservatorium, where he also taught, to see if there were any chamber groups who needed the services of a beginning cellist.

The brief affair with Juliette had one outcome involving Franz Holford. One Saturday afternoon Gorden Day visited 'Norwood', and after exchanging a brief greeting with me he closeted himself with Franz in Dr Holford's study, from where I began to hear raised voices.

Gorden Day studied piano with Franz Holford and later at the Trinity College of Music London. He founded the first Australian National Youth Orchestra, which he conducted for fifteen years. (photo from Canon)

Suddenly the study door was flung open and Gorden Day stormed into my room, shouting: 'Did *he* make you give up playing in the orchestra, Bruno?'

'No,' I protested, totally bewildered by his attitude. 'No...not at all.'

'Then why? Why are you leaving?' He was furious.

'It's because...it's just that, my age.... It's supposed to be an orchestra for young kids...and I'm...'

'Twenty-six. Yes, we've been through all that before...you *know* it makes no difference to me or the orchestra. In fact we appreciate you all the more.' He suddenly became more conciliatory: 'Are you sure you won't change your mind, Bruno? I know Juliette would love you to come back.'

'No. No, I'm sorry Gorden, I can't. For purely personal reasons, I can't.'

He bit his lip, and disbelieving, turned on his heel and walked angrily out of the house, muttering how difficult it was to get cellists for an amateur orchestra. It was the last I ever saw of Gorden Day.

******

Music on Sundays

*There is only one real happiness in life,
and that is the happiness of creating.*

- FREDERICK DELIUS

18

I was standing on a ladder cutting the hawthorn hedge when I heard the telephone ringing in *Canon's* office. A few moments later Cooie came out onto the veranda and called: 'It's for *you* Bruin...' She too found it awkward to call me by the fatuous 'Bruno', and like Juliette, she substituted the name of a bear.

It was rare for me to receive telephone calls, so I jumped off the ladder, dropped the hedge shears and ran inside – thinking it was probably someone ringing to enquire about advertising space in the magazine. The voice at the other end of the line was gruff and had a heavy foreign accent.

'I ring about advertisement in Conservatorium...my name is Vladimir and I am violin.'

I had completely forgotten about the advertisement I placed upon the Conservatorium notice board, and it took a moment for the caller's message to sink in.

'This note say Meester Harvey,' the caller continued. 'You are Meester Harvey?...You are cello?'

'Oh yes, yes I see...the note at the Conservatorium. Yes, I put it there.'

'I am violin. You are cello. We play chamber music...da?'

'Oh good!' I replied. 'Yes, yes I'd love to play chamber music with you.

'I'm Bru....umm...Fran...er, Francis...'

There. I had bitten the bullet at last, and reverted to my real name. It was the first time in my life however that I had called myself Francis.

'Da. Francis. Chamber music is good. We play. But Francis... violin, cello no good alone for chamber music. Need piano. You know any peenists?'

'No. No, not really...'

'Then I bring peenist. Trio needs peenist, da?'

A date was set for the following Sunday afternoon at three o'clock for Vladimir and his 'peenist' friend to meet with me at 'Norwood'. The conductor was never ever home on a Sunday afternoon, so I felt it unnecessary to inform him of my plans. It was not a question of seeking his permission to invite people to the house, for by now I considered 'Norwood' my home, but as Sunday drew near I became uneasy about the possibility that Franz could return early, and that he might for some reason make an unwelcome scene in front of my visitors.

I spent that Sunday morning tidying my room and clearing a space for the three of us to rehearse – banishing my large drawing board and easel to a shed at the back of the house and placing two music stands strategically behind the piano stool. It was a beautiful Spring day in September, so I opened the window to allow the scent of gardenias to drift through the house.

When everything was prepared inside I went outside to sweep the front veranda and to rake the red gravel driveway. As I was finishing I heard the latch on the front gate click and glanced at my watch. It was exactly three o'clock. I leaned on my rake at the foot of the stone steps as a young man carrying a violin and an equally young girl carrying a briefcase appeared from around the curve of the hedge.

The young man greeted me effusively: 'I am Vladimir Kalmakov, and this is my accompanist Anne.' I fancied the girl frowned at him briefly as he said '*my* accompanist', but then she turned to me, smiled and held out her hand.

'Very pleased to meet you...' she said in a soft Australian voice.

I could not take my eyes from her face, and held her hand a fraction longer than I should. She was very beautiful - petite, with auburn hair framing an almond-shaped face with grey eyes - but there was about her an air of sadness.

'I'm Frank. Or… Francis ….you can call me Frank if you'd rather, although I like being called Francis.' There was no way I could call myself 'Bruno' in front of these two and self-conscious words tumbled out as I ushered them onto the veranda and indicated three cane chairs grouped around a small outside table.

'Would you care for a drink before we play?' I had prepared some soft drinks in the kitchen and as I left to get them I paused at the bay window of the front room and observed the pair briefly through the lace curtains. The girl was remonstrating with the young man and I was still close enough to hear her say: 'I am not *your* accompanist Vladimir. I wish you wouldn't say things like that.'

When I returned they were not talking. The young man was slumped morosely in his cane chair, while the girl was admiring the yellow budgerigar which Franz kept in a small wire cage hanging from one of the veranda rafters.

'Does it have a name?' she asked.

'Mozart,' I replied. When she smiled quickly, I added: 'He likes music, and he's always singing. Mozart seems to suit…you know?' Franz had named the bird. It was one of the few of his nicknames I liked.

Over drinks they talked about themselves. Anne was nineteen, Vladimir a couple of years older, and both had attended the Conservatorium High School. Vladimir was from an émigré White Russian family which fled to Australia to escape the Bolshevik Revolution and Anne was the daughter of an Irish Catholic family living on Sydney's Northern Beaches. Her father had recently died, which explained the sadness in her mien.

The reason they were not talking when I arrived with the drinks was not the result of having an argument, but more a reflection of their mood, following a concert they had taken part in the previous day. Vladimir had been a competitor in the ABC Concerto and Vocal Competition, conducted at the Sydney Town Hall, and Anne accompanied him on piano, playing the Mendelssohn Violin Concerto. He failed to get through to the finals of the competition, and this was the reason for his despondency. While I was in the kitchen Anne had been chiding him about his playing; she continued as I reappeared.

'You were playing beautifully,' she said, 'then you got faster...and faster...and faster! In the end I could barely keep up with you!'

'I am passionate musician! I am passionate *man*!' the young Russian replied. Anne raised her eyebrows and sighed. She then turned away from him and surveyed the garden.

'What a beautiful house...what a beautiful garden,' she said calmly, and walked down the steps and onto the front lawn, in the centre of which was an oval-shaped garden bed. She pointed at a large clump of flowers.

'Oh, I *know* them,' she exclaimed. 'They're hollyhocks aren't they?'

I followed her down the steps. 'I *thought* they were called foxgloves...'

'No. No. They *look* a bit like foxgloves, but they're definitely hollyhocks. Foxgloves have a smaller flower...'

She pointed again at a row of white blossoms under the hedge: 'What are those....?'

'I think they're called crocuses,' I replied. When he planted them Franz remarked that he was planting crocuses to remind him of his 'home' in England.

'I've never seen them before. Or that tree...what is that tree with the strange bark...?' She pointed to a silver birch in a corner of the garden.

'It's a silver birch. They're a nice tree, but they belong in England. Don't do very well in Australia's climate I'm afraid....do you have a garden?'

'My parents...' she caught her breath momentarily.... 'My mother has a rose garden...and we have a lovely gum tree. We live by the sea though, so the soil is poor..you know?'

It was the Spring of 1956 and I had never been so happy in my entire life, walking in the beautiful garden of 'Norwood' in the warm afternoon sun, with a girl I felt I had known forever. From the veranda, Vladimir's voice cut through our conversation.

'Are we make music now?' She looked at me and shook her head.

'I think music is the only thing in Vladimir's life,' she said. We turned and walked slowly back to the house.

'And not in yours? Music, I mean?'

'It used to be. It used to be *everything*. Then my father died when I was fifteen and I had a breakdown. I wanted to be a concert pianist, but it became impossible. My mother needed me...still needs me. I had trouble even finishing my studies. I think I had what's called a nervous breakdown for two years, of which I can remember very little.' She suddenly snapped out of her sadness and smiled brightly again: 'But I'm better now...'

We stopped at the foot of the stone steps.

'What do you *do* now?' I asked.

'I teach music, at North Sydney Girl's High School. You know the old saying: "He who can does. He who cannot, teaches"?'

'No. Don't say that. I bet you're a great teacher. Was it Bernard Shaw who said that? He has a lot to answer for.' I replied.

I ushered them into my room, and Vladimir began unpacking his violin and caressing the bow with a block of rosin. My cello was standing ready in a corner, and as I rosined my own bow I pointed to a pile of music on the top of the piano.

'Could we begin with something really simple?' I said nervously. 'I'm sure I'm nowhere near the standard of you two...'

We settled on Mozart's Trio K498, in which the clarinet part is adapted for violin and the viola for the cello. I had been practising the cello part for weeks, spending hours a day on the work, but it became obvious from the first few bars that I was in the company of players far above my level of competence. I noticed however, that whenever I stumbled, the pianist would play my part as well as her own, to keep the music flowing. Two wonderfully stimulating hours flew by, with both young musicians brushing aside my apologies for playing wrong notes and breaking down over and over again.

Always at the back of my mind was the thought that the conductor might return at any time and not approve of me inviting strangers into the house, so at 5pm I called a halt to our rehearsal. There was also the consideration that the musicians had come to Hunters Hill by public transport, and in the case of the pianist it would take her over two hours to get home to where she lived on the Northern Beaches. Nevertheless, when I suggested having a meal before they left, both agreed eagerly and tucked in to some gourmet sausages and a glass of apple cider. As we ate in the dining room at the rear of the house, the pianist walked around the room looking at pictures hanging on the wall-papered walls.

'No family photographs....?' She observed. 'Is this your parents' house?'

'No. I actually *work* here, 'I began to explain. 'There's an office, see....It's a long story. I'll tell you next time we meet...er, that's if you both *want* to meet again...?'

To my surprise they both agreed enthusiastically, and we arranged to meet regularly at 'Norwood' on Sunday afternoons.

Kenneth Hince, Melbourne critic and Bibliophile, and Associate Editor of Canon *for several years. (Photo from* Cancn*)*

Crossroads

We are all failures - at least the best of us are.

- J M BARRIE

19

They came each Sunday for several weeks, always at the precise hour and our meetings followed the same pattern: drink on the front veranda, an almost unbroken rehearsal of two hours, concluding with a meal and the departure of the musicians at 5 o'clock. I soon found myself yearning for the week to pass, and each Sunday afternoon I would sit on the veranda half an hour before their arrival and count the minutes until I heard the familiar click of the gate latch, and the sound of their footsteps crunching up the gravel pathway.

From the very first meeting I knew I was in love with the young pianist, but the question which tormented me was whether or not she and the violinist were more than just friends. Once again I reflected that the age difference between us of more than seven years would most likely preclude the possibility of her forming a relationship with me, even if she wanted to and was free. Try as I might, it was difficult to ascertain from their body language whether their association was anything more than a professional one, so at different times during our rehearsals I attempted to find out by putting the question to them separately. Once during a rest break when Anne had left the room, I casually asked the violinist:

'So Vladimir, are you and Anne together?'

'Da. Of course!' he said, almost indifferently.

'No, but I mean…are you and she… I mean do you *love* her?'

'Of course, love her,' he said, eyeing me keenly. 'Love her…and one day maybe *marry* her!' He laughed loudly, as if he had made a joke. Then he added seriously: 'Vy you ask, Francis…?'

Before I could answer him she returned to the room and the subject didn't arise again between myself and Vladimir. However on another occasion, when the young Russian had left the room, I put the same question to her. She burst out laughing.

'Vladimir and me? Whatever gave you *that* idea?'

Her response was unexpected and I was temporarily lost for words.

'I love the way Vladimir plays the violin,' she continued, 'But that's all… we've only just finished high school.'

This was not exactly what I had wanted to hear, for it raised again the spectre of the difference in our ages, which had been such an obstacle in my relationship with Juliette. As they were leaving on this particular Sunday afternoon she stopped at the bottom of the steps and turned back, as Vladimir kept walking towards the gate.

When he was out of sight around the curve of the hedge she said softly: 'Why did you ask me if I was in love with Vladimir?'

'I didn't know whether you and he were more than….just..well, to be honest, I was going to ask if you would like to have dinner with *me* sometime…' I replied, throwing caution to the winds. 'Umm, away from here, I mean.'

'I'd love to have dinner with you,' she said, with her radiant smile.

We agreed that I should call her and arrange a time to meet. There was a restaurant opposite the Conservatorium in Macquarie Street called the Astor she said, when she could see that I was at a loss for a suggested venue. As she turned to leave, I heard the sound of a car pulling up outside and a few moments later Franz appeared around the hedge. He stopped as he saw us, and his face became clouded with suspicion and anger.

'I appear to have interrupted something…,' he said, in an accusatory tone.

'Franz, I'd like you to meet Anne….she's a pianist.' Anne stepped forward and held out her hand, which he at first ignored, then reluctantly took.

'Anne, this is Dr Franz Holford…' There was an awkward silence until I addressed the conductor: 'We've just been going through some music…'

'So I see.' He brushed past the both of us and entered the house without a further word.

I had told both Anne and Vladimir a little about my situation at 'Norwood' over the few weeks we had rehearsed together, but nothing in great detail, for as I tried to describe it to them I would become confused and self-conscious, and more aware than ever how people 'outside' the present circle of my acquaintances must have viewed my relationship with Franz Holford and the job I was pursuing at 'Norwood'.

'I don't think he likes me very much,' Anne said, as I walked her to the front gate.

'It's not *you* particularly,' I replied, 'He's very suspicious of anyone who comes to the house.'

'Why?' And why does he call you Bruno?'

As I opened the gate for her and said goodbye I shrugged. 'It's complicated. One day I'll tell you the whole story,' I said. At that time I told myself that I didn't really know the complete story.

******

In asking the young pianist out to dinner I unwittingly brought to a head a problem which I had been avoiding for some time. I would need money – and a considerable amount of it – in order to pay for such an adventure. Whenever I needed money – for any reason - art supplies, clothes, or other little luxuries – I just had to ask. Not that I was ever unreasonable in my demands, and I always felt comfortable that the work I was engaged upon deserved a lot more than I received financially. Franz never demurred, nor even questioned why I needed extra funds, and the cash would appear immediately. He never asked for receipts of what I had spent, nor did he ever require change.

However, when I asked him for ten pounds[146] in the week following the visit by my new musician friends, he stared hard at me as he reached for his wallet.

'That's a lot. Are you going out?' It was the first time he had ever queried a request for money. Grudgingly he handed me two five-pound notes.

'Yes,' I replied, returning his stare with a smile, whilst hating myself for deceiving him. For most of the time my life was an open book, but on this occasion I was determined not to tell him what I was planning, for I knew it would create a storm if he thought I was having a relationship with someone he didn't know.

We had arranged to meet at the Conservatorium on a Friday evening at 6 pm and go from there to the Astor Restaurant in Macquarie Street, where I had booked a table for dinner. After a short trip by bus down the peninsula from Hunters Hill to Woolwich, I caught a ferry at 5.30 from Valentia Street Wharf, arriving at Circular Quay just before six, from whence I walked the short distance up Macquarie Street to 'The Con' as it was ubiquitously known.

Pushing open the heavy glass doors I entered with some trepidation the large foyer of Sydney's most famous music institution and saw Anne sitting on one of the leather benches near the Box Office, chatting to a man who appeared to be in his fifties. He was smoking a cigarette and talking earnestly to her as he passed her a large brown envelope. When she saw me she smiled and beckoned for me to join them.

'I'd like to introduce you to my harmony teacher, Mr Hanson,' she said.

Raymond Hanson was a man of medium height, stockily built, with wavy grey hair and a soft, kind face. After shaking hands he paid me scant attention, addressing himself only to his student. There followed an awkward silence, and finally Anne rose, indicating her intention to leave.

'I must go.' Then she held the envelope up, and said to him: 'Thank you for this…I shall treasure it.'

It was still sunlight as we walked out of the Conservatorium and headed towards the restaurant, which was in a little lane off Macquarie Street.

As we walked past the imposing fifty-foot high bronze statue of King Edward VII, situated directly in front of the Con, I felt the need to break the silence between us and said: 'Why would they put the statue of a king on a horse outside a conservatorium of music, I wonder?'

She stopped, and we both surveyed the monument. Then she said, with a half-smile: 'Well, it *was* a set of horse stables once, wasn't it?' We both laughed, and she continued: 'Anyway, I like the trachyte base it stands on more than the sculpture.'

'The trachyte base?' I replied. 'What the heck is a trachyte base?'

'Oh, trachyte…isn't that an igneous rock?' I shrugged my shoulders in ignorance. An igneous rock? Who on earth would know a detail like that? Noting my puzzled look, she became self-conscious and frowned.

'There I go…I think it's because I like doing crossword puzzles…'

'No…no,' I responded hastily, 'I think it's…I think *you* are amazing.'

'Oh, that's good then. I'd hate it if you thought I was being a know-all. Here's the restaurant…'

We entered the restaurant by steps leading downwards into a spacious room below street level. It was directly underneath the exclusive 13-storey Astor Apartments, which had been built in 1914; the now *chic* dining room was originally an exclusive kitchen linked by service lifts to each apartment, enabling the delivery of meals direct to the Astor's residents. As the waiter seated us and gave us each a menu, I nervously felt for the ten pounds in my pocket and wondered if it was going to be sufficient to cover the cost of the meal. The pianist settled herself, looked vaguely at the menu and then put it aside and stared at the envelope she was carrying.

'Do you mind if I….?'

'Please…go ahead.' She opened the envelope and took out some sheets of manuscript paper, then gasped with astonishment. 'He's dedicated a song to me!'

'What is it? Can I see?'

She passed the manuscript across the table. It was a song to a poem by the famous Indian poet Rabindranath Tagore, set to music by Raymond Hanson and across the top of the first page the composer had written: 'Dedicated to Anne Crowe'. I felt a wave of jealousy pass through me as I read the words:

> I dreamt that she sat by my head, tenderly ruffling my hair with her fingers, playing the melody of her touch. I looked at her face and struggled with my tears, till the agony of unspoken words burst my sleep like a bubble. I sat up and saw the glow of the Milky Way above my window, like a world of silence on fire, and I wondered if at this moment she had a dream that rhymed with mine.

'He's in love with you…'

She burst out laughing. It was a full-throated belly laugh.

'He's my harmony teacher. He's an old man….'

'That's a love poem. He dedicated it to you. He's in love with you…'

She stopped laughing and looked at me seriously.

'You seem to think every man you see me with regards me as his châtelaine.'

There it was again, her choice of words: 'châtelaine'…châtelaine… I wracked my brain, trying to remember its definition. As I searched my memory, she leaned forward and looked at me intently across the table.

'Don't be silly,' she said. 'I quite like older men…' She looked at me significantly. '…but not quite *that* old!' She gave another bright laugh and returned to the menu.

'What I'd like *now* is the Filet Mignon…what are *you* going to have?'

It shouldn't have surprised me that she ate so heartily. After a performance, most musicians I had ever known were always ravenous. By the time we had finished our main course and consumed a half-bottle of wine, my mental arithmetic told me I should have enough money left for a small helping of sweets, so I asked the waiter to bring us the sweets menu.

I half-hoped that having such a tiny waistline she would decline, and perhaps settle for coffee, but again I had underestimated her.

'Oh goodee,' she exclaimed. 'Let's have the Bombe Alaska…is that all right?'

I had no idea what Bombe Alaska was, except that on the menu it was very expensive. I had just about enough money left for one dessert, so I handed the menu back to the waiter and said: 'Just the Bombe Alaska… I'll pass on the sweets, thanks.'

'No, no…' she said quickly, 'We *share* the Bombe between us…right?'

The waiter nodded. It was more than right – it was miraculous, for I could now pay for the meal in full and even leave a small tip. We both exclaimed when the waiter returned, bearing the snowy white/brown meringue dessert piled mountainously onto a large serving plate. Solemnly he poured a generous helping of cognac brandy over the sweet and ignited it with a cigarette lighter. My companion squealed with delight as the blue flame shot up in the air in a brilliant flash and died almost immediately.

'Bon appetit,' the waiter said, with the trace of a smile on his haughty, lugubrious face as he departed.

After dinner, we walked slowly down to Circular Quay, where Anne would catch the Manly ferry home, and I would take a ferry to Valentia Street wharf. It was still quite early on a gorgeous, moonlit summer night, so I suggested we sit on a bench seat in a cultivated garden nook at the Quay, overlooking the ferry terminals.

We talked incessantly. She told me all about herself, her three siblings and an Irish mother – born on the goldfields at Kalgoorlie – now a widow, due to the recent death of her husband – a clerk in the NSW Railways. The death of the father she adored had led to a nervous breakdown, and caused Anne to abandon a blossoming career as a concert pianist in order to help support the family by becoming a high school music teacher. I also spoke about my own family – the death of my mother when I was only three; my father going off to WWII and as I thought then, being killed by the Japanese in Port Moresby; of my older brother – a clarinet player, now with the Brisbane Symphony Orchestra – and of the four older sisters who raised us both when we were orphaned.

She tried several times to bring the conversation back to the reasons which had led me to 'Norwood', and the job I held with Franz Holford, but the timing was not right and I told her I needed to see her again when we could have more time together. To my delight she agreed, and we planned to make another dinner date when she came on Sunday for our regular rehearsal. I then walked her down to the Manly ferry terminal and briefly held her hands as she thanked me and said goodnight. As she walked across the ferry's gangplank she turned and waved to me, smiling her radiant smile.

With my heart singing, I caught the much smaller vessel 'Karingal' at the Hunters Hill terminal and sat on the outside deck in the balmy air of a purple Summer night, closed my eyes and dreamed of what the future might hold with this beautiful auburn-haired musician who had come so fortuitously into my life.

It was almost midnight when I let myself in the front door at 'Norwood'. The light was on in Franz's study, but I went straight to my room and prepared for bed. After a few moments his head appeared around the door.

'I can't go on giving you ten pounds every time you feel like a night out, you know,' he said in a sour voice.

'I wouldn't expect you to,' I replied.

He opened the door a little wider. 'This girl you have become enamoured of. You know if you go on seeing her it will ruin your life here, don't you?'

'Franz,' I said in a low voice, 'I have an occupation here….I don't have a *life*.'

'Oh, so you think you will find a "life" with a teenager and no visible means of support? By the way, if it's that girl I met, isn't that called "cradle snatching" these days? Surely you are too old for her aren't you?'

He had often quoted the adage 'An error of judgment is not so culpable as an error of taste'. This was clearly an error of taste, and he had descended into vulgarity. The scales had well and truly fallen from my eyes and I began to detest the stranger he had become to me. It was virtually the first really angry words we had ever exchanged, but it was the catalyst I needed, and the beginning of the end of our relationship.

I made up my mind there and then that I would immediately start looking for a paid job outside 'Norwood'.

Tailpiece for Canon

Pain

If you don't stand for something, you'll fall for anything.

- MICHAEL EVANS

20

The prospect of earning a living was never going to be easy, for I had been out of the paid workforce for almost a decade. Getting a job in Australia at this time was difficult too, due to devastation caused by floods, typhoons and bushfires, not to mention the importation of Hungarian refugees, fleeing the Soviet invasion of their country, many of whom headed for Sydney.[147] With a population of only 9.5 million in the 1950s, life in Australia under a Menzies Government was good for those who had 'made it', but as it so often happened with a conservative government, it was tough for middle and lower class wage earners.

Before looking for a job, and in view of my confrontation with Franz, I decided I should tell the one person who now constantly occupied my thoughts, what was my true work situation. I had tried many times to broach the subject with her, but could not find the appropriate words. It haunted me that she probably assumed that I either owned – or was heir to – the house 'Norwood', or at least that I was a person of independent means. If she became aware that I was virtually an unpaid servant, she would probably regard me in an entirely different light. So I made up my mind to visit her at her parents' house in Harbord.[148]

It was a Monday evening around 7 o'clock when I arrived, without making a prior engagement at her mother's house 'Tullassa' - situated a few blocks from Freshwater Beach. I knocked on the front door, which was opened by her mother, a tiny, rotund figure – unmistakeably Irish

– whose somewhat severe countenance was heightened by the use of elegant, rimless glasses.

'I'm Francis...Frank...Harvey.'

'I know who you are,' she replied tersely, 'And you'll be wanting to see my Anne I suppose?'

'Yes, if that's all right.'

'She's out in the living room, watching television....go through.'

Television had only recently commenced in Australia in that year of 1956, and virtually the only channel apart from the ABC was Channel 9.[149] Not many people as yet owned television sets, so viewing was usually a family plus neighbours affair.

The room was in darkness apart from the incandescent light of the television, but to my surprise the violinist Vladimir Kalmakov was one of three sharing a lounge with Anne as they watched. As soon as I saw him I started to back away, mumbling apologies for interrupting the family's viewing, but Anne and Vladimir both sprang to their feet, greeting me enthusiastically.

'Look, I'm sorry,' I said. 'This is really embarrassing...I came to talk. I came to talk about the trio...'

'Let's go out onto the veranda,' Anne said.

My heart plummeted when I saw Vladimir, for it was obvious that he and Anne were so close that he appeared to be accepted as one of her family. Despite her protestations to the contrary and knowing his feelings towards her, it appeared to me that there was no way they could not be emotionally involved. Rather than attempting to explain to Anne my situation at 'Norwood', I simply told both of them briefly and in a matter of fact tone of voice that I could not continue the Sunday meetings of the trio, because I had other more important work to do - adding that I was sure this also applied to them. Vladimir simply shrugged his shoulders.

'OK,' he said cheerfully, 'There is no problem Francis. I go back to TV now....OK?' He extended a hand. 'Nice meeting, Francis...maybe meet again some other time, da?'

Anne stayed. When he had left, she reached out for my hand tentatively.

'What's wrong?' she asked. 'Has something happened? It was so nice…'

I squeezed her hand. 'No, it hasn't been just "nice"…it's been *wonderful* for me, you have no idea…'

'Then why do you want to stop? Please tell me…'

'Look Anne, you know almost nothing about me. Things are…well, things are not exactly as they appear. I've tried to tell you many times, but I just can't put it into words… *I am not exactly as I appear to you*…'

'You appear to me to be a nice, kind person,' she replied softly '…who I happen to like very much. That's a good start, isn't it?'

'Let's just say that we lead totally different lives. You lead a totally different life to me. A much *better* life than mine. My life is a total fraud, believe me…and you deserve a lot, lot better. I have very little to offer which could make you happy.'

'You have yourself…'

'It's not enough…I can't do this to you. Not to *you*. I have to say goodbye, Anne, I have to go…' I squeezed her hand again and walked away.

Breaking off the relationship I had previously enjoyed with Juliette was painful enough, but, brief as it had been, parting from the young pianist was almost unbearable. I knew I would never meet a person like her again…

******

The last position I held before going to live and work at 'Norwood' was as a trainee artist with the advertising agency Goldberg in George Street in the city, so it was to advertising I returned, seeking employment.

Scanning the jobs vacant pages of the *Sydney Morning Herald* one Saturday morning I came across an advertisement from a small agency calling itself Shortridge Advertising, which looked promising. They were seeking a young man with advertising experience for their office in Hunter Street in the city. I rang the number given and was put through to the manager Bill Shortridge, who invited me to an interview.

Seeking to impress him, I put together an entire edition of an imaginary magazine – writing articles, laying out the design and even drawing imaginary advertisements, which I concocted from various glossy magazines. The idea was to show that there were few aspects of commercial publishing and advertising that I did not understand.

I completed the mock-up magazine the day before my interview and told Franz what I intended doing. We had occasionally discussed the idea of me getting an 'outside' job, which he was always very uneasy about, but I convinced him on this occasion that I could still cope with producing *Canon* and that my aspirations of becoming a professional musician would have to wait. His only real concern was that by mixing with the outside world again his own closely guarded world might become exposed to investigation. Anticipating that he would be annoyed, I was therefore surprised by his complaisance.

'Would you care for me to write you a testimonial?' he asked.

It was a generous and beautifully phrased reference, extolling my publishing and editing abilities, which he typed very professionally onto a *Canon* letterhead. Combined with my hand-drawn prototype of a 32-page imaginary magazine, it made a substantial submission, which I presented at an interview at the advertising agency office in a high rise building with a sculpture on it by Lyndon Dadswell on the corner of Hunter and Castlereagh Streets in Sydney.

******

Bill Shortridge was a commanding, ebullient, egocentric and self-made businessman who had attracted a small empire of advertising accounts, including some well-known brands and companies. His secretary – an attractive young brunette – showed me into his office, where he was holding Franz's testimonial in his hand.

'Sit down. I liked your submission – very original,' he barked. 'So, you worked on this music journal, did you? Play the piano myself…'

He put the letter down, folded his arms and leaned across the desk in intimidatory fashion.

'If everything this feller says about you is true, you'll do me. You know what salary I'm offering…when can you start?'

******

It was all too easy, it was all too quick, and it was all soon over.

The person Bill Shortridge was looking for was someone young and vital who could seek out and bring in new accounts to his advertising business, in order that he might eventually retire. After a few weeks at my new job, I would prefer to spend my lunch hours playing chess with his Dutch accountant, rather than entertaining prospective clients in pubs, and unlike several others of his employees, I was never able to work evening hours or weekends, as account executives tended to do, and still do it seems.

Shortridge lived in a large house in the prestigious suburb of Longueville, across the river from Hunters Hill. Christened 'The White House', it commanded a magnificent view of the Lane Cove River, and he would often catch the same ferry as I did when returning home from work in the city. He would never sit with me, but now and then I would notice a furtive glance from him as I alighted at Valentia Street Wharf, a couple of ferry stops before Longueville. My comings and goings were an irritating mystery to him.

My desk was in a glass cubicle within his own expansive office, from where he could monitor all my movements, and I felt uncomfortably conscious of his surveillance at all hours of the day.

After a few months – no doubt when he realized that he had made a mistake in employing me - he began to play mind games. He would hold his wrist high in the air, pull back his shirt cuff and glare at his wristwatch if I was more than a minute or so late; he would engage in a loud, prolonged cough if I spent too long on the telephone. On another occasion when I wasn't looking he dropped a five pound note on the floor just outside the office door, hoping I would pocket it so that he could then accuse me of theft; to his chagrin I picked it up without thinking and gave it to his secretary.

After six months we had both had enough and my job was terminated by mutual consent. It was the only position in my whole working life from which I received the equivalent to the sack, and from it I learned a good lesson – never to work at a job which I did not enjoy for its own sake.

******

The advertisement read simply: 'Editor required for outdoor magazine'.

In the latter half of 1956, armed only with Franz's reference, I presented for an interview with the Managing Editor of a small publishing business in Kent Street. Rodger Hungerford was a tall man in his fifties, with a genial countenance, whose most striking physical feature was the absence of his left arm at the shoulder. I never asked him how he lost the arm, but his secretary informed me that it had been taken by a shark. He had written a book unambiguously titled *How to catch a fish*[150], which had sold so many copies he had built upon it a unique publishing business. The book is still published today.

We chatted for more than an hour on the pleasures of writing, editing and publishing in general, until he finally pushed his chair back, stood up and said:

'You are the new editor of *Angler's Digest*. Welcome to my small team.'

It was a totally unexpected result and I found myself suddenly put on the spot. He was such an honest, direct person that I felt obliged to blurt out:

'I should tell you that I know absolutely nothing about fish or fishing, apart from what I used to do as a kid…'

'That doesn't matter, you can refer to anyone here. We're all experts. As long as you're a good writer and editor, that's what we need.'

He went on to point out that he knew of only two ways to appoint editorial staff: choose an expert in the area of expertise and train them to write, or appoint a good journalist and allow them to train as a specialist. The staff he referred to consisted of only three people - himself, 'Big' Bob, who sold all the advertising for his publications and his receptionist/secretary Jan.

Angler's Digest was a no-nonsense, practical monthly magazine, packed with true-life stories and piscatorial advice, avidly read by a wide circulation of professional and amateur fishermen. Certainly my new magazine couldn't be compared to the new weekly *Nation* magazine which had just appeared in Sydney, nor a literary quarterly such as *Quadrant* or *Meanjin*, but it was a great way to re-start my career in the commercial publishing world.

In the final analysis, it was a well-paid full time job in a friendly environment, and I was fortunate to have a position at last as a professional journalist. I commenced work the week following my interview and was delighted to find myself given carte blanch with the magazine's editorial, for which Big Bob chased up all the advertising and provided valuable leads for stories. I edited and wrote all the articles and reviews, and even took black and white photographs on assignment for the magazine, and from my first month's pay I bought Franz a 48-piece Wedgwood dinner service for 'Norwood' and myself a brand new, twin lens reflex *Rolleiflex* camera.

******

(Left) Alfred Cortot (1877-1962), famous Swiss pianist Franz Holford claimed to have studied with in Paris. (Right) Robert Teichmüller (1863-1939), German concert pianist and music educator, he also claimed as his teacher. (Below) Felix Weingartner (1863-1942), famous Austrian conductor, whom Franz Holford claimed as his uncle. (Below right) Kaiser Wilhelm II (1859-1941), in whose service Holford claimed his father was the royal household's surgeon. (Photos from Canon)

Rise and demise of *Canon*

Man is not what he thinks he is, he is what he hides.

- ANDRÉ MALRAUX

21

Ever since he entered my life in the 1940s at St John's Church Woolwich, Franz Holford had been an enigma. I sensed from the beginning that the this was also the opinion of others with whom he came into contact – notably the Champ family. Here was a good pianist, who rarely gave public concerts; a good - though somewhat erratic - teacher, who had only a handful of pupils; an excellent conductor, who never conducted any recognized choirs or orchestras and a prolific, if somewhat dilettante composer whose compositions were rarely heard beyond the soirées held at the Champ's residence in Hunters Hill.

Yet he was prepared to claim that he was descended from German royalty, was born and educated in Heidelberg, where he claimed to have attended universities there and later at Oxford; that he held a doctorate in music and two other disciplines, and that his piano teachers had included the great Alfred Cortot and the German concert pianist Professor Robert Teichmüller.

He had even gone to the trouble of once showing the author a 'class photo' taken at Oxford University in which he claimed to be pictured, although the individual faces were so small they were impossible to identify.[151]

People believed him simply because they had no good reason to think otherwise, and because of his own personal charisma. He was a commanding figure – tall and well built, with handsome features and a genial smile, and a cultivated voice which eschewed vulgarity of any kind. He dressed elegantly whatever the company he kept, and wrote in a beautiful, calligraphic hand – on the best quality writing paper for his correspondence, often using deep purple ink. He quoted freely from poets such as W H Auden, Gerard Manley Hopkins, Synge, Keats, Shelley and Byron and his favourite composers were Chopin, Rachmaninov, Schumann and Delius. He possessed valuable original scores and manuscripts of the latter, which had been sent to him by Delius' amanuensis, Eric Fenby.

When I finally became aware of the truth of his lineage, as portrayed on his mother's death certificate I was staggered, and found it almost impossible to believe. I had given up a career to go and work for him virtually unpaid at 'Norwood'. I had not been drawn to him as a substitute father, but as a man who appeared to be the embodiment of the romantic artist – a cultivated foreigner living in a country starved of culture. I was fascinated as to how anyone could live such a life in Australia, and as the evidence of his real background kept accumulating - I hoped secretly that none of it would ultimately prove to be true. As for confronting the great man with what I knew, and seeking an explanation, it was unthinkable; Franz Holford was not the kind of person who could ever be proven wrong in the slightest detail, let alone be unmasked as a fraud.

One extraordinary aspect of events at the séance held at the Champs' residence was that no one, to my knowledge, ever broached this subject again with Franz Holford, nor he with them. It all passed as if nothing at all untoward had occurred and no one was prepared to question the great man on the subject.

I never mentioned to Franz Holford or anybody else what I had discovered about his background, but I became increasingly aware and understanding of the duplicity in his life which caused him to act in all manner of strange ways. I was to discover for example that not being in possession of a legitimate birth certificate can complicate one's life enormously.

******

My work on *Canon* continued, but now it had to be confined to evenings and weekends because of the full-time job I had taken in the city. By cutting out most other activities, such as practising piano, cello and music copying, I found I could keep pace with producing the magazine, but could not continue the arduous and time-consuming task of selling advertising, most of which had to be conducted during business hours. I was also loth to give up the one small area of my activities which actually brought in a little money – music copying – but with the advent of John Antill's 'Music Writer' and other emerging technologies, the laborious process of hand-copied manuscripts was in any case gradually being replaced by other, more efficient means.[152]

Franz Holford would never again replicate the privileges he enjoyed during the years 1950 to 1954. At that time he had an unpaid staff of six people who worked unofficially on *The Canon*: Associate Editors Kenneth Hince[153], and Wolfgang Wagner[154], Secretary John Champ, Assistant to the Editor Gordon Clarke, Doris Eddey as the magazine's representative in Melbourne, and the author. In addition there were many regular music critics such as Keverell McIntyre, Jeffreys Scherek, Roger Covell, Max Harris, Ernest Briggs, Desmond O'Shaughnessy, Roy Davies, Robert Dalley-Scarlett and a host of erudite writers contributing articles to the magazine. To my knowledge, none of these contributors – apart from Kenneth Hince - ever received any payment for their services.[155]

The whole project appeared to be underwritten from the start by the steel tycoon Reginald Champ and the many readers who responded generously over the years.[156]

Meanwhile, on the personal side of his life Franz enjoyed such privileges as paying a peppercorn rental for a magnificent house, having the free services of a housekeeper, regular meals at the Champ's residence, and travelling in a Bentley car with the attractive Gwen Champ as his personal chauffeur. He paid no income tax, nor any of the business expenses of running *The Canon* and he received an endless supply of books, music scores and recordings submitted to the magazine for review. Many of these he on-sold, or used as gifts to ingratiate himself with new acquaintances, or he gave them away to friends.

******

For the first three years of its life, I had little to do with producing *The Canon* - my contribution being the drawing of little dinkuses or tailpieces, which were used to complete empty spaces at the conclusion of articles, or as decorations for uncials. However, when I went to live at 'Norwood' I gradually became more and more involved with the production of the magazine, which required writing and editing articles and reviews, selling advertising and liaising with the printer. For all my efforts, Franz Holford was apparently loth to acknowledge the contribution I made and not only failed to include my name on the editorial title page, as he had done with others such as Kenneth Hince and Wolfgang Wagner, but insisted that I use absurd pen names on my articles and initials only on reviews of concerts, records or publications, as if for some reason he felt he had to disguise my very presence; it was one of his many idiosyncrasies which other people beside myself just accepted. It didn't worry me then, and it worries me even less today.

The most valuable contribution *Canon* made to Australia's musical life was to record the number of outstanding musicians who visited this country across the years, and in many cases to publish articles by and about them. One of the most important of these was Eugene Goossens, who was welcomed in 1946 with the words: 'We give you greeting, Mr Goossens, may your sojourn with us be a happy one, and may we appreciate the tremendous opportunity you are giving us…'[157]

Upon his arrival, Goossens amazed everyone by declaring that among his reasons for deciding to take up the post of conductor of the Sydney Symphony Orchestra was that through his mother he was the great great great grandson of Captain James Cook, the discoverer of Australia![158] Eugene Goossens was to feature prominently in the pages of *Canon* during his stay in Australia, and a special commemorative edition was devoted to him in July 1952 to mark his five years in this country.[159] Another notable international visitor reviewed in the first edition of *Canon* was the great Chilean pianist Claudio Arrau, who enjoyed considerable success in Australia, but whose subsequent visit was marred by a scandal which involved his being arrested in a public toilet in Hyde Park. He was given a nominal fine of £5 for 'offensive behaviour'[160], in what proved to be an echo of the Goossens scandal, which had happened in the previous year.

The Boyd Neel Orchestra was also a visitor in 1947, and this proved propitious for *Canon*, for Dr Neel gave the little magazine a public commendation, which was picked up in the media, ensuring some valuable publicity.[161]

In that edition, Boyd Neel said that impresarios were 'sabotaging' serious music in England by giving the public innumerable performances of such compositions as the Tschaikowsky B Flat Piano Concerto, with 'flashy' pianists as soloists. He said that the scheme was entirely commercial, and the majority of the audiences attended, not for the intunsic value of the concerto, but because '…they have heard it in a film'.[162]

Neel concluded by saying: 'My visit to Australia gave me fresh hope for music, when I saw the enthusiasm and genuine appreciation of the great music that exists in your country. England has a lot to learn from you in this respect.'

******

The early editions of *Canon* were filled with conversational articles and reviews which largely philosophised on the nature of music, without providing much in the way of an in-depth analysis of the contemporary Australian musical scene. Individual writers occasionally contributed more scholarly or colourful articles, such as Eric Fenby – amanuensis to Delius – with whom Franz struck up an ongoing friendship[163] and Isabelle Moresby.[164] The latter was a published author who had written a book on New Guinea; in 1948 she wrote another: 'Australia makes Music'[165], which was reviewed in *Canon* by Dr Robert Dalley-Scarlett, another musician with whom Franz struck up a long-term friendship. Sadly, Dalley-Scarlett dismissed Moresby's book in two lines:

> I opened the book with the highest anticipations, and I closed it with profound regret.[166]

Among the early reviewers of records, music and concerts was George Wollaston, who conducted a regular session on Radio Station 2SM, 'Afternoon with the Classics'. A valued regular columnist, his death in

The Canon often lacked consistency of design, especially in its covers and logo, and basic publishing information was sometimes omitted. Nevertheless, editions like the Olympic Number (Bottom left) and Music of Israel (Top left) were popular.

July 1948 was a great loss to the little music journal. A constant theme throughout the various reviews in *Canon* of concerts in Australia was the lament on the size of our concert-going audiences. It is the same today as it was then.

The twenty-eight editions of *Canon* published between August 1948 and November 1950 were the halcyon years of the journal in terms of editorial content and consistency of production. The editorial team of of which I was a part: Franz Holford (Editor), Gordon Clarke (Assistant to the Editor) and John Champ (Secretary) found increasing maturity in writing and editorial skills, and achieved a modest – but consistent – format.

Canon began attracting contributors of high quality to the monthly journal, among the first of whom was Eugene Goossens, whose article 'Where are the scores?'[168] may be said to have led to the first performance of John Antill's ballet *Corroboree* in 1950. In the same edition, Sir (then Mr) John Barbirolli contributed 'The art of conducting', which ran across two editions of *Canon*, by courtesy of *Penguin Music Magazine*.[169] This led to a friendship between Franz and Ralph Hill (Penguin's Editor), which resulted in the great English musicologist contributing on a regular basis to *Canon*. Franz in turn also contributed an article to Hill's magazine on the state of music in Australia in 1950. It was a fair, if somewhat generalised appraisal of the then current state of Australian music, and contained a very interesting prognostication on Goossens' campaign to establish a 4,000-seat opera house on Bennelong Point. Franz concluded the article with a typically patronising statement on Australia:

> Australia is musically one of the most enthusiastic countries in the world. But her enthusiasm is coupled with a youthful impetuosity that inclines towards an attitude of pseudo-superiority. When her enthusiasm becomes tempered with a keener discrimination and her regrettable hostility to criticism with a willingness to accept advice, the future of Australia as a great musical nation will be assured.

Following the success of Barbirolli's series 'The art of conducting', Franz obtained the rights to serialise Nicolas Slonimsky's book 'The road to music' from the publishers Dodd, Mead & Co of New York, which ran across five editions, from March to July 1949. Around about this time two names began appearing regularly on reviews, the bearers of which would have a significant influence on the development of the magazine – Wolfgang Wagner and Kenneth Hince.

******

By far the most important edition of the magazine in these early years was the Schoenberg edition, produced in September 1949[170], which was the brainchild of Wolfgang Wagner, whom Franz appointed Associate Editor. Franz had met Wagner quite by accident in Grahame's Bookshop in Sydney and assumed that he was the brother of Dieter, both of whom were grandsons of Richard Wagner. He immediately invited him to write for *Canon*.

Wolfgang Wagner was however no relation to the renowned German composer, but was born in Czechoslovakia in 1904, the son of a Dr Karl and Lili Wagner. He had emigrated to Australia in 1939 aboard the *Oronsay* with his wife Charlotte and two daughters, in order to avoid the war in Europe and he eventually became the regular music critic for the old *Sun* newspaper, in Sydney.

After reading a book by Dika Newlin: *Bruckner, Mahler, Schoenberg* – Wagner wrote to the authoress, who was a pupil of Schoenberg, requesting her help in preparing a tribute edition of *Canon* for the composer's 75th birthday.

Newlin responded immediately and with enthusiasm, for she relished the opportunity to further the work of the extraordinary composer whose pupil she had been as a young student - one of his last.[171] The result was a most comprehensive survey of the man and his work by such authorities as Newlin, Leibowitz, Steuermann, Otto Klemperer, Alban Berg, Alma Mahler and of course Schoenberg himself, who contributed a stunning article on Mahler, with whom Schoenberg had studied.

In Australia at this time, Schoenberg's music was, to quote one contributor, 'an unopened book'. Music houses, when approached, admitted to stocking none of his compositions. Musicians therefore had little opportunity to form an opinion for or against Schoenberg's 12-tone works, which were so controversial at the time. Following this edition of *Canon*, Eugene Goossens announced his intention of performing Schoenberg's *Five Pieces for Orchestra* in Sydney. Of the composer, Goossens said: 'He remains the least understood, and almost the most neglected composer of his generation'.

The Schoenberg edition of *Canon* received considerable acclaim from music critics. The following review appeared in *The Age*, under the heading 'Atonalism in music':

Autographed copy of Arnold Schoenberg's photo portrait, sent by him to Associate Editor Wolfgang Wagner, in appreciation of the special 75th Anniversary edition of Canon, featuring the great German composer, whose works were almost unknown in Australia at the time. (Papers of Wolfgang Wagner, Mitchell Library MLMSS10642)

> The Australian monthly journal of music Canon has devoted its September number to an appreciation of Arnold Schoenberg the composer, as a tribute on his 75th birthday. Schoenberg is the archpriest of atonalism in music and the twelve-tone scale, and the journal has done music some service, by seeking to explain in various articles by prominent musicians just what this pioneer of a new music is driving at. One of the most interesting things in this symposium is Schoenberg's own appreciation of Gustav Mahler, although his long analysis of Mahler as composer and conductor may, still leave many people doubting.[172]

******

A continuing feature of the magazine was the symbiotic relationship between the *Canon* and the Organ Society of New South Wales, beginning with its first contribution (Volume 4, Number 10, May 1951) until the last (Volume 9, Number 1, August, 1955). This relationship saw *The Canon* acting as a vehicle for the bulletin of the Organ Society (which subsequently became known as The Organ Music Society), publishing valuable and knowledgeable articles on aspects of organ building and construction, techniques of playing, acoustics, new music publications, interesting repertoire, composers of organ music, in fact articles of interest to all organists and lovers of the instrument. It even published the Society's Minutes of meetings.

Whether Franz had a financial arrangement with the Organ Society, or whether both parties had agreed to share their limited circle of readers is unknown, but the partnership added substantially to *Canon's* subscription base, and produced some very scholarly articles for the delight of lovers of the organ. This popularisation of the organ reached its peak in Australia with the visit of the great Italian organist Fernando Germani, organist to the Pope, in 1956.

Other important contributions which *Canon* made to the musical literature of Australia were articles such as James Hall's *History of Music in Australia*, which was serialised in instalments across three volumes of the magazine, commencing with Vol 4 No 6 in January 1951. The author was a distinguished journalist, whose father was Chairman of the Adelaide Advertiser in 1954, and later James became Features Editor of

The Australian in 1972. The twenty-four instalments were subsequently bound as photocopies into a book *A History of Music in Australia*, by James Hall and deposited in the library of the Australian Music Centre.[173] This important piece of research has, over the years, been frequently used as a reference on Australian music by researchers and scholars.[174]

******

In 1954 Queen Elizabeth II visited Australia. Always having an eye to the main chance, Franz composed two works, *The Fair Elizabeth*, for choir, harp and oboe and *An Australian National Anthem*, which his good friend Robert Dalley-Scarlett included in a free concert by the Handel Society in Brisbane entitled 'Royal Occasions' in February 1954.

Franz's two compositions for the occasion received a very favourable review from Roger Covell, who would later go on to contribute further editorial material to *Canon*.[175] The concert also featured Coronation Music of Elizabeth I, plus a major work by Robert Dalley-Scarlett.[176]

Franz had previously brought out an edition of *Canon*, which appeared in June 1953 (Vol 6 No 11) with a photo of the young Queen Elizabeth II on its cover, entitled the 'Coronation' edition, in which the magazine hailed the arrival of the monarch and promised a special edition soon after she reached Sydney on 3 February 1954. Unfortunately, apart from an article 'Coronation Thoughts' by the ever-faithful Dalley-Scarlett, the promised edition failed to materialise. The June 1953 edition did however produce a little poetic gem in praise of the new Queen, from *Canon's* Brisbane critic Ernest Briggs:

ELIZABETH, WHO PLAYED THE VIRGINALS

Elizabeth, who played the virginals,
And set great men to great adventuring,
And put composers to their madrigals,
And poets to their art's indenturing;
To bring such deftness to the lyric line,
Such elegance, and wit so quaint and terse,
That still those testaments of ardour shine
from that renaissance of immortal verse.

Grant us your grace, that in your namesake's years
The stricture of the liberating word
may bring our souls where revelation sheers;
By midnight spires and timeless towers that heard,
From that pure height where only eagles fly,
The gyring eagle's great nocturnal cry.

- ERNEST BRIGGS

******

One of the ideas for widening the scope of *Canon* and making it more attractive for potential advertisers was to feature the music of selected countries and devote an entire edition to them. This was done by approaching the various embassies and gaining their collaboration in sourcing both editorial contributors and lists of potential advertisers.

Change of format from B5 to A4 size, from the Christmas edition 1954 to accommodate more flexible advertising. This author's article on carols was written under the pseudonym 'H R Francis', illustrated with an imitation woodcut.

For seven years from the first edition, *Canon* was published in a B5 size format, but with the Christmas edition 1954 we decided to enlarge the size of the journal to A4, in order to give potential advertisers a greater flexibility for their advertisements. No less than 15 pages of advertising were sold for this edition of 48pp. We also lightened the mood of the magazine by introducing musical crosswords (with prizes) and featuring cartoons such as those by Gerard Hoffnung, for which we obtained serial rights from '*Punch*' magazine in London. We increased the cover price from 1/6d to 2/- and for the first time the magazine actually began to show a profit.

The first of the special editions of the magazine highlighting the music of different countries featured the music of Switzerland.[177] We approached the Swiss Consulate General, who was delighted to provide an eloquent Foreword and who put us in touch with Dr William Tappolet from the University of Geneva; Dr Tappolet commissioned a splendid list of articles on leading Swiss composers: Arthur Honegger (André Jural), Paul Müller (Peter Mieg), Conrad Beck (Peter Bergen), Frank Martin (Hans Ehinger), Jean Binet (William Tappolet), Robert Oboussier (Peter Mieg) and Willy Burkhard (Paul Volkhardt).

Dr Tappolet also provided a valuable list of potential advertisers, and amongst others I was able to obtain the Belvedere Hotel ('Sydney's only Swiss hotel'), some Swiss insurance agencies and the Swiss Music Catalogue of Oxford University Press. The record companies Decca and Coronet also promoted their artists Eugene Istomin and Ernest Ansermet and took advertising space in this edition.

This 62pp edition of *Canon* was very successful both in terms of advertising revenue and an increase in sales, and we promised readers that we would deliver further special issues on a quarterly cycle, beginning with an 'All Nations' edition to celebrate the up-coming Olympic Games in Melbourne in November 1956.[178]

The Olympic Edition of *Canon* proved to be a remarkable publishing achievement for such a small group of dedicated people. Twenty-two countries were represented: Italy (Fernando Germani), Aboriginal Australia (A P Elkin), Norway (Olaf Thorvaldsen), America (Ernest Llewellyn), Switzerland (Hans Ehinger), Canada (Helen Creighton),

Spain (Catherine Mackerras), Germany (K H Ruppel), India (Yehudi Menuhin), Holland (Jan Peeters), Israel (Peter Gradenwitz), Finland (David Cherniavsky), Roumania (David Penfold), Greece (Jean Faquis), Russia (Joseph Waldon), Philippines (Dina Tead Michaelis), Britain (Peter Heyworth), Czechoslovakia (Gordon Clarke), Indonesia (R W Benn), Denmark (William Hansen), Poland (Jan Mieczlow), Latin America (Paula Fiera), India II (A H Fox Strangways), Britain II (Peter Heyworth).

The Olympic edition set a high editorial standard, with eminent contributors such as A P Elkin, Yehudi Menuhin, Fernando Germani, Ernest Llewellyn, A H Fox Strangways and Peter Heyworth giving their imprimatur to the journal.

The intention thereafter to feature the music of different nations every quarter (*Canon* being a monthly publication) was a venture of such comparative magnitude that it could never be sustained with such small resources. Nevertheless, six special issues were produced: Switzerland, 'All Nations' (Olympic edition), Sweden, Denmark, Israel and Germany, in addition to the famous Schoenberg edition and an issue devoted entirely to Musica Viva. *Canon* also assisted in the launching of Sydney University's journal *Musicology* - which became *Musicology* Australia - by 'piggybacking' its very first edition on the back of *Canon's* list of 2,000 subscribers.

With the publication of the Music of Sweden number in 1958, Franz Holford decided that since the magazine appeared to be prospering – largely due to the dramatic increase in paid advertising – he would remove its address from the Champ's residence at 18 Woolwich Road and set up an independent publishing company. He called it Norwood Publishing Co, and its address became 27 Woolwich Road.[179] The venture lasted only one edition. Franz had no expertise in running a company, however small, and nor did I. The Norwood Publishing Co quickly faded into history and the magazine began to decline.

Around this period Wolfgang Wagner had a huge falling out with Franz Holford. Ever since the great success of the Schoenberg edition of *Canon* Wagner had been bombarded by questions from his colleagues, both in Australia and from overseas, seeking information about the famous editor who had collaborated with him to produce such a remarkable tribute to Schoenberg. It was the same scenario as Eastwood in the 1930s, following his first piano recital. Musicians in Europe and America were asking questions. Who was he? Where had he come from? Who taught him?

Wolfgang Wagner could not understand why Franz would not allow him to write a major article – if not a *book* – about him. His constant refusal to cooperate irritated the Czechoslovakian journalist and eventually turned nasty and heated exchanges took place. Eventually Holford wrote Wagner a letter, inviting him to resign from *Canon* (not that it was a paid position!). Amongst other things, he wrote:

> My dear Wolf,
>
> I am always most difficult – I think Eva will agree with me – but I have not even the *slightest* desire to hurt you, and when I do (it seems pretty frequently) I am most sorry.
> But you *don't* understand (admit it) and I cannot do any more than stay within myself. I *don't* want to talk about *myself* and I beg you to realise this. Your advice is very valuable (I have no doubt) but I cannot accept it, because it would take you too long to tell my story – and I don't intend to do that…..(Then he laid down the following challenge to Wagner):
> Don't worry about me. If I hurt you and oppress you then resign from *Canon* and forget all about it. I am so sorry to be such a nuisance to you.
> Immer
>
> Franz

My Dear Wolf –

I am always most difficult — I think Eva will agree with me — but I have not even the slightest desire to HURT you, & when I do (it seems pretty frequently) I am most sorry. But you dont understand (admit it) & I cannot do anymore than stay within myself. I dont want to talk about myself and would beg you to realise this. Your advice is very valuable (I have no doubt) but I cannot accept it because it would take far too long to tell my story — & I dont intend to do that.

Pinwell of Scotch College has been attended to. Some weeks ago I personally sent him the 20/- plus Canon et et.

Dont worry about me if I hurt you & oppress you then resign from Canon & forget all about it.
I am so sorry to be such a nuisance to you.

Immer

Franz

Letter from Franz Holford to Wolfgang Wagner in 1953

Wolfgang Wagner *did* resign from *Canon* and died a few years later, in 1969. His departure was a great loss to *Canon*. He was a fine writer, and so devoted to music that in his youth he wrote articles for sports magazines, gossip columns etc to earn money to buy tickets for himself to pursue his love of opera. Music criticism was an area where *The Canon* had proved its greatest service to Australian music and Wagner's authoritative voice had bought verisimilitude to the little music journal.

A number of music critics had their first starts with the magazine, including Ernest Briggs, Fred Blanks, Martin Long and Roger Covell; professional journalists such as Wolfgang Wagner and Kenneth Hince also benefited from making contributions to the magazine, as did musicologists such as Robert Dalley-Scarlett, Andrew Macredie, Professor Donald Peart and many others.

After sixteen years of monthly publication in 1963, and shortly before its demise, the editor decided the time had come to thank all those who had laboured – mostly in an honorary capacity – to promote the cause of classical music in Australia through the little journal's pages. Through his editorial 'The Overture' he wrote:

> Sixteen years is a long time to be running a journal of *this* nature in *this* country and the moment is appropriate to salute those who have made definite contributions to the life-line. Our printer and our subscribers come first, for without the printer the subscribers would never have seen a copy; and without the copy we would have no advertisers. Then the many contributors who have constantly written and kept us in touch with the vast world of music outside the Commonwealth of Australia, together with those who consistently write of musical events in Australia.

Some of those 'contributors', such as the Champ family, Gordon Clarke, Kenneth Hince, Wolfgang Wagner, Andrew McCreadie, Doris Eddey and others may have felt it rather churlish not to be actually named in this tribute by the editor as an acknowledgment of all their idealistic service across the years. I know this author did.

******

From the Christmas edition of 1964 the magazine began to falter, and its publication became erratic. This edition was designated Volume 17

Number 1, but the next number did not appear until the following year, in April 1965, and should have been either Volume 17 Number 2, or Volume 18 Number 1, but instead was imprinted Volume 17 Number 3. A fourth edition in Volume 17 appeared in July 1965 and a fifth edition in October of that year.

The last year of *Canon* saw the publication of only one edition, in April 1965. In a last attempt at keeping the magazine alive after I had left, Franz Holford engaged with Professor Donald Peart of Sydney University and it was agreed to merge *Canon* with a new publication from the Musicology Department of the University, calling it *Musicology 1*. It was edited by a panel of university academics comprising Dene Barnett, Doreen Bridges and the music critic Martin Long. The 44pp edition contained some fine articles, including an excellent contribution from Martin Long on the Elizabethan lutenist Francis Cutting, which featured a complete list of this 16th Century composer's compositions.

Evelyn Rothwell, English oboist and her husband John Barbirolli helped prepare several major works of Franz Holford for publication and broadcasting, as well as contributing articles to The Canon. (Photo from Canon)

One of the reasons for the erratic numbering of the final editions was that the faithful G W Hall refused to print any more copies after Volume 17 Number 2. The printer who had carried the magazine for over sixteen years apparently amassed a debt which could no longer be sustained, and without the backing of the Champ family it decided to call quits to the venture. The Musicology edition was printed by Wighton and Simpson, a Sydney publisher/printer renowned for its publication of art books. After one issue the magazine was moved again, and the last four editions were printed by that venerated bibliophile and espouser of lost causes Walter Stone, through his Wentworth Press.

The magazine ceased publication in 1966.

******

Les Adieux

Never touch your idols: the gilding will stick to your fingers.

- GUSTAVE FLAUBERT

22

It was 1959 and three years had gone by since those magical few weeks spent in the company of the pianist from the conservatorium. She had gone from my life, leaving a huge void. At times I sat on the veranda of 'Norwood' staring vacantly at the wisteria and crataegus bushes and wondering how different things might have been had the relationship continued.

For the first time in almost ten years I began reviewing my life at 'Norwood' and realised what a mess it had become. I was approaching twenty-nine, and though I now had a permanent job in the city, I had no money saved, virtually no possessions, no real friends and after a full-time job in the city there was an out-of-hours job producing *Canon* which took up all my spare time. I had long since arrived at the conclusion that I would never be a professional musician, nor an artist, nor perhaps even a writer in the sense of a novelist or playwright.

A few days before Christmas 1958, a card arrived in the mail at 'Norwood' and I immediately recognised the handwriting. It was signed simply 'In memory of happy Sunday afternoons, love Anne'. My heart leaped at the possibility that she might still be free, so I picked up the phone immediately and with the card still in my hand rang her home phone number. At the other end the cold and unwelcoming voice of her mother informed me that her daughter was away with friends aboard a businessman's yacht on Sydney Harbour. She could not be sure when she would be back. Disappointed, I left a message that I had rung and waited for days for a return telephone call which never came. I assumed that the card had been nothing more than a polite recognition of times past by a friendly but passing acquaintance and went back to work, trying to put it out of my mind.

******

In the spring of 1959 the English tenor Christopher Lodge invited Franz Holford to spend a weekend at his farm 'Rosewyck', in the little township of Milton, inland from Ulladulla on the south coast of New South Wales. He also invited Dr Scougall, with whom he had established a friendship through the Champ soirées and myself. We would be travelling there in the famous surgeon's car.

Dr Scougall duly arrived to pick us up at 'Norwood' early on a Saturday morning in his late model black Bentley and the first thing I saw on entering it was a glamorous young blonde sitting in the driver's passenger seat. Dr Scougall introduced her as one of his nurses, working at St Vincent's Hospital. There was no explanation for her presence, as Franz and I took our seats in the rear of the vehicle, but it quickly became obvious that she had a very special relationship with the Macquarie Street specialist.

During the journey 'Dr Holford' regaled his captive audience with extracts from poetry, his music and the usual fanciful stories of his past – growing up in a royal family in Heidelberg, studying at Oxford University, and the special relationship he enjoyed with the great Alfred Cortot and Felix Weingartner. I had heard it all before, and quietly dozed with my head ensconced in the car's luxurious upholstery; in fact I soon fell into a deep sleep, and only awoke as we pulled in to the country town of Orange for lunch.

At a restaurant in the main street a middle-age German male waiter of swarthy complexion who walked with an exaggerated limp welcomed us and ushered us into our seats. Dr Scougall paused before sitting down and studied the man thoughtfully. As the waiter hovered expectantly to take our order, Scougall said in a lazy, almost disinterested voice: 'Show me your leg…'

'Vot? …. Mein leg?' said the astonished waiter.

'Yes man, pull your trousers up and show me your leg…sit in the chair there…!'

Under Dr Scougall's imperious gaze, the waiter slowly sank into one of the café's bentwood chairs and meekly rolled up the trouser on his left leg.

'Put it out in front of you,' Scougall commanded. 'Thaaat's right. Now this may hurt a bit…'

Whereupon the doctor took hold of the leg by the calf and the ankle, pulled it towards himself, twisting violently as he did so. The waiter let forth a piercing scream, causing several of the patrons in the restaurant to leap to their feet in horror.

Scougall ignored the man's scream and said: 'Now….stand up…..there… how does that feel?'

The man stopped screaming and stood to his feet shakily. He stared at the Australian doctor, his eyes wide, face white with shock. Then he took a step forward on his left leg, his eyes never leaving Scougall's face.

'It feel…..it feel….a…*mazing*! he cried. He started hopping around on the pavement, yelling at the top of his voice. Then he rushed at the doctor, put his arms around him and began jumping up and down. 'Amazing! Amazing! You a vonderful man…!' He looked around at all the patrons, who began smiling and spontaneously started to applaud.

'This man….this man….he do miracle! My leg been bad for years….now it…it amazing!'

Stuart Scougall smoothed down his safari jacket unsmilingly, sat down and addressed the man in a slightly exasperated tone:

'Yees…well you should have seen an orthopaedic surgeon earlier shouldn't you… now stop that please and take our order, will you?'

But the man was ecstatic. He flung his arms around the doctor's neck and kissed him, saying: 'Everything on the house for you and your friends, herr Doktor!'

The blonde girl, whose name I still did not know, smiled knowingly and leaning across the table, kissed Scougall lightly on the lips.

'You're such a show-off Stu…' she murmured.

Christopher Lodge came out of the house to greet us as Dr Scougall turned the car into the picturesque driveway of Lodge's sheep farm 'Rosewyck' at Milton. His wife stood behind him in the doorway. He briefly introduced her, then ushered us all into his loungeroom, where stood a baby grand piano in one of the bay windows. Franz immediately sat down on the piano stool and played some flashy chords and scales, affirming the real reason for us all being in the countryside….for him to rehearse several of his newly composed songs with Christopher Lodge.

Leaving the rapt blonde in the curve of the grand, with Dr Scougall and Christopher Lodge looking on admiringly, Mrs Lodge directed me to one of the bedrooms with the overnight luggage we had brought. She said there were three bedrooms, pointing out her husband's, then indicated the one that Dr Scougall would sleep in whereupon she turned to me with a quizzical look:

'Is the….young lady staying…?'

I thought: unless she is prepared to walk back to Sydney, the answer must be in the affirmative.

'I don't know. Well yes, I guess…'

With obvious embarrassment, she went on: 'Well, I suppose she will be sleeping in there too.'

She pointed out the third bedroom: 'Dr Holford will sleep in here…..and you too?'

'No, no,' I shot back. 'It's only one night. Can I use the lounge?'

'Of course dear…I'll get out some bedding for you.' She smiled weakly. A small, birdlike creature – the ying to the yang of her husband, who mixed being a wealthy and powerful farm owner with his busy life as a tenor.

After settling in, Christopher Lodge began going through the music, with Franz at the keyboard. Dr Scougall decided to take his young nurse out on a tour of the property, and asked me to join them. Since it was quite cold outside, I decided to stay by the lounge room fire, keeping it stoked with the neatly cut blue gum logs stored on the hearth in a beautiful copper storage bin. After a simple dinner, which Mrs Lodge prepared and then cleared everything away to the kitchen without anyone else offering to help her, there was a brief recital by Chris Lodge and everyone retired early to their respective bedrooms. I noticed that throughout the animated discussion over dinner and afterwards, Christopher Lodge's wife barely uttered a word and her husband scarcely even looked at her; it was as if she was some ghostly, silent maidservant, waiting upon us all.

At around 2am I awoke, feeling extremely cold and found that the fire had died down to a few glimmering coals. Using a pair of iron tongs, I stirred the fire and added some more kindling until it was blazing again. Having dozed most of the afternoon, I was not feeling very tired, so I sat in one of the armchairs near the hearth, staring vacantly into the fire. After some time the door to the Lodge's bedroom opened softly and Mrs Lodge emerged in her dressing gown. Without a word she sat down in a chair alongside me and also gazed into the fire.

There was total silence throughout the house, until we both became aware of moans and grunts coming from Stuart Scougall's bedroom. When the girl's cries rose to a crescendo, Mrs Lodge glanced at me briefly, then averted her eyes again to the fire.

'Have you got a girlfriend, love?' she asked in a low voice.

'Not really,' I replied. 'I used to…'

'Love doesn't last very long with some I'm afraid,' she continued, almost to herself. 'And marriage can be very cruel…'

Back in Sydney several months later I learned that Mrs Lodge died shortly after our visit, and Christopher Lodge immediately married the young daughter of a wealthy landowner in the district. Stuart Scougall was divorced in the late 1960s.

******

In 1959 it was suggested by Hugh Hunt that I compile a yearbook on the Australian live theatre. The success of Ray Lawler's play *The Summer of the Seventeenth Doll* four years earlier had sparked a major revival of live theatre in Australia, and there was an opportunity to coincide the launch of such a volume with the opening of Lawler's second play *The Piccadilly Bushman*, which was to be premiered at Melbourne's Comedy Theatre in September 1959.

When I told Franz what I was planning, he was at first enthusiastic and suggested that I incorporate the yearbook as a companion to *The Canon* in the Christmas edition of 1959. When I demurred, saying I would rather handle this project entirely separately and on my own, he flew into a violent rage, the like of which I had not witnessed before – accusing me of ingratitude and of betraying the ideology of *Canon* which he had striven for years to achieve. Then, to my utter astonishment he stepped forward and slapped me hard across the face.

I stared incredulously at him for a few moments. I had no idea that he could ever have taken such an action. In all the years I had known him, he had never really lost his temper, or been entirely out of control. Certainly not to this extent – and even though my cheek stung from the blow, I found myself almost admiring him because of it. He was revealing a very vulnerable side to his nature. He was also trembling with rage, and fear showed in his eyes as he tried to ascertain what my next action might be. After what seemed an eternity, I turned on my heel and without a word went to my room.

I gathered up my cello, stuffed some music in its back pocket and picked up a green backed copy of Bach's organ chorales which Fernando Germani had once given me as a present, took one last look around my room - at the piano, books, music, records and art paraphernalia which had been my entire life for the past ten years and walked out the door, onto the veranda, down the red gravel path and out the front gate of 'Norwood'. Without looking back, I turned to the right and headed in the direction of the only other home I had known, in Woolwich.

******

It was ten o'clock on a balmy summer evening as I walked slowly down Woolwich Road. I stopped at Kelly's Bush, where I used to play cricket in my youth, and there amongst the salt bush scrub stood the scout hall, where my brother used to practice his clarinet – out of sight and sound of any neighbours. It was of course deserted at this hour of night and locked, so I lay my cello down on the thick carpet of grass surrounding it. I took off my shoes and taking the cello out of its fur-lined case I slid myself in it up to the waist, and using my coat as a pillow, lay down and went to sleep.

It was 7am when I awoke to the sound of magpies singing loudly in the gum trees of Kelly's Bush. My limbs were stiff and my back hurt from lying on the hard ground, but as I got to my feet and walked around, the blood began circulating freely and the soreness disappeared. I ate a handful of pink berries from a nearby lilli pilli tree to refresh my mouth, then I re-packed my cello, sat on the steps of the scout hall and pondered the events of the night before.

I knew that I would never return to 'Norwood'…I knew that my life there was finished. Strangely, I began to experience a profound sense of relief. Relief from the falseness of that other state of existence – the lies and the uncertainty…. the pretension of it all. It was as if I had just stepped off a roller coaster at Luna Park, and the ground suddenly felt steady beneath my feet again. What would I do next? Where would I find a place to live? I still had my job in the city, but nowhere to stay. Luckily the imbroglio with Franz had happened on a Saturday night, and it was now Sunday morning and I had no need to go to the office in the city.

I remembered that my brother had given me his telephone number about six months ago, when I met him on the steps of the Sydney Town Hall after a concert. I found it in my wallet, and began walking down to the Pier Hotel, which had a public telephone nearby and I rang him. My brother could always read me like a book. He knew that I was in trouble.

'What's up? He said immediately.

'I've left Norwood,' I replied.

'Where are you?'

'The scout hall.'

'What the bloody hell are you doing at the scout hall?' he exploded. 'Never mind. I'll come and get you.'

Within the hour my brother's battered Toyota Crown drew up outside the scout hall. I put my cello on the back seat and sat beside him in the passenger seat. He knew immediately that I didn't want to engage in small talk.

'Where do you want to go?' he asked quietly.

'I don't care. I thought you might have some ideas?'

He looked at me and slowly shook his head from side to side. 'Frankie…. Frankie….Frankie…'

'You mean "Bruno" don't you?' We looked at each other for a brief moment, then burst out laughing. We laughed and we laughed, till my face was wet with tears.

'You idiot,' he said. 'You bloody idiot!' Putting the car into gear, we drove off. As we passed 'No 27' Woolwich Road, neither of us looked to the left. My brother was silent, and still asked me no questions.

******

His car pulled into a private car space outside the pavilion to the North Sydney Cricket Ground. My brother turned off the ignition, and as he opened the door to hop out of the car he turned his head back: 'Come on,' he said. 'I've got something interesting to show you…'

Taking a key from his pocket, he opened an outer door to the pavilion, over which a sign read: 'To Kiosk' and beckoned me inside. There was a large open public space, with a long bar in the middle, with refrigerators full of soft drinks and ice creams and racks of chocolates and sporting memorabilia. He went behind the bar and beckoned me again and opened another door, revealing a spacious room which was obviously a living space, with a double bed, wardrobes, a table with four chairs and a refrigerator; in one corner stood an upright piano, beside which was a music stand and a wire rack containing several clarinets.

'Welcome to my cave,' he said drily.

We sat at the table drinking a half spent bottle of red and he related the story of his own fortunes. 'Or misfortunes I suppose…' he added ruefully.

After many years of practice, and with the aid of an excellent teacher at the Sydney Conservatorium, following my departure to live at 'Norwood', my brother pursued a successful career as a clarinettist. Though a late starter, he achieved the distinction of being appointed clarinettist with the Queensland Symphony Orchestra – a position he held for some time.

As was the case in those days the State symphony orchestras would often lend and borrow principal players as the need arose to boost a particular program. Thus, when my brother received a call to join the Sydney Symphony Orchestra for a casual assignment he was delighted to accept, since it meant he could be reunited with his Sydney family again, however briefly. He was totally unprepared for what followed.

The program for the SSO concert contained some of the most difficult orchestral music in the repertoire, and to compound the problem for my brother he was given only one rehearsal before the performance. Inevitably he made some small mistakes, whereupon the principal clarinettist would tut-tut, snort loudly and shift in his chair, instead of attempting to help my brother through the difficult passages, as is the responsibility of orchestral principals.

By the time of the evening concert my brother was a bundle of nerves, and when he made a small slip during *Till Eulenspiegel's Merry Pranks* the principal gave vent to an audible expression of disgust and shook his head vigorously. During the intermission in the Green Room behind stage, my brother packed up his instrument and prepared to leave. The principal clarinettist stood in the doorway barring his exit and said: 'Where are you going? We're on again in the second half...' My brother looked at him with contempt, and without uttering a word pushed him roughly aside and walked out.

With his mind in turmoil, he drove to Palm Beach, the furthermost of Sydney's northern beaches and slept that night in his car, overlooking the calm and beautiful Pittwater peninsular. When dawn came he jogged on the beach and took a cleansing dip in the ocean. He felt an immediate sense of peace, and as he returned to his car he saw a kiosk which sold refreshments to surfers, bearing a sign reading: 'For Sale', and giving a telephone number. Using all his savings he ultimately bought the kiosk, and within a few months he had revitalised it into a profitable little business. Encouraged by his success, he began obtaining the catering rights for various outdoor sporting venues, including Prince Alfred Park in Sydney, Belmore Oval and most recently North Sydney Cricket Ground. With all his ventures burgeoning, he was rapidly becoming a very wealthy man.

'So you see old son, when one door closes……now what's *your* story?'

The English composer Martin Mather was looking for accommodation, so he threw in his lot with my brother and me and we rented a three-bedroom house in the south eastern Sydney suburb of Pagewood. It was large and rambling and gave each of us plenty of space – for Martin's piano, for my brother's clarinet practice and for my publishing interests. Martin had a full time job at the Mitchell Library and my brother had his flourishing catering businesses, and I had a good job editing my fishing magazine.

However, recently I had become obsessed with the idea of publishing the yearbook on theatre which Hugh Hunt had suggested, and I was sure I could not handle the two jobs at once. My brother as usual had the immediate solution: 'Go on your own,' he said. 'Start a publishing business, I'll help you pay your part of the rent.'

Resigning from *Angler's Digest* was a totally different experience to leaving 'Norwood'. The director of this small publishing business Rodger Hungerford was unhappy at my leaving and said he had plans for extending the company which included offering me a partnership in it if I stayed, but when he could see I was resolved to leave he patted me on the shoulder and said: 'Well, good luck young fella…it's been a joy having you around.' I left with tears in my eyes.

I rented two good sized rooms in the city, in the Crystal Palace Arcade in George Street opposite the Regent Theatre and above a shop making and selling ballet shoes, run by an incredibly industrious woman Joan Barrie and her large be-whiskered husband. A handsome man of enormous girth, Alec Barrie had been an RAAF pilot during WWII, with no particular expertise in anything *after* the war, except for throwing parties and consuming huge quantities of whisky during business hours.

He informed me that he was in charge of 'public relations' for Barrie's Ballet Shoes and gave me the two rooms above the shop for a peppercorn rental, in exchange for me agreeing to handle the shop's advertising, which was a pleasant and not too time-absorbing task. For her part, Joan Barrie was too busy designing and making her pointe shoes (which were enormously popular amongst ballerinas and their students) and running the shop, to be concerned with anything but making the considerable sums of money necessary to enable Alec to be kept in the style to which he had grown accustomed.

******

It took six months to publish *Australian Theatre Year 1959-60*. With the support of Hugh Hunt, the Elizabethan Theatre and J C Williamson, I was able to attract leading writers, theatricals and critics in the Australian live theatre as contributors, including John McCallum, Hugh Hunt, Robert Quentin, Hayes Gordon, Dorothy Helmrich and the critics Lindsay Browne, Max Harris and Roger Covell, with a foreword by Sybil Thorndike. My brother helped me fund the publishing of the book and we were lucky to have Martin Mather with his Mitchell Library experience as proof-reader.

Significantly in the 160pp edition there were 30pp of advertising, which produced a handsome revenue, in addition to its cover price. It was also possible to print a feasible number (10,000), to enable it to be distributed through a leading distribution company, Gordon & Gotch, something which had not been possible to achieve with *Canon*. The edition sold out and was so successful financially that it encouraged me to found a monthly magazine *Theatregoer*, to commence publication in 1960, with a circulation of 5,000, using the same distributor, Gordon & Gotch.

******

In early August 1960 an order for six copies of the Yearbook came from the Education Department in Sydney. Normally I would have passed the request on to the distributor Gordon and Gotch, but for some reason I decided to deliver the copies personally. The head office was in Bridge Street, so I caught a bus from Pagewood to Wynyard and walked up Bridge Street towards the imposing sandstone building. As I paused at the imperious entrance I noticed a figure approaching from further up the street towards the Conservatorium. For a brief moment I fancied that it was the pianist from our one-time trio, but dismissed the thought and entered the building.

As I was placing the parcel of books on the table of the concierge, I heard a soft voice behind me:

'Hello, what are *you* doing here?'

It was her, wearing a simple white blouse and a brown herringbone skirt and carrying a brown leather briefcase. I was totally at a loss for words for her unexpected presence was overwhelming. I yearned to just take her in my arms and smother her in kisses, from the sheer joy of seeing her again.

'Anne……my God! I was just….just delivering a parcel,' I stammered, then recovering somewhat, asked: 'What are *you* doing here?'

'Oh I come here to collect my pay…' There followed an awkward silence. I'm a teacher…remember?

'I sent you a card…' she added hesitantly.

'I got it, and I rang, five minutes after receiving it…..I spoke to your mother…'

'You *did*?'

'She promised to…hang on….she didn't *tell* you I rang?' She shook her head slowly.

'My mother….hmmm…' then she smiled a broad, rueful smile. '*Now* I understand.' 'That….er, that just might have been a mistake…'

'She never told you?'

'She never told me.'

'God, I should have realised…I wanted to…I wanted you to…' I looked at her in desperation. 'Look…are you free? I mean, free *now*… for a coffee or something…?'

'As soon as I collect my cheque, yes I'm free…and I'm just dying for a coffee.'

We walked down to Circular Quay, and sat on the same bench as when first we met. As previously, we spoke non-stop, and I was delighted to learn that apart from one brief liaison, she had never married; it was a liaison with a certain opera singer that had gone nowhere - an older man, she said - at which we both laughed, remembering our previous conversations. As she sat alongside me on that park bench, in all her warmth and beauty and wonderful intellect, I realised with a shock that I had never even kissed her, but I also knew that I would never walk away from her again, until I had asked her the one all-important question. Her answer was yes.

We were married in St Mary's Cathedral on 27th August 1960 and in 2025 celebrated 65 years of happy marriage. Our union produced four remarkable offspring: Dr Michael Kieran Harvey, Dr Dominic Gerard Harvey, Dr Bernadette Anne Harvey and Rowan Harvey-Martin, all of whom continue to make their own special mark on the history of music in Australia.

Woodcut by Eva Sandor, for Canon.

(Left) Anne Theresa Crowe, Music Mistress North Sydney Girls High School, 1956.

(Right) Anne Harvey, marriage at St Mary's Cathedral Sydney 1960

Postlude

*Wretched the man whose fame
makes his misfortunes famous.*

- LUCIUS ACCIUS

23

Following my decision to leave 'Norwood' in the autumn of 1959 and re-enter the world I had left behind almost ten years before, I lost track of Franz Holford, *The Canon*, the Champ family and all the chimera of a life few would believe could happen to anyone. To my great happiness - after leaving the house where I had lived and worked for almost ten years - from the moment of our marriage, I scarcely spared a thought for anything but the future of my own family.

Many years passed before a chance meeting with my old friend Donald Newton revived our mutual interest in Franz Holford and *The Canon*. Don's wife Marjorie had achieved a doctorate, which included a special interest in family history. It was she who painstakingly put together - with the aid of official certificates - the true facts of Franz's life and ancestry. Later still I was able to determine the denouement of his final years and death with the aid of an excellent memoir: 'Franz Holford as I knew him', given me by an ex-colleague at Macquarie University, the author Olive Lawson.

A few years after I left 'Norwood' there was a breakdown in relationships between Franz Holford and his principal benefactor the Champ Family, following a decision by the d'Apice Family to evict Franz from 'Norwood', where he had lived as a protected tenant for over twenty years. The d'Apices eventually sold the house and Franz was forced to ask Reg and Gwen Champ if he could move in with them. By this time

Franz, the *Canon* and the whole paraphernalia of music making in the Champ residence had become such an alarming drain on the family's financial resources that they decided to end their relationship with him. Their solution was to sell 'Threlkeld' and buy a house in Mosman, cutting all ties with Franz Holford.

Olive Lawson could not recollect exactly when she first heard of Franz, but it was shortly after I left 'Norwood' - probably in 1959 - for in that year she met the New Zealand music historian John Mansfield Thomson, who was staying in Sydney while researching the life of Australia's then Grand Old Man of music, Alfred Francis Hill then nearly 90.

For some time, John Thomson stayed at the Hill's home at 37a Raglan Street, Mosman, to facilitate daily discussions with Alfred. Alfred Hill's grandson Tony Pollett – whom Olive Lawson later married - took her to meet his grandfather and thus she also met the New Zealand composer John Thomson.[180] It was the latter who introduced them to 'Dr' Franz Holford.

The previous year, Thomson had contributed an article for an issue of *Canon*[181], then being published by Franz from the premises of J Albert & Son in King Street, Sydney.[182] The patriarch of the Albert family, Alexis, had been a friend of Alfred and Mirrie Hill for decades; it was no doubt through them that John Thomson, who was also a music editor and writer, was put in touch with the occupier of Albert's top floor office, Dr Franz Holford.[183]

At this time Don Newton, Franz's pupil from 1944-1953, was working as National Sales Manager for Albert's, and he encouraged Ted Albert to publish The Albert Edition, consisting of solely Australian works in all genres.[184] Newton began recruiting serious Australian composers for Albert's, signing Nigel Butterley, Ian Cugley and Margaret Sutherland - among others - the genesis of The Albert Edition. Newton balanced the catalogue with an education list, publishing among other top-selling items Victor McMahon's recorder tutor and a very successful music appreciation course, *Listening Alive*, by Roger Heading.

To help with the selection and editing of works for The Albert Edition, and wanting to do a good turn for the financially-strapped Holford, Newton introduced him to Ted Albert, an introduction which resulted in

Albert's appointing Franz as Editor of The Albert Edition, over the head of Don Newton who had created it!

Newton soon became increasingly concerned, as Holford began publishing a growing number of his own compositions which Newton knew would undermine the financial viability of The Albert Edition. Franz published from 1967-1972 at least eighteen small-scale compositions under the pseudonym Gaetano Tesoriero, which he sent out free to all NSW secondary school music teachers in the hope of capturing the music education market.

According to one high school music teacher on the receiving end of this flood of 'educational material' from Albert's, it all ended up in her wastepaper basket. In 1968 the situation escalated into an Agreement, drawn up between Franz Holford and Albert's, to publish a huge list of Franz's own compositions: 44 songs, a choral work 'The Englishman', cello and piano pieces, 10 oboe pieces, four works for violin and piano, two trios, five negro spirituals, 18 piano pieces and 30 various arrangements of folk songs.[185] Most of these works had not even been written.

As his dream for Australian music publishing gradually collapsed, Don Newton could only look on with anguish and despair, for Franz managed to forge such a close personal relationship with Ted Albert, that he could be placed under no restraint when making his ill-chosen editorial decisions. When Newton expressed his mild concern at the direction in which the Australian Catalogue was going, his former mentor replied coldly: 'Well then, you had better leave.'

This was a dreadful reward for a former loyal student who had influenced Ted Albert into taking Franz Holford into the company in the first place as an editor when the composer had fallen on hard times.

In 1973, Albert's became associated with the American company Music Sales, and the disillusioned Don Newton took the opportunity to move on to Rose Music (Yamaha) the following year. As the years passed he watched with chagrin and heartache as his brain child The Albert Edition disintegrated. Adding to his frustration was seeing all his groundbreaking and meritorious work in establishing the catalogue being attributed to his former teacher and mentor, Dr Franz Holford.

The Albert Edition eventually accumulated a large debt, and was finally closed down. When his position inevitably became untenable, Franz left Albert's, but not before borrowing from Ted Albert a sum of money, upon the assurance that it would be repaid from the forthcoming sale of a house he supposedly owned in England. It was a ruse he had employed previously in attempting to borrow money from wealthy friends and acquaintances, including Sir Bernard Heinze. No such house existed of course, and the loan – along with the debt incurred by The Albert Edition – was ultimately written off.

Both Edwin (Ted) Carr and John Thomson intimated to Olive Lawson in conversations they had over many years that they had found Franz suspect. When living in Britain, Ted Carr checked the alumni records at the Oxford Colleges and found no record of anyone called Franz Holford had ever been an undergraduate there.[186]

Shipping records confirmed the Franz Holford had never left Australia.

Olive Lawson (Far right), granddaughter of Henry Lawson, with the author (Left) and staff at Macquarie University in the 1980s. (Photograph by courtesy Macquarie University)

Postlude

In the late 1980s, when Ted Carr was staying with Lawson in Sydney, he told her quite firmly that in his opinion Franz Holford was a charlatan.[187]

******

Olive Lawson had two significant meetings with Franz Holford a few years after she returned from a time in London to live again in Sydney. At the beginning of 1974 she rented a flat in Cremorne and renewed her friendship with Mirrie Hill, who was then sharing her home in Mosman with her brother, Eric Solomon. Olive was 40, widowed and living tenuously on an income derived from intermittent, casual, and freelance work as either music teacher or writer/editor. Concerned for the unsatisfactory nature of her friend's income, but unbeknown to her, Mirrie broached the matter to Franz, and described Olive Lawson as someone she saw having influence amongst the music fraternity of Sydney. Mirrie knew that music was Olive's first love, and she thought that Franz might be the very person to help her find a suitable job. Later, Mirrie excitedly telephoned her friend to say that Franz had said he would be able to give her a position at Albert's, and within a day or two Franz himself rang, inviting Lawson to lunch with him in the city.

Olive Lawson had never met Franz Holford until that meeting for lunch at the Carlton Hotel just off Martin Place. She described the meeting thus:

'Waiting for me at the entrance, he might have just stepped out of a Saville Row tailor; faultlessly groomed, although large and rather stout and heavily bespectacled.

'He seemed to know the doorman and the dining room staff at the very expensive Carlton, where it appeared that he had an ongoing account. He behaved in a completely gentlemanly manner, but rather too clearly, to my judgment, was trying to impress me by nonchalantly waving aside the menials who were at his disposal.

'He asked me nothing about my experience, nor did he mention anything about the position I believed to be awaiting me at Albert's. Throughout the meal he talked entirely of himself, telling me the main events of his life. It was as though he needed to establish his credentials with me.

'What I remember of his monologue was that he said he had been born in Heidelberg, Germany. There was no mention of his mother, but his father had been a doctor, closely associated with the Kaiser. He was also Felix Weingartner's nephew.' (Here he digressed in order to ascertain that Lawson had heard of the conductor.)

'As a young boy he had been either adopted or fostered by Weingartner, who oversaw his musical education and later sent him to study in Oxford. He had studied piano in Paris with Cortot.'

At their first meeting, according to Olive Lawson, Franz did not give any evidence at all of being interested in her career, nor in what skills she could bring to Alberts. It was her belief however that he occupied a position with the music firm which gave him authority to find and appoint anyone he needed for their publishing side. This is also the impression he had given Mirrie Hill.

After lunch at the Carlton, Franz asked Lawson to come to see him again, at his office, and they made an appointment for a few days later. At their second 'interview' she met him as planned, in an upstairs room at Alberts.

'It was more or less filled with a grand piano.' Lawson recalled, 'There was a chair by the window, on which I sat to wait. There seemed no sign of any general office furniture, so I assumed that whatever job was available must be in some other part of the business premises.

'I ventured a question or two about the available position,' she continued, 'With a flick of the hand that I later noticed was characteristic, he brushed off my enquiry with some remark about there being "no need to go into that - they would have lunch first".'

Franz had reserved a table at the French restaurant one or two doors further up King Street. Warren Thompson, then on the staff at the Conservatorium, was waiting for them. Franz had invited him to meet her. Why? she wondered.

'I could not help but conclude that Franz thought I should meet his acquaintances in Sydney's musical hierarchy.'

Olive Lawson said that all she could contribute to the conversation were a few remarks about her experience as a student in the 1960s at the Sydney Conservatorium. She remembered little of the conversation between Warren Thompson and Franz, except that it amounted to disjointed remarks being passed across the table, nothing that Lawson ought or ought not to have heard. What Lawson did not know was that at this time Franz Holford was negotiating with Thompson to secure the famous Urtext Catalogue for Albert's, and he wished to show off his credentials.[188]

There seemed to Olive Lawson that there was no point to this meeting except for Franz to either show Lawson off, or to show Warren Thompson off. Again there was no mention of any position for which she was being assessed.

'It did not occur to me then (not until thinking over these events for this memoir) that he might have wanted Warren Thompson's opinion of me. At that time I was very gullible and trusting, and was never suspicious of others' motives, especially of the person such as Dr Franz Holford, who was so highly regarded by Mirrie.'

Little did Lawson know that she had good reason to be suspicious of Warren Thompson's motives. She was certainly unaware that Thompson had been removed from a boy's college in Melbourne and was gaining a reputation amongst the musical fraternity of Sydney for being a paedophile.

After the meal Warren Thompson had to rush back to the Conservatorium, so Franz and Olive returned to his upstairs office and again she ventured to ask about the position. He dismissed the enquiry and said he had to take her downstairs to meet someone to whom they needed to talk. Olive assumed this would be the person responsible for staff. In an office that finally looked like an office, she was introduced to a Mr Peachey. They sat in a semi-circle. Mr Peachey said absolutely nothing and appeared to have no interest whatever in the fact of Lawson being brought to meet him. She gave Mr Peachey a summary of her work experience, and told him that she would be very happy to accept a position with Alberts, but that she needed to know what was required. She asked if he had a job description, and what the salary would be. Mr Peachey looked very ill at ease.

Lawson received no reply from either of them.

Franz Holford then leaned across, placed his hand upon her knee, and said that 'because of the very great affection between us' there was no need for her to worry about those details.

'Thus ended the interview,' Lawson said. 'When we parted outside in King Street, I asked him directly what was to be the arrangement. He said he would let me know.'

He never did so. It did not cross Olive Lawson's mind that there was in fact *no* job; nor that Franz was his own master and that neither his work nor his entourage had anything whatsoever to do with Mr Peachey or with Albert's employees. Lawson concluded that the whole meeting had been a charade.

Having heard of her through Mirrie Hill, Franz saw her as potential; qualified in music, young and presentable, an all-purpose companion and general assistant. Unpaid. Perhaps he was trying to fill the vacancy *this* author had left.

'These lunches were evidently preliminaries to some kind of a "relationship"', Olive Lawson assumed.

'I suppose that in Holford's calculations I fitted the bill because of the Hill's long association with Alberts, and that my friendship with Mirrie gave me some special eligibility.'

Olive Lawson could not telephone Mirrie Hill until she knew the outcome of her 'interviews'. However, Mirrie was *expecting* the courtesy of a call. She finally phoned Lawson about a fortnight after she had first mentioned that Franz had a job for her. When she asked why Olive had not contacted her, Lawson had to say that Franz had not offered her any position. Lawson did not recount any of the details, as she did not think Hill would believe her. The regrettable affair was the cause of a marked coldness thereafter in Mirrie Hill's attitude to Lawson and for a long time there remained a feeling that the unquestioning friendship the two women had enjoyed over twenty years had been damaged.

Mirrie Hill had regarded Olive Lawson as one of Alfred's many grandchildren, to whom she had given her friendship; she was then

Postlude

nearly 90 and Lawson simply did not have the courage (or the cruelty) to destroy her belief in Franz. His persona had great authority with people of Mirrie's generation in Sydney's music world, particularly because of the prevailing reverence for German Romanticism and the 'great German conductors', with whom she had been told many Sydney musicians believed Franz Holford had direct connections.

******

Some time after Eric Solomon's death, when Mirrie was living alone, Franz moved into her home. The details are similar to those in the other instances of his taking over the domestic life of an elderly, wealthy woman living alone; securing her total trust and then exploiting her financially.

A situation developed based on Mirrie's sympathetic hospitality to Franz, who had had to leave 'Norwood' when the property was sold by the owner in the 1960s. He had been making use of Mrs Beatrice Smith, widow of a wealthy businessman. (Mrs Smith was 'Auntie Bea' to the three daughters of the Nisbet family, then friends of Olive Lawson).

Over a period of several months Franz ingratiated himself with Mirrie Hill, first asking whether he might stay for a night or two, and then suggesting that he might stay permanently and attend to the shopping and housework, at a time when it was becoming clear that Mirrie would soon need help of this kind. She gradually entrusted him with general household matters. It seems that he had no income, so he had worked out a way of living without it. According to Lawson he was paid handsomely. Mirrie Hill either gave him her cheque book, or perhaps signed blank cheques, for the payment of her bills, the purchase of food and other household necessities.[189]

He took over, attending gradually to the provision of meals, and generally looking after her in a way she could no longer do for herself. Because of this - a tremendous help to a frail old woman - Alfred's family and her friends put up with a situation they found very suspect. In a note obviously intended to allay the family's fears, Mirrie wrote: 'I wish to remain in my home. This means being looked after as to food and a certain amount of medical care. My friend, Franz Holford supplies this need…'[190]

During these few years, Franz made several trips to Melbourne and to Brisbane, to see other composers, such as Margaret Sutherland, ostensibly to assist them in musical matters; among these women was Betty Beath.[191]

After Franz moved into Mirrie's house, Olive Lawson saw much less of her friend.

Mirrie Hill, Australian composer was one of three Solomon children, born in Randwick, 1889. She studied at the Sydney Conservatorium under Henri Verbrugghen and with the New Zealand composer Alfred Hill, whom she later married. Hill conducted her Rhapsody for Piano and Orchestra at the Sydney Town Hall in 1914 when Mirrie was 24. (Unknown photographer)

Postlude

'Holford seemed to be jealous of her friends,' Lawson recalled. 'Typically he would answer the phone and say Mirrie was not available, or was resting.

'However, there were a few occasions when she invited me over to have lunch with her, usually when Franz was out for the day.' Olive Lawson recalled two such occasions, when he returned and joined them in her sitting room.

'He used the opportunity to try to impress by being boastful,' she remembered.

One of these conversations was about Sir Eugene Goossens. Contrary to what is generally believed, it was not his 'good friend Gene' but Franz himself (he claimed) whose recommendation – or perhaps mere agreement - was that Bennelong Point would be the best site for the Sydney Opera House. (This world-shaking decision was apparently made in conversation with Gene, while they were being driven about, seated together in the back seat of an ABC car).

The second of the two remembered conversations Lawson found alarming, even after twenty-five years.

'Franz was in an open, friendly mood,' Lawson said. 'Sitting back in one of Mirrie's comfortable armchairs, sipping a drink, and reminiscing. His remarks were addressed to me, as though Mirrie were not there.

'He told me how he used to go up to the Blue Mountains for weekends with Gene and "all the boys". Apparently someone had a place up there,' Lawson added.[192]

'We had "some nice little boys"', Holford confessed.

Olive Lawson said it was not possible to tell whether he was trying to shock her, or was just demonstrating his 'open-mindedness'. Mirrie either did not care to listen, or just let him ramble on into his whisky. She was very Victorian in her attitude, Lawson said, but told her friend on one occasion that 'nothing shocked her'.

Make of it what one will, Olive Lawson concluded, this incident was either a fantasy under slight intoxication or an admission of paedophilia, if not as a participant, then as a collaborator.

In the early 1980s, Mirrie rang Lawson to ask her to visit. After some general conversation the ageing composer asked Lawson whether she could tell her what had happened to her money. When Lawson replied that she had no idea, Mirrie Hill's only comment was that 'Franz would not take it'. Such a thing was quite outside Hill's knowledge of Holford. Her Bank Manager had drawn her attention to the state of her account. For reasons probably connected with her great age and perhaps some memory loss, she evidently had not been checking her bank statements, or possibly had not seen them, because Franz collected her mail on his way down to the house. She did not often climb the fifty steps to the street and the letter-box any more.

As a shrewd business-minded woman, Mirrie Hill had always managed her affairs with the greatest economy. It was inconceivable that she would have allowed her money to fritter away. Lawson gathered that over a fairly short period a very large sum had disappeared, presumably in a series of cash withdrawals Hill did not know about.

'He was so cunning that he might also have gained access to her investments,' Lawson said.

Sometimes deceitful people can sense another's scepticism. Lawson's worst suspicion - though not till much later - was that Franz's resentment of her failure to be swept off her feet by him had caused him to suggest to Mirrie that *she* might have in some unspecified way gained access to her money. Instead, it was obvious to everyone that he had been using it for his own purposes for years, as her executor told the family after her death.

Olive Lawson's final clash with Franz Holford occurred at a luncheon he organised for Mirrie, her family and friends. It was at about Christmas time, and must have been her 95th birthday, in December 1984. Franz did all the preparations, and the party was a great success. After the meal everyone sat around with coffee and chocolate mints, and Franz sat down at Mirrie's piano to entertain the guests. He had moved his own (or Albert's) grand into Mirrie's sitting room, but it stood out of the way, behind hers.

Postlude

According to Lawson, his playing was a demonstration of his great facility and musicality - a medley of classical and operatic pieces all run together with great panache. Mirrie and Olive were seated closest to him, near the end of the keyboard. During the performance, Lawson asked Mirrie, in a low voice, if she might take her coffee cup. Franz stopped playing and sprang to his feet, then turned and hissed angrily at her for daring to speak.

'*You*…Olive Lawson!' he spluttered. Then, red-faced and infuriated, he slammed the lid of the piano down, turned his back and walked out of the room. After a couple of moment's stunned silence, people resumed their coffee and conversation. Mirrie then took Lawson to one side and quietly said 'I cannot apologise to you for the behaviour of another person; but I *do* apologise to you because that occurred in my home'.

Holford remained at Mosman for a year or so after that. At the end of April in 1986 a minor stomach ailment began to worry Mirrie. Presumably at Franz's insistence she was hospitalised, and died in Royal North Shore Hospital on 1 May 1986.

It is not known exactly when Franz Holford moved out of Mirrie Hill's home, but he must have arranged to finalise his affairs in Sydney very close to the time of her death. Following this, he went to Brisbane to live out his final years in the care of the composer Betty Beath.[193]

He died in a Brisbane hospital 5th December 1994.

******

How does one assess the life of such a man? Opinions of him range from that of Eric Cuckson, who described him as a vampire sucking money from his victims, to a loveable old rogue who cynically exploited the vulnerability of many people, mainly women.

For myself – having lived and worked at 'Norwood' for almost ten years and perhaps being one of only a very few who saw Franz Holford at such close quarters over such a protracted period – I do not share Phillip Wilcher's idealistic view. However, as a quite prolific composer - which the catalogue of his compositions in this book reveals - some musicians believe that the considerable portion of his compositions deserve a permanent place in the pantheon of music.

In his obituary in *The Australian,* 3rd January 1995, James Murdoch wrote:

> 'He leaves some substantial works that have not been heard for generations, but may yet come back into fashion.

If this book inspires future musicians or musicologists to revive the compositions of Franz (William) Holford (especially his songs) no one would be happier than this author.

Even though my association with *Canon* was largely as an unpaid volunteer who was not given the courtesy of a by-line for his services and even if my life as an amanuensis was virtually that of an unpaid servant, the riches I gained from living in such exquisite surroundings, the personages I rubbed shoulders with and the freedom I had to develop as a writer – not to mention the happiness of meeting the person I have spent the past 65 years of my life with - more than compensate for any disadvantages I suffered because of my association with Franz William Holford.

******

The Canon remains the longest-running classical music journal in the history of Australian independent publishing.

END

Appendix 1

Typical of the misinformation surrounding the life and times of William Franz Holford, is the following extract from a publication providing heritage information on various aspects of Hunters Hill, emanating from the local community:

This house was built by Charles Edward Jeanneret in 1893 on the Wybalena Estate. George S Mackenzie lived here from 1895 to 1910 and called the house Rosenan. S G Lavers was the occupant from 1914 until at least 1933 and the name of the house was changed to (Norwood) in 1916. In later years the property was leased by an apparently eccentric gentleman called Franz Holford (1907-1994) a prominent musician, who composed many works for instrument and voice. Born in Heidelberg, Germany, on 9 November 1907, he moved to Australia in the late 1930s after having studied both in Paris and at Oxford University with Alfred Cortot (piano), Jack Westrip *(sic)*, Hans Bekker and Sir Hamilton Harty. His compositions were subsequently performed by renowned musicians in England and Europe. In 1948, his interest in the development of Australian music led Franz to found the Australian Journal of Music, *The Canon*, and he continued as its editor throughout its seventeen years of publication. He was well known in Hunters Hill as the local piano teacher and would conduct lessons in the library at the front of the house, greeting his pupils' parents on the front stairs, always impeccably dressed in a suit.

Appendix 2

FRANZ HOLFORD COMPOSITIONS

*Denotes location in the Fisher, Sydney Conservatorium, National and Mitchell Libraries

TITLE	MEDIA	PRINT	RECORDING	PUBLISHER	FISHER	S.CON	NATIONAL	MITCHELL
Andy's gone a'droving; The Wild Colonial Boy (1964)	Voice/P	*		J Albert	*		*	
Arabesque (1970)	Oboe/P	*		J Albert	*	*	*	
Aubade (Australian Music for Strings), includes Autumn Oaks	Strings		CD JADCD1069	Jade	*			
Autumn Oaks (1969)	Cello/P	*		J Albert	*	*	*	
Ballade in Db Major for Piano, Parts 1 & 2, Franz Holford	Piano		+PRX2402 SX6432/3				*	
Capriccio (1960), Franz Holford	Piano		CD (2)	J.Albert/2MBS-FM				*
Columbine in Spring, Gordon King	Voice/P		+PRX2211 SX6192/3				*	
Come Away Death (1970)	Voice/P	*		J Albert	*	*	*	
Compact; Plough (1944), Horace Fuller	Voice/P		CD (2)	J.Albert/2MBS-FM			*	*
Cottage Song	Voice/P					*		
Dance of a Gnome (1959)	Oboe/P	*		J & W Chester	*	*	*	
Delian Fantasy for Piano, Parts 1 & 2, Franz Holford	Piano		+PRX2404 SX6598				*	
Delian Fantasy for Piano, Parts 3 & 4, Franz Holford	Piano		+PRX2404 SX6599				*	
Dreamland (1969)	Oboe/P			J Albert	*	*	*	
Expectancy (1977)	Voice/P	*		J Albert	*	*	*	
Fair Elizabeth (1954)	Voice/P	*		J Albert				
Felicity (1946), William Herbert	Voice/P	*	CD (2)	J.Albert/2MBS-FM			*	*
Five Elizabethan Songs; June Midnight, The Coming of Spring; The Girl in Green, Horace Fuller	Voice/P		CD (2)	J.Albert/2MBS-FM	*			*
Giga (1974)	Oboe/P	*		J Albert	*	*	*	

Francis Ravel Harvey

TITLE	MEDIA	PRINT	RECORDING	PUBLISHER	FISHER	S.CON	NATIONAL	MITCHELL
Goblin (1958) Oboe/P, Ian Wilson	Oboe/P		CD	J.Albert/2MBS-FM				*
I have a bonnet trimmed with Blue (1970)	Voice/P	*		J Albert	*	*	*	
In the Woods; January Dusk, Gordon King	Voice/P		+PRX2211/2 SX6194/5				*	
June Midnight (1976)	Voice/P	*		J Albert	*		*	
Kew in Lilac Time, MLC Choir, Hope Donaldson, Piano	Choral		+PR1032 S1926/7				*	
Love's Philosophy (1947), William Herbert	Voice/P	*	CD (2)	J.Albert/2MBS-FM	*		*	*
Madrigal (1973)	Voice/P	*		J Albert	*		*	
Mamble (1944), Horace Fuller	Voice/P		CD (2)	J.Albert/2MBS-FM				*
Mamble, MLC Choir, Hope Donaldson, Piano	Choral		+PR1032 S1926/7				*	
Mangers (1970)	Voice/P	*	CD (2)	J Albert	*	*	*	*
Minuet (1976)	Clarinet/P	*		J Albert	*	*	*	
Moonlit Apples (1944), Ereach Riley	Voice/P	*	CD (2)	J Albert	*	*	*	*
Music when Soft Voices Die (1971)	Voice/P	*		J Albert	*		*	
My Youth, Horace Fuller	Voice/P		+SX5762 CD (2)				*	*
Night is fallen (1938) William Herbert	Voice/P		CD (2)	J.Albert/2MBS-FM				*
Nocturne (1975)	Clarinet/P	*		J Albert	*	*	*	
Not Wise as Cunning (1944), Horace Fuller	Voice/P		CD (2)	J.Albert/2MBS-FM				*
Nunc Dimittus; Cotswold Love; She walks in beauty; Moonlit apples; Felicity; The pledge; Under the snow; Night is fallen; Ereach Riley	Voice/P		+PRX2194 SX6152				* (Also in Uni of WA)	
On a Lake (1944), Horace Fuller	Voice/P		CD (2)	J.Albert/2MBS-FM				*
On the Tide (Australian Music for Clarinet/Piano) Includes Lullaby	Clarinet/P		*		*			
Pastorale: Goblin (1959)	Oboe/P		CD (2)	J & W Chester	*	*	*	*

Appendix 2

Title	Instrument		Catalog	Label				
Plough (1944), Horace Fuller	Voice/P		CD (2)	J.Albert/2MBS-FM				*
Poet's Song (1944) Horace Fuller	Voice/P		CD (2)	J.Albert/2MBS-FM				*
Prelude E Minor, FH (1960), Franz Holford	Piano		+SX6295/6				*	
Preludes F Minor & Db Major, Franz Holford	Piano		+PRX2261				*	
Prelude in G Minor (1941), Franz Holford	Piano		CD (2)					*
Proud insolent June (1944), Horace Fuller	Voice/P		CD (2)					*
Rain (1944), Horace Fuller	Voice/P		CD (2)	J.Albert/2MBS-FM				*
Saraband (1974)	Oboe/P	*		J Albert	*	*	*	
Scherzo Bb Minor for Piano, Franz Holford	Piano		+SX3480/1				*	
Scherzo C# Minor for Piano (1940) Franz Holford	Piano		+SX6295 CD (2)				*	*
Scherzo D Minor for Piano Franz Holford	Piano		+PRX2350				*	
Scherzo F# Minor & Prelude E Minor for Piano, Franz Holford	Piano		+SX6295/6				*	
Ships of Grief, Gordon King	Voice/P		+PRX2212				*	
Slumber Song (1969)	Oboe/P	*		J Albert	*	*	*	
Sonata C Minor for Piano, Parts 1 & 2 Franz Holford	Piano	*					*	
Sonata D Minor, Violin & Piano, Robert Patterson	Violin/P		+PRX2324 SX6432/6433				*	
Sonata No 3 for Oboe and Piano (1952)	Oboe/P		CD	J.Albert/2MBS-FM				*
Sonata No 4 for Oboe & Piano (1971)	Oboe/P	*		J Albert	*	*	*	
Sonata No 1 D Minor for Two Pianos, John Champ & Franz Holford	Piano		+SX6294				*	
Southampton Bells; Nunc Dimittus; Cotswold love, Ereach Riley	Voice/P		*PRX2194 SX6153				* (Also in Uni of WA)	
Summer Madrigal (1974), Ian Wilson	Oboe/P	*	CD (2)	J Albert	*	*		*
Summer Madrigal (1957)	Oboe/P	*		J & W Chester	*			
Syncopation (c. 1978) William Lovelock	Piano	*			*	*		
The Coming of Spring, (1944), Horace Fuller	Voice/P	*	CD (2)	J.Albert/2MBS-FM	*	*		*
The Englishman (1973)	Choral	*		J Albert	*	*		

The Girl in Green (1944), Horace Fuller	Voice/P		+PRX2008 SX5766/7				*	
The Poet's Song								
The Keel Row (1970)	Voice/P	*		J Albert	*	*	*	
The Merry Month of May (1944), Horace Fuller	Voice/P		+PRX2008 SX5766/7				*	
The Rainbow (1944), Horace Fuller	Voice/P		+SX5762 CD (2)				*	*
The Stolen Child, Parts 1, 2 & 3 MLC Choir, Hope Donaldson, Piano	Choral		+PR1031 S1924/5				*	
The Tollgate (1943), Ereach Riley	Voice/P	*	CD (2)	J Albert	*		*	*
The Whitethroat & the Holly (1944), William Herbert	Voice/P	*		J Albert	*		*	
Three Lyric Songs: Autumn, Molly, The Gnome & the Penguin (1969)	Voice/P	*		J Albert	*		*	
Three Songs: Cottage Song; The Poet's Song; Plough (1950)	Voice/P	*		Chappell & Co	*		*	
Time for Playing: Three 3rd Grade Piano Pieces for Recreation (1966)	Piano	*		J Albert	*	*		
Toccata for Piano	Piano		+PRX2409 SX6608/9				*	
Under the snow (1945), Ereach Riley	Voice/P		CD (2)	J.Albert/2MBS-FM			(Also in Uni of WA)	*
Variations on a Lute Dance (1957), Franz Holford	Piano		CD (2)	J.Albert/2MBS-FM				*
Variations on a Theme of Paganini, Franz Holford	Piano		+PR2353 SX6486/7				*	*
Wily Cupid (1973)	Voice/P	*		J.Albert	*	*	*	
Winter Landscape (1949) Franz Holford	Piano		CD (2)	J.Albert/2MBS-FM				*

* *All recordings marked with a cross + are Columbia Process Recordings (78 rpm 12"), with relevant serial numbers; they are in the possession of The National Film and Sound Archive, Canberra.*

Appendix 3

COMPOSITIONS BY 'GAETANO TESORIERO' AKA FRANZ HOLFORD

(Copies of this Catalogue are held in the State Library of New South Wales, Call # Q784.62406/3A1 and in the National Library of Australia)

Ave Maria : Piano solo
Sydney : Albert & Son *circa* 1969 3pp

Ave Maria : Voice, with piano or organ accompaniment
Sydney : Albert & Son *circa* 1969 3pp

Bells : Piano Solo
Sydney : Albert & Son *circa* 1969 3pp

Birds & Animals : Four Little Piano Pictures : Piano solo
Sydney : Albert & Son *circa* 1971 4pp

Bird in the Cherry Tree : Voice & Piano
Sydney : Albert & Son *circa* 1971 2pp

Catchin' fish : a merry song : Voices, chime bar, recorder & piano
Sydney : Albert & Son *circa* 1969 5pp

Caught on a string : three open-string pieces : Strings
Sydney : Albert & Son *circa* 1969 3pp

Gelsomino Jasmine : Piano solo
Sydney : Albert & Son 1970 3pp

Little Suite : Bb Clarinet & Piano
Sydney : Albert & Son 1970 7pp

Lullaby – *Buona sera* **:** Voice & Piano
Sydney : Albert & Son *circa* 1970 2pp

Minuet & Gavotte : Violin solo
Sydney : Albert & Son *circa* 1969 3pp

Natale : Christmas Song Voice & Piano
Sydney : Albert & Son *circa* 1967 3pp

Ninna nonna : An Italian Christmas Song (2 parts) Voice & Piano
Sydney : Albert & Son *circa* 1967 3pp

Olympic Games : Five Fun Finger Exercises Solo Piano
Sydney : Albert & Son *circa* 1969 3pp

The Young Traveller : 8 Adventurous Excursions Solo Piano
Sydney : Albert & Son *circa* 1969 2pp

Wedding Song : Voice, Piano or Organ
Sydney : Albert & Son *circa* 1970 4pp

Youngsters : Music for singing & movement Simple Percussion
Sydney : Albert & Son *circa* 1972 10pp

Appendix 4

FRANZ HOLFORD PROCESS RECORDINGS (3) – COLUMBIA (Aust) PL

Title	Matrix	Type	Performers	Format
Sonata C minor "Allegro con brio" Pt.2	PRX 2407 SX6605	Piano	Franz Holford	78 r.p.m 12"
Sonata No1 D minor for two pianos 3rd mov. "Vivace" Part 2	SX 6294	2 pianos	Franz Holford & John Champ	78 r.p.m 12"
Toccata Part 1	PRX 2400 SX6608	Piano	Franz Holforf	78 r.p.m 12"
Toccata Part 2	PRX 2409 SX6609	Piano	Franz Holforf	78 r.p.m 12"
Scherzo C# minor & Prelude E minor	PRX 2261 SX6295	Piano	Franz Holforf	78 r.p.m 12"
Prelude F minor & Db major	PRX 2261 SX 6296	Piano	Franz Holforf	78 r.p.m 12"
Columbine in Spring & January Dusk	PRX2211 SX6192	Vocl	Horace Fuller & Franz Holford at piano	78 r.p.m 12"
June Midnight & Elizabeth Ann	PRX 2211 SX6193	Vocl	Horace Fuller & Franz Holford at piano	78 r.p.m 12"
Sonata D minor Violin & Piano 2nd mov. Part 2 & 3rd mov. Part1	PRX 2324 SX 6432	Violin & Piano	Robert Patterson violin, Franz Holford piano	78 r.p.m 12"
Sonata D min Violin & Piano 3rd mov. Part 2	PRX2324 SX 6433	Violin & Pi	Robert Patterson violin, Franz Holford piano	78 r.p.m 12"
The Stolen Child Pt 1	PRX 2816 SX7189	Choral	Warick Singer & Linda Parker Soloist with Piano Acc. John Champ	78 r.p.m 12"
The Stolen Child Pt 2	PRX 2816 SX7190	Choral	Warick Singer & Linda Parker Soloist with Piano Acc. John Champ	78 r.p.m 12"
Sonata C minor Allegro Moderato Pt. 1	PRX2405 SX 6600	Piano	Franz Holford	78 r.p.m 12"
Sonata C minor Allegro Moderato Pt. 2	PRX2405 SX 6601	Piano	Franz Holford	78 r.p.m 12"
The Pledge & The White Throat and the Holly & Vagabond	PRX 2196 SX6156	Vocal	Ereach Riley (tenor) Franx Holford Piano	78 r.p.m 12"
Carol & Nigh is Fallen &Down by the Sally Gardens	PRX 2196 SX6157	Vocal	Ereach Riley (tenor) Franx Holford Piano	78 r.p.m 12"
Moonlit Apples	PRX2213 SX 6196	Vocal	Gordon King Baritone & Franz Holford at piano	78 r.p.m 12"
Blackbird & Dusk	PRX 2213 SX 6197	Vocal	Gordon King Baritone & Franz Holford at piano	78 r.p.m 12"
The Rainbow & My Youth & Rain	PRX2006 SX5762	Vocal	Horace Fuller & Franz Holford at piano	78 r.p.m 12"
Roundels of the year Part 1	PRX2006 SX5763	Vocal	Horace Fuller & Franz Holford at piano	78 r.p.m 12"
Variations on a Theme By Paganini Part 1	PRX2352 SX 6484	Piano	Franz Holford	78 r.p.m 12"

Variations on a Theme By Paganini Part 2	PRX2352 SX 6485	Piano	Franz Holford	78 r.p.m 12"
Sonata No1 D minor for two pianos 1st mov. Allegro Moderato Pt1	PRX 2259 SX6290	2 Pianos	Franz Holford & John Champ	78 r.p.m 12"
Sonata No1 D minor for two pianos 1st mov. Allegro Moderato Pt2	PRX 2259 SX6291	2 Pianos	Franz Holford & John Champ	78 r.p.m 12"
Sonata No1 D minor for two pianos 2nd mov. Lentemente	PRX 2260 SX 6292	2 Pianos	Franz Holford & John Champ	78 r.p.m 12"
Sonata No1 D minor for two pianos 3rd mov. "Vivace" Part 1	PRX 2260 SX 6293	2 Pianos	Franz Holford & John Champ	78 r.p.m 12"
Sonata D minor Violin & Piano 1st mov. Pt 1	PRX 2323 SX 6430	Violin & Piano	Robert Patterson violin, Franz Holford piano	78 r.p.m 12"
Sonata D minor Violin & Piano 1st mov. Pt 2 & 2nd mov. Pt1	PRX 2323 SX 6431	Violin & Piano	Robert Patterson violin, Franz Holford piano	78 r.p.m 12"
FOUR SONGS: 1.Dream Pedlary (T. Beddoes) 2. O Men from the Fields (Padraig Calm) 3.Innisfree (W. B. Yeats) 4.Spring (Anon 17th cent.) Iberian Sketches Nos.1,2,3 & 4 (Piano solo)	PRX5487 EMI	Vocal & Piano Solo	Mary Blake Soptano Franz Holford piano	33 r.p.m 12"
Iberian Sketches Nos.5 & 6 SIX SONGS:1. Autumn (F. Holford) 2.The Sally Gardens (Yeats) 3.Winter (Shelley) 4. June Midnight (John Drinkwater) 5.The Robin's Cross (G. Darley) 6.Vagabond (John Drinkwater)	PRX5487 flip side	Vocal & Piano Solo	Stewart Harvey baritone Franz Holford piano	33 r.p.m 12"

Copies of these mainly 78 rpm vinyl recordings exist in the National Film and Sound Archive in Canberra, in private collections and in some music institutions. The late Donald Newton had a complete set of these Columbia recordings, privately pressed by Columbia for Franz Holford, and used by him for radio broadcasting – where he could gain acceptance for their public use by the ABC.

Sources and acknowledgments

Obviously the main source of reference for this book was the music magazine *The Canon*, on which I worked for many years in an unofficial capacity as production assistant, sub-editor, writer, illustrator, music copyist, advertising salesman and personal assistant to the editor. If I had given any consideration to my future retirement, in that wild and thrilling period of years, I would have had the foresight to save a couple of copies of each edition and await the passage of time until I could sell them as 'collectibles'. Currently on Ebay for example, copies of the Schoenberg Jubilee Edition (Volume 3 Number Two, September 1949) sell for around $100 each, and the others from $10 to $70 each; I estimate the value of a complete set of *Canon* today at around $20-$30,000. The problem is of course that few – if any – complete sets exist. The State Library of NSW's set from which I worked was unfortunately missing numbers 4, 5 and 6 of Volume One. However, during a visit to Canberra in June 2016 I visited the National Library and was allowed to make scans of these three missing editions, which have been given to the NSW State Library, so that it now has a complete set of the magazine.

What both Library's collections of *Canon* lacks (which would have been a godsend in the writing of this book) is an index. I commend this as a project to some aspiring young musicologist with an interest in the history of Australian music. Someone may enjoy the complicated and time-consuming task of cataloguing some sixteen years of Australian music commentary. Who knows, it might even lead to the acquisition of a subsidised phD.

I am deeply indebted to the late Donald Newton and to Dr Marjorie Newton for their excellent research, and the use of letters, articles, photographic and other materials. Professor Robert Cuckson also sent me useful recollections from America, and of course the author Olive Lawson's memoir was enormously helpful for a description of Franz

Holford's later years. Olive also agreed to review my manuscript, in exchange for me reviewing her excellent book: *Alfred Hill: Beloved Landmark* .

I am grateful to Canberra music teacher Suzanne Hewitt for lending my wife and me her lovely house for three weeks in 2016 to enable me to complete my research at the National Library. To thank my dear wife Anne for her encouragement in getting this book 'done' is almost axiomatic. It has taken so long, and she has been so patient, as well as having an unerring eye for solecisms.

Lastly I wish to thank the NSW State Library, the University of Sydney, the Australian Music Centre and the National Library Canberra for access to their collections, and to some research assistance (NLA) in researching various Australian singers and musicians.

Francis Ravel Harvey

May 2025

******

ENDNOTES *Prelude Two*

1. *A Franz Holford Miscellany: including his Middle See* compiled and edited by Jennifer Hill and Kerry Murphy. (Centre for Studies in Australian Music, University of Melbourne, 2001)
2. Ibid.
3. Wilcher, Phillip '27', in *Music Teacher Magazine*, Vol 9 No 1, November/December 2001
4. Murdoch, James, in *The Australian*, 3 January 1995. Murdoch concludes his obituary with some perhaps prescient words: 'He leaves some substantial works that have not been heard for generations, but may yet come back in fashion'.
5. Donald and Marjorie Newton Papers concerning Franz Holford 1938-2008, State Library of NSW, MLMSS 7943.
6. Harvey, F R 'A shadow without substance', *Music Forum* May-July 2004 (Music Council of Australia, Sydney, 2004).

ENDNOTES CHAPTER 1 *Woolwich*, 1944

7. Our mother died in 1933, and our father had vanished in New Guinea during the war. My brother and I were left in the care of our four sisters and an adopted aunt..
8. John Edgington was General Manager of a company which imported the Floating Dock to Woolwich in 1888.
9. *Adelaide News*, Adelaide, SA, 25 August 1945.
10. Victor Roy Massey (–) was music master at Scots College in 1943 and organist and choirmaster at All Saints Church, Woollahra from 1920. He was organist at St Mark's Church, Darling Point, but dismissed in 1944. Victor Massey was also a composer and author of the 'Austral' method of chanting.
11. Wilcher, Phillip, '27', in *Music Teacher Magazine*, Volume 9 Number 1, Nov/Dec 2001

ENDNOTES CHAPTER 2 *Lineage*

12. English Birth Indexes, 1861 First Quarter, Vol 6b, p.576
13. Death Certificate states 'About 60 years in NSW'. He was in England for the 1881 Census, so presumably arrived about 1882. Not on NSW Assisted Immigrants Index.
14. B.*circa* 1828 in County Kildare, Ireland.
15. Marriage Indexes 1887/841.
16. John Perkins died at the Holford home, 51 Andreas Street, Petersham in 1905.
17. Births Index NSW, Reg No 7599/1910. The author remembers the date of 9th November as the day each year on which Franz Holford celebrated his birthday.
18. Marriage Certificate, BDR, 31st October 1914.
19. Laws concerning adoption were not introduced into NSW until 1923.
20. A Franz Holford miscellany: including his Middle see / compiled and edited by Jennifer Hill and Kerry Murphy [Melbourne]: Centre for Studies in Australian Music, University of Melbourne, 2001 x 90 p., ill., ports ; 21 cm.
21. Ibid.
22. Philip Webster Holford, a grandson of William Webster, visited Fanny and Albert Youngs when he was a child, and recalls that: 'Fanny played the piano well, as did her daughter Edna May...' (Notes of a telephone conversation with Philip Webster Holford, 16th November, 2003)
23. A biography of George de Cairos-Rego can be found on the *Music Australia* website: www.musicaustralia.org.
24. Conversation with Gordon Smee, April 2010.
25. Barrie (John) Brettoner (1913-1993) born in Yorkshire, England, he came to Australia at the age of 12. In 1930 he was made a Fellow of the Trinity College of Music, but to earn a living during the Depression he became a professional Wurlitzer organist, playing at major cinemas in Sydney. He played at the opening of the *Civic* Theatre Auburn in 1934 and at all the major Sydney cinemas, and was resident organist at the Savoy at Hurstville in 1940. (The *Rosicrucian Forum*, 1957)
26. *The Sydney Morning Herald* 10 February 1930 p 6.

27.	Wunderlich, Ernest Julius (1859 -1945). He introduced German stamped metal ceilings to Australia and erected some of his earliest imports in Sydney Town Hall and in the piano showrooms of Octavius Beale and William Paling. An enthusiastic musician and composer, he criticized Percy Grainger's 'free' music and published an album of songs and numerous piano pieces, some showing the influence of J S Bach. Ernest helped to establish the New South Wales State Conservatorium of Music and endowed exhibitions there; his friends included Henri Verbrugghen, Joseph Bradley and William Orchard.
28.	*Sydney Morning Herald*, 9 February, 1934, p 8.
29.	Holford, William *Sydney Morning Herald*, Letters, 14 February, 1934, p11
30.	Sitsky, Larry in *Australian Chamber Music with Piano*, (ANU Epress, Canberra, 2011)
31.	Don and Marjorie Newton Papers concerning Franz Holford 1936-2008. State Library of NSW, MLMSS 7943.
32.	Felix Weingartner, Wikipedia.
33.	The *Northern District Times*, 1 July 1937, p5.
34.	'Australian Stage Gossip', from *The Otago Witness*, 8 December 1894.
35.	'Australian Stage Gossip', from *The Otago Witness*, 8 December 1894.
36.	*The Northern District Times*, 4th November 1937, p.4.
37.	Amy Carey regularly sang with local groups such as the Hurlstone Choral Society in performances of *Messiah* and other well-known oratorios.
38.	*The Northern District Times*, 14 April 1938.
39.	A Franz Holford miscellany: including his Middle See / compiled and edited by Jennifer Hill and Kerry Murphy [Melbourne]: Centre for Studies in Australian Music, University of Melbourne, 2001.
40.	I have witnessed this letter in *The Northern District Times*, but failed to locate it for this publication - *Author*
41.	NSW Marriage Index, Reg No 1939/021856.
42.	NSW Death Index, Reg No 1942/18449.
43.	Franz Holford always gave the impression that he owned 'Norwood'. Perhaps the generous ongoing rental by the d'Apice Family was their response to an act of musical generosity of his, or sympathy for a fellow artist.

ENDNOTES CHAPTER 3 *Hunters Hill*

44.	The Italian artist Dattilo Rubbo, who lived in Hunters Hill at one stage, was interned for a short period in 1940 on the outbreak of World War II, for making donations to an Italian club.
45.	He told several people, including the author, that during WW2 he worked for the 'War Office' and in the British Intelligence Service in 'Medical Records', and that he was issued with a revolver for his protection.
46.	Holford, Franz *The Building of Goblin Town*, (Sydney, Deaton & Spencer, 1937) NLA BibID: 2979006
47.	Holford, Franz *Through the Casement*, (Sydney, Deaton & Spencer, 1941) NLA BibID: 927298.
48.	Holford, Franz *Tone Poems*, (Sydney, Deaton & Spencer, 1941) Don and Marjorie Newton Papers concerning Franz Holford 1936-2008. State Library of NSW, MLMSS 7943.
49.	The author recalls sitting on the veranda of 'Norwood' with Franz Holford as he read one of his short stories, entitled *Spinny*, the story of a little orphan girl taken in to his home by an English gentleman and who dies tragically in a house fire.
50.	Gordon Smee: Conversation with the author, April 2010. He informed the Rev Gordon Smee upon meeting him that he had acquired all his doctorates overseas, at overseas universities, including Oxford and Heidelberg.CHAPTER 6
51.	NSW Death Index, Reg No 1942/18449.
52.	NSW Probate Indexes show that neither William Webster Holford (d.1942), Annie Elizabetholford (d.1951) or John Perkins (d.1905) left any property. None of the three appear on the indexes, which means that they did not own any real estate, substantial cash, stocks and shares or jewellery etc.

53. Later, when he was working as an editor for Albert's, Franz would write a little 'piano method' and dedicate it 'To Sue'.
54. New pianos were rare at this time, in fact it was not till after WW II, in the more affluent period that new pianos became more available.

ENDNOTES CHAPTER 4 *There came a company man*
55. Gwen Champ's nephew Gordon Clarke also became a pupil of Franz Holford
56. John Champ was a well known ABC accompanist, and created an ABC radio series 'The Way of Music'.
57. Don Newton recalls Franz Holford telling him that he 'dandled John on his knee when only a few years old'. (Don Newton letter to the author, May 2010)
58. See his lengthy biography in *Who's Who in Australia* (1929).
59. Dr J G Dingle 'Silk Production in Australia: A Report for the Rural Industries Research and Development Corporation' (RIRDC Publication No 00/56, May 2000).
60. Papers of Reginald Champ, State Library of NSW MLMSS 9473.
61. Perhaps they lived for a period in Medindie, which is a suburb of Adelaide, and named their Hunters Hill house after this suburb.
62. Presumably he was living at his parents' house 'Melton' in Drummoyne Ave, Drummoyne.
63. Lysaght's was a subsidiary of an English company, and was started in Newcastle in 1885. Reg's father was given the job of General Manager in 1905 at the Bridge Street, Sydney office of the company, and was appointed Managing Director in 1926.
64. John's sister Judith had been born in 1930. She was educated at Methodist Ladies College, where in 1946 she played hockey in the MLC First Team. In 1945 she played Thisbe in the college's production of *A Midsummer's Night Dream*, and she would ultimately go on to a moderately successful professional acting career.

ENDNOTES CHAPTER 5 *Threlkeld*
65. In this period he wrote the words and music for a charming little song for the Champ children called *The Gnome and the Penguin*, which he sang as he accompanied himself on the piano in the style of Nöel Coward.
66. Music Minus One was founded in 1950 by Irv Kratka, a 24-year-old US college student.
67. Davies, Stephen, *Themes in the philosophy of music* (London, OUP, 2003).
68. However, many teachers believed that the use of Music Minus One led to 'untidy' playing – where the pianist runs the risk of not spending the necessary time to acquire an appropriate technique for large works such as concertos.
69. Phil Holford, Franz's 'nephew', recalls Franz Holford giving him a stack of records and a record cutter, when Phil was 12 years old. (Conversation with Marjorie Newton, 16th November 2003)
70. Franz Holford, Letter to Don Newton, 10th August 1947. Don and Marjorie Newton Papers concerning Franz Holford 1936-2008. State Library of NSW, MLMSS 7943.
71. Shipping List, 1947.

ENDNOTES CHAPTER 6 *Evenings with the rich and famous*
72. Scougall, Stuart, *Consider the Lilies* (Sydney, Ure Smith, c.1953). This was a private press publication, of which only 200 copies were printed, paid for by Dr Scougall. and illustrated with wood engravings by Eva Sandor. Rare copies are sold through the internet for around $A200.
73. Franklin Bennett was a very good local artist who made a living painting the homes of the rich and famous in and around picturesque Hunters Hill, then knocking on their doors and selling the paintings to them.
74. Holford, Franz, *Elegy* (G W Hall, Sydney 1948). Copies of 'Elegy' appear for sale from time to time on the internet. A recent listing by Amazon.com offered a single copy of the book at £UK249.90 ($A525.46).

75. *Ibid.*
76. 'Visit of Professor Georg Schneevoigt', in *Burnie Advocate*, 27 May 1940
77. Helen Bainton later wrote a book *Remembered on Waking* (Sydney, Currawong Publishing Co 1960) which she dedicated to Franz Holford. It contains many references and anecdotes about him.
78. It was the 1938 version of the *Pathétique*, with the Berlin Philharmonic Orchestra, conducted by Wilhelm Furtwangler.
79. Stuart Scougall had views on health which included brushing himself instead of washing, and rubbing oil all over his body. He slept with his feet uncovered to the ankles, even in the depths of winter.

ENDNOTES CHAPER 7 *The Canon*
80. Rex Cairos de Rego eventually abbreviated his name for convenience, to Rex de Rego.
81. Gordon Smee, conversation with the author, March 2010.
82. Holford, Franz, *Mamble*, SATB (1944) words by John Drinkwater. He later adapted it to a song for soprano voice. Papers of Franz Holford MS 8809.
83. Holford, Franz, *The Stolen Child*, SATB (1945) words by W B Yeats. Papers of Franz Holford MS 8809.
84. Hector White went on to school music teaching, and subsequently published a text book on music.
85. Refer to p.107 *Delius as I knew him*, by Eric Fenby.
86. Letter from Franz Holford to Reg Newton, 17th August 1945. Don and Marjorie Newton Papers concerning Franz Holford 1936-2008. State Library of NSW, MLMSS 7943.
87. Letter from Franz Holford to Don Newton, 24th July 1946. Don and Marjorie Newton Papers concerning Franz Holford 1936-2008. State Library of NSW, MLMSS 7943.
88. Robert Dalley-Scarlett (1887-1959) at the time was conductor of the choir of the Brisbane Handel Society (1932-59). He was a respected international Handel authority who continually encouraged all forms of music-making at both amateur and professional levels.
89. *Messiah* program, 15th December 1950. Don and Marjorie Newton Papers concerning Franz Holford 1936-2008. State Library of NSW, MLMSS 7943.
90. The skilful cellist Alison Battarbee (Mother of Margaret Throsby) played the solo trumpet part in the upper register of her cello, to great effect.
91. *Messiah* program.
92. The first edition appeared in August, 1947.
93. *The Canon*, Vol 1 No 1, August 1947.
94. $3 approximately in present currency.
95. Boyd Neel spoke glowingly of the magazine to an Australian newspaper during his visit in 1947.
96. During the co-editorship of Kenneth Hince (1951-1954).

ENDNOTES CHAPTER 8 *Amanuensis*
97. I later discovered that the recording was in fact was by Artur Rubinstein, which he made in 1932, with John Barbirolli conducting the London Symphony Orchestra.
98. Homosexuality between consenting males was forbidden in Australia since settlement. It was finally decriminalised in NSW in 1984.

ENDNOTES CHAPTER 9 *Isolation*
99. Gwen Champ's nephew Gordon Clarke, who became his pupil, was nicknamed 'Googs'.
100. In an undated letter to Don Newton, shortly before dispensing with her services, Holford wrote: 'If you telephone please give me a three-call sign as I am dodging Cooee at the moment, as I cannot nurse her and myself.' Letter from Franz Holford to Reg Newton, *circa* 1955-6.

	Don and Marjorie Newton Papers concerning Franz Holford 1936-2008. State Library of NSW, MLMSS 7943.
101.	Holford, Franz *The Stolen Child* (Choir and Piano, 1948)
102.	Franz and Marjorie divorced sometime in the late 1950s.
103.	Newton told the author that Franz had never made any inappropriate gestures towards him as a student.
104.	Don Newton also recalled stumbling accidentally upon Franz and Gwen Champ kissing passionately in the hallway of 'Threlkeld' on one occasion.
105.	John Champ spent his latter years living with a male partner in Mosman.
106.	The original business address for the journal was the Champ's house 'Threlkeld', 18 Woolwich Road, Hunters Hill.
107.	The first edition was dated August, 1947.
108.	British composer, pianist and teacher (1792-1871), who met Beethoven and whose tenth symphony in G minor was praised by Richard Wagner.
109.	See List of Compositions, p149*ff*.
110.	Holford, Franz – Correspondence: Letters from Sir Eric Fenby. National Library. NLA MS 8967

ENDNOTES CHAPTER 11 *The Apocalypse*

111.	Goossens arrived in Australia in July 1947 and his arrival was heralded in the first edition of Canon (Vol 1 No 1, August 1947). He featured in many other early editions of the journal.
112.	Goossens wrote an article describing *The Apocalypse*, entitled 'World Premiere' in the October 1954 edition of Canon.
113.	*Canon*, January 1955, p.251ff.
114.	*Canon*, Vol. 9, No 9, April 1956, p 249

ENDNOTES CHAPTER 12 *Cut down to size*

115.	Letter to Don Newton, 31st August 1954. Don and Marjorie Newton Papers concerning Franz Holford 1936-2008, State Library of NSW, MLMSS7943.
116.	*Canon*, December 1957, p 140.
117.	The invention of this 'cumbersome but efficient machine' is attributed to Murray Parker, a music librarian with the ABC, Melbourne. Mss for a Treatment *Music in Australia*, 1948, Papers of Kenneth Hince, 2691/10148, Australian National Library.

ENDNOTES CHAPTER 13 *The narcissist*

118.	In his heyday, which was before WW2 and some 25 years after it, Leslie Flint was one of Britain's best-known Spiritualists. He claimed to have communicated with many famous people, from Archimedes, Chopin and Ghandi to Marilyn Munro. The recordings of Flint's séances are now stored at the University of Manitoba. The collection contains around 2,000 audiotapes and 300 books.
119.	*Canon*, Vol 1 No 1, August 1947.
120.	The famous Hungarian born pianist arrived in Australia in 1945, and gradually re-established her international performing career from this country.

ENDNOTES CHAPTER 14 *The séance*

121.	Champ, Judy *Revelations: Conversations with sages and seers, a journey into the psychic* (Book House, Sydney 2002)

CHAPTER 15 *'Glorious John', and others*

122.	Among his friends, Barbirolli became known as 'Glorious John' after Ralph Vaughan Williams wrote the epigraph across the title page of his Eighth Symphony prior to its premiere in 1956.

123. Goossens spent nine years in Australia, from 1947 to 1956. He conducted the Sydney Symphony Orchestra and other groups, and was the director of the NSW State Conservatorium of Music. He held these positions until March 1956, when the scandal erupted which forced him to resign only a year after being knighted.
124. Emigrants to Australia at this time were given a variety of names under the White Australia Policy: 'White Aliens', 'Aliens', 'New Australians' and finally just plain 'migrants'.
125. Whilst in Australia, he would arrange for the test cricket scores to be sent up to him at the conductor's podium, during rehearsals. *Adelaide Advertiser*, 5th January 1951, p9.
126. There is some doubt as to whether this work is altogether by Bach. Some scholars maintain it was the work of his son Phillip Emanuel who transcribed a passage of improvisation on the organ by his father, hence the relative brevity of the composition.
127. Mather, Martin 'The role of science in modern composition', in *The Canon* Vol II, No 3, October 1957.
128. Now Artistic Director of the Huddersfield Contemporary Music Festival.
129. 'Martin Mather', in Canon Vol 11, No 3, October 1957.
130. Inspired by working at the Mitchell Library, since he could not support himself as a full time composer.

ENDNOTES CHAPTER 16 *Caught out*

131. *Canon*, Vol 6 No 1, August 1952, pp 10-11.
132. In a subsequent interview I discovered that Gerhard Willner and his wife were living in New Zealand at the time I met them, where they had been given British nationality after only 20 month's residence, in recognition of the value of their services during WWII to the British forces in the Middle East. The Willners gave up successful careers in Europe in 1932 and fled from Hitler to Egypt, finally getting married in Alexandria. The concentration of British troops in Egypt in preparation for the Middle East campaign brought them their opportunity for war service in their own field, with Gerhard Willner's appointment as director of the 'Music for All' section of the army education program for the British forces. They gave over 400 concerts throughout the Middle East, touring desert camps and living under similar conditions to the troops. New Zealand troops encamped not very far from their home at Maafi, a suburb of Cairo, and they made many friends among the New Zealanders.

ENDNOTES CHAPTER 17 *Love in the afternoon*

133. The Elizabethan Opera Co was established by the Australian Elizabethan Theatre Trust (formed in 1954 in honour of Elizabeth II, who visited Australia in this year). The Trust was the brainchild of H C ('Nugget') Coombs. In 1967, Coombs also persuaded Prime Minister Harold Holt to legislate to create the Australian Council for the Arts (now the Australia Council) as a body for the public funding of the arts, and in 1968, he became its chairman. He worked closely with Prime Minister John Gorton to secure funding for an Australian film industry. Coombs also became Chancellor of the Australian National University, which he had helped found in 1946.
134. 'Ambassador for Opera', by 'F B R Harvey' in Canon, Vol 11, No 9, May 1958.
135. 'Beecham lashes at "nitwits" in Covent Garden Trust', in *The Newcastle Sun*, 9th January, 1949.
136. 'Australian singers have captured London', Neville Cardus, in *Sydney Morning Herald*, 27th November 1954
137. *Brisbane Courier*, 12th May 1931, p10
138. Beecham went on to say: 'I would bet £100 to a farthing that no such voice exists in the British Empire.'
139. Beecham, Sir Thomas 'Conductor's wager...', by HTH in *Courier-Mail*, 13th January 1934.CH
140. Quentin had been in the Secret Service of the Royal Navy and had visited Sydney in 1945.
141. Australian Theatre Year 1959-60 (FP Publications, 1960)
142. Robert Cuckson is a British-born composer/teacher (1942-), who emigrated to Australia at the age of seven. He studied at the Sydney Conservatorium and gained his Diploma (in piano)

in 1960. Cuckson followed this with private studies in piano, composition and theory in the UK and the US, his teachers including Ilona Kabos and Carlo Zecchi (piano), Georg Tintner and Peter Racine Fricker (composition). In 1968 he worked towards a BS in composition at the Mannes College of Music in New York. (Cont p.121) (Cont) He followed this with three degrees in composition from Yale University: MM (1971), MMA (1974), and DMA (1979). A resident of the United States since 1974, Robert Cuckson took US citizenship in 1983 and is presently Dean of Composition at Mannes College, New York.

143. Now known as Yooung Performer of the Year.
144. In a letter to the author, 16 April 2010, Robert Cuckson wrote: 'At some point he (his father) had become entirely disillusioned with Franz. He saw that there would be no end to his financial demands and fairy stories, and to feel that he had got himself into the clutches of a vampire.'
145. The National Youth Orchestra was formed in 1954 and was supported by the Smith Family, where initial rehearsals were held. Later it received sponsorship from the British Motor Corporation (BMC) and moved to Paling's Building in Angel Place. Gorden Day conducted the orchestra for more than fifteen years, until it was superseded by the Sydney Youth Orchestra in 1973.

ENDNOTES CHAPTER 19 *Crossroads*

146. This was prior to Decimal Currency in Australia, which was adopted in 1996.

ENDNOTES CHAPTER 20 *Pain*

147. In the mid-1950s, Australia welcomed about 15,000 Hungarians by recruiting them from migrant camps run by the UN's International Refugee Organisation (IRO). Their fares to Australia were funded by the Australian Government. Among them was Tibor Paul (Pál) (1909-1973), conservatorium teacher, musical director, and conductor of international fame.
148. The name Harbord was changed to Freshwater in 2009.
149. Australian commercial television was launched when Bruce Gyngell uttered the famous words "Welcome to television" on TCN 9 in Sydney on the evening of 16th September 1956.
150. *How to catch a fish* was re-printed into at least six editions over a period of some twenty years. It is still available on Google Books or eBay.

ENDNOTES CHAPTER 21 *Rise and demise of 'Canon'*

151. This same photograph was featured in the monogram *A Franz Holford Miscellany: including his Middle See*, compiled by Jennifer Hill and Kerry Murphy (Centre for Studies in Australian Music, University of Melbourne, 2001).
152. With the arrival of computers and programs such as 'Sibelius' and 'Finale', the use of hand copied manuscripts for performance has virtually disappeared. It has been replaced by the Ipad.
153. Hince joined *The Canon* as Associate Editor in 1951 (Vol 4 No 6) and left in 1954 (Vol 8 No 3).
154. Wagner helped put together the Schoenberg edition in 1949 (Vol 3 No 2) and the Goossens edition in 1952 (Vol 5 No 12), then joined as a regular Associate Editor in 1953 (Vol 6 No 10), leaving at the same time as Kenneth Hince in 1954.
155. He would include a £1 note occasionally in letters to Hince, amidst profuse apologies that he could not afford more: *Papers of Kenneth Hince*, MS 2691, NLA.
156. On more than one occasion he gave to different people a bill of sale over his grand piano, but it seems no one ever forced him to surrender the beautiful Blüthner grand.
157. *Canon*, Vol 1 No 1 August 1947, p 22
158. Article: 'Eugene Goossens is descendant of Captain Cook' in *The Sydney Morning Herald*, 20 August 1946.
159. *Canon*, Vol 5 No 12, July 1952.
160. *Canberra Times*, 29 August 1957, p17

161. 'Boyd Neel reflections' in *The Argus*, Melbourne, Victoria, 27 December 1947
162. Ibid
163. Fenby, Eric 'The well contains – the Fountain overflows', *Canon*, Vol 1 No 8, March 1948. Franz Holford corresponded regularly with Eric Fenby, and at one stage suggested that he go to England to live with Fenby and his family.
164. Moresby, Isabelle 'Ancient Music of the Australian Aborigine', *Canon*, Vol 1 No 8, pp17-19.
165. Moresby, Isabelle 'Australia makes Music' (Longmans Green & Co, Melbourne, 1948).
166. *Canon*, Vol 2 No 4, November 1948, p 166.
168. *Canon*, Vol 2 No 1, August 1948.
169. Ibid
170. *Canon*, Vol 3 No 2, September 1949.
171. Dika Newlin (1923-2006) was variously described as pianist, professor, musicologist, composer and punk rock singer, one of whose last roles was as a leather-clad, bright orange-haired punk rocker and Elvis impersonator.
172. *The Age*, Melbourne, Victoria, 15 October 1949.
173. Australian Music Centre, Ref: 780.994/8. The book is for reference only and is not available on loan.
174. *Canon* was acknowledged as source material most recently by Graeme Skinner for his doctoral thesis at Sydney University in 2011.
175. *Courier-Mail*, Brisbane, 18th February, 1954.
176. Dalley-Scarlett, Robert, *The Armada*, for chorus, tenor & orchestra; a setting of Thomas Babington MacAulay's 19th Century ballad.
177. *Canon*, Vol 10, Number 1, August 1956.
178. *Canon*, Vol 10 Number 4, November 1956.
179. *Canon*, 'The Music of Sweden', Vol 12 Number 2, September 1958

ENDNOTES CHAPTER 23 *Postlude*

180. New Zealand born and educated, John Mansfield Thomson (1926–1999) spent most of his working life as a musicologist, editor, and music commentator in London, where he accumulated a deep reservoir of experience, not least from founding and editing the journal *Early Music* for Oxford University Press, and editing a number of influential books, including Charles Rosen's *The Classical Style*.
181. 'A note on Russian music', by J M Thomson, in Canon, Vol 12 No 3, October 1958.
182. When the Champ family moved from Hunters Hill to Mosman, 'Threlkeld' ceased being the address of the journal. Whether Franz Holford found another benefactor for the magazine in Ted Albert is not known.
183. John Thomson contributed several articles to *Canon*, and his association with Franz certainly continued; perhaps in connection with John's own music journals, published in London and Wellington in the 1970s and 80s.
184. It was Don Newton who introduced Billy Thorpe and The Aztecs to Albert's, an association which ultimately culminated in the movie *Strictly Ballroom*.
185. Papers of Franz Holford MSS 8809, Piece 3, NLA.
186. One of Franz Holford's claims was that the eminent German conductor Felix Weingartner had sent him to study at Oxford.
187. In a letter to Lawson years later, her friend John Mansfield Thomson also expressed his reservations about Franz, referring to him as '…that old reprobate'.
188. Thompson later invited Franz onto the adjudicating panel for the first Sydney International Piano Competition.
189. Amongst papers found after her death was a document in Franz's handwriting, signed by Mirrie, giving him carte blanche over the withdrawal of funds from Mirrie Hill's account with the Bank of New South Wales, Mosman. (Hill Family Papers and Music, *Correspondence 1960-1984*, MSS 6357 ML)
190. Ibid

191. The author approached Betty Beath for a recollection of her time with Franz Holford, but she declined.
192. A report of six months' investigation by the police which led to the Goossens arrest in 1956 is believed to disclose details of 'parties' in bohemian King's Cross and this secluded mansion in the picture-postcard Blue Mountains. A senior police official said at the time: 'The names of many important people in business, the Government, and society are mentioned in the papers we have.'
193. In a letter to Franz from Betty Beath in 1983, she had written: '…I do hope you are planning a visit to Brisbane…I miss having you close.' Papers of Franz Holford, MSS 8809, Piece 4, NLA.